DO-IT-YOURSELF BIBLE STUDIES

JOHN

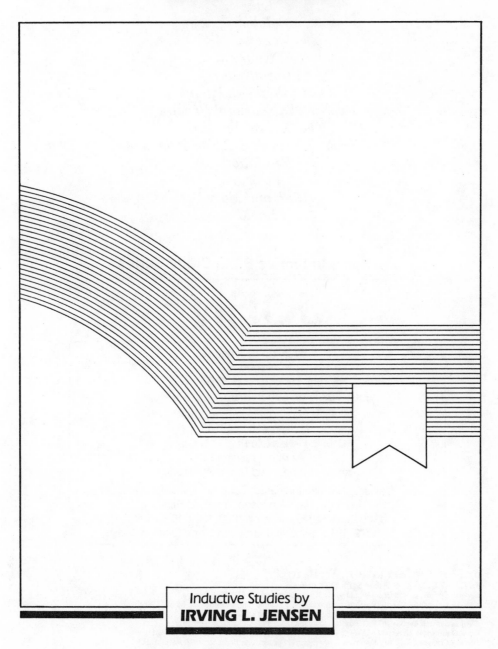

Inductive Studies by
IRVING L. JENSEN

Here's Life Publishers, Inc.
San Bernardino, California

Other books available in the Irving Jensen Do-It-Yourself Bible Study Series

Matthew
Mark
Luke
John
Acts
Romans
1 Corinthians
2 Corinthians/Galatians
Hebrews/The Pastoral Epistles
The General Epistles
The Prison Epistles/1 & 2 Thessalonians
Revelation
Psalms
Ruth and Mary
David

Jensen's Inductive Bible Study Series

JOHN

by Irving L. Jensen
Published by
HERE'S LIFE PUBLISHERS, INC.
P.O. Box 1576, San Bernardino, CA 92402

Fifth Printing, November 1989
ISBN 0-89840-051-1
©1983, Here's Life Publishers, Inc.
All rights reserved
Printed in the United States of America

For More Information, Write:
L.I.F.E.—P.O. Box A399, Sydney South 2000, Australia
Campus Crusade for Christ of Canada—Box 300, Vancouver, B.C., V6C 2X3, Canada
Campus Crusade for Christ—Pearl Assurance House, 4 Temple Row, Birmingham, B2 5HG, England
Lay Institute for Evangelism—P.O. Box 8786, Auckland 3, New Zealand
Campus Crusade for Christ—P.O. Box 240, Colombo Court Post Office, Singapore 9117
Great Commission Movement of Nigeria—P.O. Box 500, Jos, Plateau State Nigeria, West Africa
Campus Crusade for Christ International—Arrowhead Springs, San Bernardino, CA 92414, U.S.A.

CONTENTS

PREFACE

No one can read and study the Gospel of John without being a changed person when he has finished. If you are an unbeliever, this Scripture can lead to spiritual new birth. If you are a believer, as a disciple of Christ you can mature day by day, beholding afresh your Savior Jesus and all His wonderful works. Open your heart and mind to all that God wants you to learn from this portion of His Book.

Preface

INTRODUCTION

The purpose of this study guide is to lead you to a discovery of many wonderful truths of God recorded by John. In the course of your study you will learn methods of personal, independent Bible study, so that you will gain more confidence and direction in the full Bible study process.

Your attitude will determine in large measure how fruitful your study is. Consider these three determinants for Christian students:

1. *Time.*

Be willing to spend time—that precious commodity!—in all your studies. A. W. Tozer once said, "God has not bowed to our nervous haste nor embraced the methods of our machine age. The man who will know God must give time to Him." Diligent Bible study demands work, but it is wonderfully rewarding. Read Hebrews 5:11–6:2, which warns that a Christian will not grow spiritually if he does not advance from the "milk" to "strong meat" stage of instruction.

2. *Hunger.*

Be hungry for the spiritual food of God's Word. It has been well said, "If you want food for your soul, you must have soul for the food."

3. *Dependence.*

Let a dependence on the Holy Spirit underlie all your Bible study. He who inspired the Scriptures wants to enlighten you as you study those Scriptures so that eternal fruit will be produced in your life. (Read John 16:12-15 and 1 Corinthians 2:12-13.)

The applications urged by this study guide are geared mostly to the Christian student, who can identify with Jesus' disciples throughout the gospel narrative. If you are not a believer when you begin this study, you can be assured that the Lord wants you to believe and receive the eternal life which He is offering you even now. (Read John 20:30-31.)

Book Study

As someone commented, "Study the Bible the way God wrote it—BOOK BY BOOK." This is the natural way of a long-term, day-by-day pattern, keeping in mind that the Bible is a lengthy book and Bible study is for a lifetime. For the New Testament, this approach involves twenty-seven book studies. There are various orders in which you could study the books, depending on your needs and desires. However, it makes sense to start with one of the four gospels since they contain all the historic facts of *The Christ-Event.*

The procedure of book study is simple: After learning the book's background, get an overview (survey) of the whole book to see the large and general movements and emphases. Then proceed slowly with the full Bible text (analysis), beginning at the first chapter and moving along verse by verse (sentence by sentence), paragraph by paragraph, and chapter by chapter. This is the normal way of studying any book, and it is the way each biblical author put his thoughts into writing as he was undergirded by the Holy Spirit (2 Peter 1:21). (Actually, the original author did not use chapter or verse divisions to show his thought patterns.)

This study guide begins with the background and survey of the Gospel of John. All the remaining units are studies of each consecutive segment of the Bible text. Your approach will always be to let God reveal through John *what* He wants to say and *how* He wants to say it. Your task will be to observe just that, to understand its meaning, and so be prepared to apply the Word to your life.

Inductive Bible Study[1]

This manual uses the inductive approach of studying, because it is a basic, natural way of analyzing the Bible text. There are three stages in inductive study, in this order:

1. Observation—What does the text say?

2. Interpretation—What does that mean?

3. Application—How can I apply this?

It can be seen from this order that conclusions are not arrived at until the latter part of the study. This follows the important principle of letting the Bible speak for itself, rather than imposing conclusions on it prematurely.

In the inductive method the observation stage is crucial if there is to be sound interpretation later. In your study, try to observe *everything*—the apparent insignificant items as well as the strong and weighty truths. The principle here is that each part of the Bible text is important and should not be overlooked.

Develop personal study habits that are suited

to your own abilities and inclinations. The following elements are basic to effective study, whatever the method:

a. Schedule: Set aside *time*—a *regular* time.
b. Desire: Guard this with all your strength.
c. Text: Spend most of your time with the Bible text itself. Don't read into the text any meaning that is not there.
d. Context: Let context—the surrounding words and phrases—be your ally in interpreting a passage.
e. Observation: See for yourself *what* the Bible says and *how* it says it. Train your eyes—physical and spiritual—to keep seeing things in the text. Don't be content with a casual, quick glance. Comprehensive analysis can be the most enjoyable part of your study.
f. Recording: Keep your pencil busy. This is one of the main emphases of this self-study guide. "The pencil is one of the best eyes."
g. Application: Be continually on the lookout for spiritual lessons in the passage. These include your relationship with God and with other people, commands to obey, sins to confess and avoid, promises to claim, paths to pursue, and warnings to heed. In the *Applications* section of each study unit, do more than is asked for.

How to Use This Study Guide

Each numbered unit of study appears on two facing pages. The overall pattern of your study of a unit moves from left to right. Follow the suggestions given below, for each study unit.

1. Observe at the top of the pages what the Bible passage is, and the title assigned to it, suggesting its theme.

2. Read the SETTING description to get a feel for what brought on the present passage.

3. Refer to the survey chart of the book of John and note where in John the passage of your study unit appears. The shading shows the location. This preliminary exercise is intended to help you recognize the general *context* of your passage.

4. Read and study the textual re-creation of the Bible text (NASB) as it appears in the chart of the left page. This "talking text" preserves the thought patterns of the Bible text to help you in the observation stage. The two main things it shows are *emphases* and *relationships* of words and phrases. These are the best clues to what the biblical author is writing. For *emphasis*, a word may be shaded, or printed in large letters, or circled. The *relation-*

ship between two phrases may be made by a connecting line, or similar print, or similar location (e.g. three items listed in group form). Noting emphases and relationships is a large part of the observation stage. You are encouraged also to make other markings on the printed text with your pencil to show other emphases and relationships. The importance of diligently studying this textual re-creation cannot be overstated. It is a key to effective Bible study.

5. Move now to *Key Words and Phrases*. Have pencil in hand for marking and recording. Read the textual re-creation again and mark words and phrases which you think are key ones in the segment. Things which identify *key* quality include: repetition, importance (e.g., a strong doctrinal phrase like "died for you"), sharpness, uniqueness, cruciality. One key word is shown for each unit, as a starter. Record others that you see, using the suggested verse locations.

6. Read the *Segment Survey*, referring to the charted text as you read. The purpose of this exercise is to get a feel of the entire segment as a whole, before examining the parts.

7. Now you are ready to launch into the main part of the OBSERVATION stage, the *Paragraph Analysis*. Your study will move paragraph by paragraph, as indicated on the pages. Record answers to questions when these are called for. Some of these questions are simple yet basic; for example, *Who? What? Where? When? How?* and *Why?* Use notebook paper to record extensive answers.

8. Note the list of *Related Verses*. Sometime during the observation stage, read these verses in your Bible and record the main parts of the verses in the spaces shown. You will have reason to refer to these on your own in the three stages of your study (OBSERVATION, INTERPRETATION, APPLICATION).

9. Now that you have seen what the Bible text *says*, you are ready to think about what it *means*. This is the INTERPRETATION stage. The Bible is its own best interpreter, so you will find that many, if not most, of your interpretations will come from your observations of the Bible text. When questions are given in this section, answer these to the best of your ability, using the Bible text as the basis of your answer. This is the inductive part of your interpretative study. Much of this section contains brief commentary on things not answerable from the text, but it is given to help you in your total study. Your own inductive study remains as the most important part, however.

10. All Bible study should ultimately reach the APPLICATION stage. At this part of your study it will be very helpful for you to recall what you have learned about the ten basic steps toward Christian maturity described by Bill Bright, in *Ten Basic Steps Toward Christian Maturity*.[2] These are listed here:
    1. The Christian Adventure
    2. The Christian and Abundant Life

3. The Christian and the Holy Spirit
4. The Christian and Prayer
5. The Christian and the Bible
6. The Christian and Obedience
7. The Christian and Witnessing
8. The Christian and Stewardship
9. Old Testament highlights
10. New Testament highlights

Read the unit's Bible text again and see if any of these steps appear in the text, either directly or indirectly. If they do, ask yourself how you can apply the passage to your personal life. (Reference to the Basic Steps will be made at times with a notation like this: TBS#4.)

Use notebook paper to record applications when more space is needed.

11. The purpose of the two parts, *Summary* and *Memory Verse(s),* is to let you take one final, brief look at the passage you have studied, and carry away with you at least one memorized verse.

12. The last section, *Looking Ahead,* introduces the subject of the next unit. Thank the Lord for His help in studying the unit you have completed, and pray for His continued light and inspiration as you move to the next unit.

Note: The following abbreviations are used in this study guide:

TBS—Ten Basic Steps
NASB—New American Standard Bible
NIV—New International Version
LB—Living Bible

Suggestions for Group Leaders

Group Bible study can be thoroughly enjoyable and spiritually productive if a few basic guidelines are followed. Group members will learn valuable Bible study skills and communication skills, too, as they share their insights, questions, and life-impacting decisions with one another.

1. *Organize Your Group Carefully and Prayerfully*

Ask God to direct you to several persons who want to develop a deeper relationship with the Lord through group Bible study. These may include new Christians, friends at work, neighbors, or fellow students. Tell them specifically why you want to form a Bible study group; stress the non-threatening, friendly aspects of the meetings; and indicate the place and time of the study. Assure each prospect that the spiritual benefits to be obtained through this kind of Bible study are outstanding.

Generally, six to ten persons comprise an effective group. Each session should be held in an informal setting: a comfortable living room, a private room in a restaurant, or a dormitory room. Light refreshments may be served at either the beginning or close of the study session.

How you arrange the seating is crucial. Ideally, each group member should be able to see everyone else in the group. So, if possible, arrange chairs in a circle or semi-circle. Discussion will be aided by seating a timid person directly across from an outgoing person.

2. *Build a Supportive Atmosphere*

Spend a few minutes at the beginning of each session as a get-acquainted time. Encourage your students to talk about their victories and concerns. Ask two or three persons to pray with praise and requests based on these victories and concerns.

Convey to the group the assurance that no comment or question raised during a sesion will be ridiculed or ignored. Students should feel secure about entering into discussion as cherished and respected members of the group. Thank your students for participating and compliment them on their openness and their learning. If you find that someone has a tendency to dominate discussions, you may find it helpful to make the rule: "No one may answer more than two questions consecutively without giving another person the opportunity to respond."

Conclude each session with a brief summary of your group's progress—what was learned and how the group plans to apply the truths gained from the study. This will give everyone a sense of accomplishment as well as a sense of accountability to be doers of the Word.

3. *Serve as a Discussion Leader*

Your role in group Bible study is that of a discussion leader. A wise discussion leader does not lecture throughout a session, nor does he act as the expert answer-man. Instead, he relates to the group in a manner similar to that of a coach to his team. Just as a coach helps to develop his players' skills and to motivate them, so a discussion leader shows his students how to study the Bible and apply it to daily living. Further, a discussion leader motivates his students to study the Bible diligently and enthusiastically.

4. *Lead Your Group Through Each Section of Every Lesson*

These instructions are based upon the students' doing the assignments during the group Bible study session. However, the assignments are readily adaptable to a do-it-at-home-first system, if you prefer.

Setting

Ask a student to read this "Setting" section aloud from the study guide. Then, direct the group's attention to the organizational survey chart so they will see where this setting fits into the whole course. Ask if anyone needs further clarification of the setting before you proceed to the next section.

Key Words and Phrases

Instruct the group to read the Bible text silently. It is given in full in the study guide. After reading it, each person should determine its key words and phrases and write these in the "Key Words and Phrases" section. Answers may vary, so don't be alarmed by the different opinions. Ask for volunteers to tell why they made the selections they recorded. The important aspect of this assignment is that your students conceptualize what is happening in the text and think about its significance.

Segment Survey

This section provides some secure pegs on which your students can fasten their grasp of the passage or segment of Scripture. Help them to think through the question(s) in this section. Let volunteers share their answers and tell why they answered as they did.

Paragraph Analysis

It is important to study Scripture paragraph by paragraph, for this helps to see everything in context. Fanciful interpretations, as well as other wrong interpretations, are likely to experience a quick death when a student understands the context of a passage.

Since assignments are more enjoyable when served in bite-size chunks, let the students proceed through the "Paragraph Analysis" section one paragraph at a time, sharing answers and discussing each paragraph.

Related Verses

As your students complete this section, they can see at a glance how Scripture compares with Scripture, and how each passage reinforces the message of the segment under study. Encourage your students to tell how each verse relates to the Bible text.

Interpretation

In this section, the group will find helpful explanations, and they will be able to do some serious thinking about what is being taught in a passage of Scripture. Let your students share their answers. Also, if they wish to raise questions of their own, based on this passage, let them do so. And, whenever possible, let the answers to these questions come from the group.

Applications

Here the mind and heart team up to meet issues, needs, and concerns of daily life. Challenge the group to answer each question thoughtfully, relating it to their own lives. Encourage them to make a few firm decisions about implementing what they have learned. They each should ask themselves:

"How can this information change my attitudes?"

"What changes should I make in my life, based on this information?"

"What specific things can our group do for God's glory, based on what we have learned today?"

You may wish to ask the group to set a few spiritual goals. Then call for progress reports in succeeding study sessions.

Summary of Passage

Ask a student to read this section out loud, or ask the group to summarize the Bible text in their own words.

Memory Verses

Learning a verse or two of Scripture in connection with each passage studied is excellent spiritual discipline. Take a few minutes of each session to accomplish this. Congratulate those who commit the verse to memory.

Looking Ahead

Before you conclude the study session, refer your students to the "Looking Ahead" section so they will anticipate the next segment of the course.

Time Frame

How much time your group devotes to each section of a lesson depends upon whether the write-in assignments are done at home or during the sessions. The following time frame is suggested for the latter. Be flexible in altering the time slots to fit the preference of your group.

SECTION	TIME
Setting	3 minutes
Key Words and Phrases	6 minutes
Segment Survey	5 minutes
Paragraph Analysis	30 minutes
Related Verses	10 minutes
Interpretations	10 minutes
Applications	15 minutes
Summary of Passage	4 minutes
Memory Verse	5 minutes
Looking Ahead	2 minutes
Total:	**90 minutes**

If you are a student or group leader and desire fuller explanations on how to use this Bible study, the publisher will be happy to send you a free guidebook, *How to Use Irving Jensen's Do-It-Yourself Bible Studies*. Write Here's Life Publishers, P.O. Box 1576, San Bernardino, CA 92402, for your copy.

BACKGROUND OF JOHN

Before we study the Bible text itself, we need to learn some things about the background of the book of John—its original setting.

A. **Author**

In many of the Bible books, authors are not named in the text itself. This is so in the case of the Gospel of John. The traditional view is that John the apostle, sometimes referred to as John the evangelist, was the author. Read John 21:20-24, where the phrase "the disciple whom Jesus loved" appears (cf. 13:23; 19:26; 20:2; 21:7). This may be interpreted as referring to the apostle John.

A thumbnail sketch of this apostle follows:

1. John was a son of Zebedee (21:2) and Salome (cf. Matthew 27:56; Mark 15:40; John 19:25). If Salome was a sister of Jesus' mother Mary, Jesus and John were cousins. This would partly explain the close association between the two.

2. John was a brother of the apostle James. They and their father Zebedee were fishermen, on the Sea of Galilee (Mark 1:19,20).

3. John may have been a disciple of John the Baptist when Jesus called him into His service (Mark 1:20). John's age at that time may have been around twenty-five, and he lived to be one hundred.

4. John was a Palestinian Jew, a close companion of Peter, and a contemporary of the events of his gospel. He became a leader of the Jerusalem church (Galatians 2:9).

5. John wrote three epistles and Revelation in addition to his gospel.

6. There are only a few historical references to John after the events of the gospels. Read these:

Acts 4:1-22; 8:14-15 —John with Peter

Galatians 2:9 —One of John's contacts with Paul

Revelation 1:1,4,9 —John's exile experience, around A.D. 95

B. Place and Date of Writing

For the last years of his life John lived near Ephesus. The other three gospels had been written, and the church was reflecting more and more on the significance and interpretation of Jesus' mission and teachings. According to divine schedule, time had come for a fourth and final gospel record, which would include, among other things, more interpretations and more long discourses of Jesus. Around A.D. 85 the Holy Spirit guided John to write this inspired gospel.

C. Original Readers

By the time John wrote this part of the New Testament, the church had matured in its transition from a Jewish exclusivism (cf. Acts 10) to a universal outreach. Hence it was natural for this fourth gospel to be directed to a universal audience. This is why John translated Hebrew and Aramaic words (e.g. Siloam, 9:7; Gabbatha, 19:13; and Golgotha, 19:17), and why he explained Jewish religious practices (e.g. the burial custom of 19:40). It is interesting to observe also that the word "world" appears seventy-eight times in the book.

D. Purposes of Writing

John identifies specifically in 20:30-31 his primary purpose of writing: to win *unbelievers* (Jews and Gentiles) to a saving faith in Jesus as Christ,

the Son of God. Related to this is the ministry of confirming *believers* in their faith, so that the church would have a stronger witness.

John also had other purposes in mind, subordinate but related to those mentioned above. One was to refute the heresy of Docetism, which denied the true humanity of Jesus (observe John's "answer" in 1:14). Another was to expose the unbelief of Judaism (e.g. "He came to His own, and those who were His own did not receive Him," 1:11).

SURVEY OF JOHN

Survey first, then analyze. This is the standard approach for studying a book of the Bible. So, before we analyze each unit (segment) of the book, we will scan the book as a whole, in a skyscraper view.

A. Main Features and Overall Structure

Refer to the accompanying survey chart as you read the observations and descriptions that follow. Note: This survey chart will appear at each unit of your analytical studies to remind you of the location of the unit's passage in the scope of the whole book.

Book of John: LIFE IN JESUS, THE SON OF GOD

P R O L O G U E	SIGNS WROUGHT			SELF REVEALED			E P I L O G U E 21: 24 25
	PUBLIC MINISTRY -3 YEARS-		(GREAT) (PAUSE) ▶	PRIVATE MINISTRY -FEW DAYS-			
	ERA OF INCARNATION BEGINS	YEARS OF CONFLICT	DAY OF PREPARATION	HOUR OF SACRIFICE		DAWN OF VICTORY	
1:1	1:19	5:1	12:36b	18:1		20:1	21:1

1. John has 21 chapters. Scan the pages of your Bible and note the comparative lengths of the chapters.

2. The first eighteen verses set the tone for the book, introducing Christ as God. This is the PROLOGUE (1:1-18).

3. The concluding chapter (EPILOGUE) reports the last appearances of Jesus to His disciples. Read the concluding two verses (21:24-25).

4. John divides the public ministry of Jesus into two main parts. How does this show on the chart?

5. Generally speaking, to whom is Jesus extending His ministry in 1:19–12:36a? What do you think is meant by "private ministry" and to whom is it extended according to 12:36b–21:25?

6. Observe the outline SIGNS WROUGHT; SELF REVEALED. Actually, in both main divisions of the book Christ reveals who He is. In the last division, however, He presses His claim more explicitly and reveals it fully in His death and resurrection.

7. The time of 12:36b has been called "The Great Pause." Note this on the chart. Read 12:36b in your Bible. To see how it is a turning point, observe the "they" of 12:37 and "his own" of 13:1.

8. Compare the time periods of both sections of John. Note also the temporal references: "era," "years," and so forth.

9. With whom do you think Jesus was in conflict (5:1ff.)?

10. What section reports Jesus' death?

11. What section reports Jesus' resurrection?

B. Key Words and Verses

There are many key words in John, most of which are repeated often. Among these are "believe" (appears 98 times), "world" (78), "Jew" (71), "know" (55), "glorify" (42), "My Father" (35), "love" (30), and "light" (23).

Among the verses which could be called key verses are 20:30,31, which state the gospel's theme.

C. Title and Theme

John was written to lead the reader to belief in Jesus as the Christ, the Son of God, which results in eternal life. Appropriately, the title assigned on the survey chart is "Life in Jesus, the Son of God."

D. Some Prominent Subjects

Among the prominent subjects of John are: the prologue (1:1-18); Jesus' meeting with Nicodemus (3:1-21); farewell discourses (14:1–16:33); high priestly prayer (17:1-26); hour of sacrifice (18:13–19:42; and resurrection (20:1-31).

The New American Standard Bible

Why is the *New American Standard Bible* (NASB) the text used for these DO-IT-YOUR-SELF study guides?

This question is answered best by identifying the objectives of the Bible Studies. Here are the main objectives:

1. To make a detailed study of the Bible book, carefully analyzing its paragraphs and segments (groups of paragraphs).

2. To identify with the Bible authors as closely as possible by finding the answers to these questions: "What are you saying?" and "What do you mean?"

3. To learn not only *what* the Bible author wrote (content), but *how* he wrote it (form). Once these things are discerned, we are ready to ask him: "*Why* did you write it?"

4. To apply the Bible text to our personal living, as it originally was intended by that author.

The NASB supports those objectives in the following ways:

1. It is a precise, accurate translation of the original languages. F.F. Bruce says: "It retains many of the features of the ASV [*American Standard Version*, 1901], especially that precision of rendering which made that version so valuable for *detailed textual study.*"[3] Regarding its accuracy, William S. LaSor writes that it is "exceptionally faithful to Hebrew and best Greek texts."[4]

2. The precision of the NASB translation lends itself to a breakdown of its phrases and lines into a "talking text." This gives the student an excellent view of *how* the original author arranged what he was inspired to write.

3. The NASB, though far from the King James in its literalness, is nevertheless the most literal of the modern versions. It is not paraphrastic and casual, yet the text is in clear, readable contemporary English. This allows the serious Bible student to make accurate OB-SERVATIONS in the course of his study.

Notice where the NASB stands in the following comparative list of major English Bible versions, moving from the very literal to the very paraphrastic (from my book *How to Profit From Bible Reading,* p. 24):

1. *New King James Version*   (NKJV, 1982)
2. *New American Standard Bible*(NASB, 1971)
3. *Revised Standard Version*   (RSV, 1952)
4. *New Berkeley Version in Modern English* (Modern Language Bible)   (MLB, 1959)
5. *New International Version*   (NIV, 1978)
6. *Good News Bible* (Today's English Version)   (TEV, 1976)
7. *New English Bible*   (NEB, 1970)
8. *Jerusalem Bible* (Roman Catholic)   (JB, 1966)
9. *New Testament in Modern English* (Phillips)   (Phillips, 1958)
10. *The Living Bible*   (TLB, 1971)

Conclusion: Today we are blessed with having many good Bible versions. I have found the NASB to be the best version for the analytical studies of this DO-IT-YOURSELF series. As you study the UNITS, the text of other versions (e.g., the excellent *New International Version*) will be cited for clarification or alternate reading.

FOOTNOTES

1. For further description of textual re-creation (talking text), see Irving L. Jensen, *Enjoy Your Bible,* pages 76-82.

2. Bill Bright, *Ten Basic Steps Toward Christian Maturity* booklets, or *A Handbook for Christian Maturity*—a compilation of the TBS booklets.

3. "Bible Versions and Bible Enjoyment," *Eternity Magazine,* 1974, page 42.

4. *Ibid.*

THE GEOGRAPHY OF JOHN'S GOSPEL

THE GREAT SEA

GALILEE

Capernaum •   • Bethsaida

SEA OF GALILEE (TIBERIAS)

Tiberias •

• Cana

Mount Carmel ▲

Kishon River

• Nazareth

Yarmuk   River

Salim? •
Aenon? •

SAMARIA

▲ Mount Ebal

Samaria •

Sychar •

Jabbok River

Jordan River

PEREA

Mount of Olives ▲
Jerusalem ★   • Bethany

• Bethany Beyond Jordan

JUDEA

Bethlehem •

DEAD SEA

Arnon River

Scale of Miles

0   10   20   30   40

Zered River

Map adapted from *JOHN*, by Irving L. Jensen, 1970. Moody Press,
Moody Bible Institute of Chicago.

PROLOGUE
and ERA of
INCARNATION BEGINS
JOHN 1:1–4:54

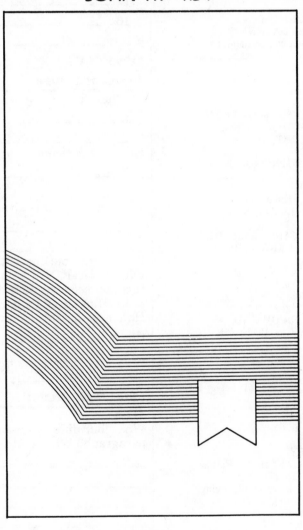

SETTING John introduces Jesus to his readers in a prologue of eighteen verses that is one of the highest points of Scripture. He reveals Jesus as God, the Word, Creator and Savior, and he describes the glories attending His coming to this earth. The era of Jesus' incarnation begins. (See survey chart.)

Book of John: LIFE IN JESUS, THE SON OF GOD

P R O L O G U E	SIGNS WROUGHT			SELF REVEALED		E P I L O G U E
	PUBLIC MINISTRY -3 YEARS-		(GREAT) (PAUSE) ▶	PRIVATE MINISTRY -FEW DAYS-		21: 25
	ERA OF INCARNATION BEGINS	YEARS OF CONFLICT	DAY OF PREPARATION	HOUR OF SACRIFICE	DAWN OF VICTORY	
1:1	1:19	5:1	12:36b	18:1	20:1	21:1

THE TRUE LIGHT

1 In the BEGINNING was THE WORD,
      and THE WORD was WITH GOD,
      and THE WORD WAS GOD.
2 He was in the BEGINNING WITH GOD.
3 All things came into being
      by Him;
    and apart from Him
nothing came into being
    that **has come** into being.
4 In Him was LIFE,
    and the LIFE was the LIGHT of men.
5 And the LIGHT shines in the DARKNESS,
    and the DARKNESS did not comprehend it.

(margin: CREATION)

6 There came a **man**
      sent from God,
    whose name was JOHN.
7   He came for a WITNESS,
    that he might bear WITNESS of the LIGHT,
that ALL MIGHT BELIEVE through him.
8   He was NOT **THE LIGHT,**
    but came
      that he might bear WITNESS of the LIGHT.

(margin: WITNESS)

9 There was the TRUE LIGHT
      which, coming into the world,
      ENLIGHTENS EVERY MAN.
10 He was in the WORLD,
    and the WORLD was MADE through HIM,
    and the WORLD did not KNOW HIM.
11 He **came to HIS OWN,**
    and those who were HIS OWN
      did **not receive Him.**
12 BUT as many as **received Him,**
    to them He **gave the right**
      to become **CHILDREN OF GOD,**
  even to those who BELIEVE in HIS NAME,
13   who were born
    (1) not of blood,
    (2) nor of the will of the flesh,
    (3) nor of the will of man,
    (4) **but OF GOD.**

(margin: SALVATION)

14 And THE WORD
      (1) became FLESH, and
      (2) dwelt among us,
  and **we beheld HIS GLORY,**
    glory as of the only begotten from the Father,
      full of GRACE and TRUTH.
15 John bore witness of Him, and cried out, saying,
    "This was He of whom I said,
      'He who **comes** after me
        has a **higher rank** than I,
      for He **existed** before me.'"
16 For of HIS FULNESS we have all received,
      and GRACE UPON GRACE.
17 For the LAW was given through MOSES;
  GRACE AND TRUTH
      were REALIZED through JESUS CHRIST.
18 No man has **seen GOD** at any time;
    the only begotten GOD,
      who is in the bosom of the **Father,**
  HE HAS EXPLAINED HIM.

(margin: INCARNATION)

Key Words and Phrases

1:1 _____ "Word" _____

2 _____

4 _____

6 _____

7 _____

9 _____

11 _____

16 _____

others: _____

OBSERVATIONS

Segment Survey

1. Where in the segment is Jesus identified by name? _____

How else does John identify Him? _____

What paragraph is about another person? _____

2. Note the outline CREATION; SALVATION; INCARNATION. Try to account for the order of these subjects, as John writes about them.
3. In what three paragraphs does *light* appear? How are the three paragraphs interrelated by this subject? _____

Paragraph Analysis

1:1-5
What four different words identify Jesus in this paragraph? What truth does each teach?

_____

1:6-8
1. What was John, and what was he not?

_____

16

2. Compare the words "was" (first paragraph) and "came" (this paragraph). _____

_____

1:9-13
1. How does the first word "There" focus attention on Jesus? _____

2. What two rejections of Jesus does John cite?

_____
_____

3. How does a person become a child of God?

_____
_____

4. How is this "rebirth" described in verse 13?

_____
_____

1:14-18
1. In what different ways does John describe Jesus? _____

2. Who are the "we" in verses 14 and 16?

_____

According to this paragraph, what do believers see and receive? _____

_____
_____

Related Verses
John 14:6,8,9 _____

_____

Ephesians 1:7,8 _____

_____

Philippians 2:5-11 _____

_____

Colossians 1:16 _____

_____

Titus 2:11 _____

_____

Hebrews 1:2,3 _____

_____

1 John 1:1-3 _____

_____

INTERPRETATIONS
1. What word in this passage describes the plight of the world of sinners? What statements imply a spiritual need? _____

_____

How is Jesus the solution?

_____

2. "Comprehend" (1:5). Some versions translate the Greek original as "overpower."
3. "John" (1:6). This was John the Baptist, not John the apostle.
4. "Enlightens every man" (1:9). This is not universal salvation. What is the intention of the phrase? _____

5. "He came to His own..." (1:11). This is the intent of the original text: "He came to His own [things, place], and those who were His own [people, the Jews] did not receive Him."
6. "Grace upon grace" (1:16). NIV translates, "one blessing after another." What is your definition of grace? _____

7. What do verses 12 and 13 teach about being born again? _____

_____
_____

APPLICATIONS
1. Compare John 1:1-3,14a with Philippians 2:5-11. Write in your own words what it means for you to "have this attitude in yourselves."

_____

How can you work on the shortcomings?

_____

2. What does the truth of 1:16 do to you?

_____

3. What do you learn from John the Baptist about witnessing? (TBS#7). _____

_____
_____

Summary of Passage
Jesus was in the beginning, before anything else existed. He was the Word; He was with God; He was God. He created all things. For death, He is life; and for darkness, He is light.

John the Baptist came to bear witness of Jesus as the light of the world.

All who believe in His name become children of God, and begin to receive blessing after blessing from the fullness of His grace.

Memory Verses   1:12,13
Looking Ahead
John the Baptist introduces Jesus to the multitudes, as the Lamb of God.

SETTING John is busy baptizing people (cf. Matthew 3:5) in the Jordan River at Bethany, when a deputation of Jewish religious leaders come from Jerusalem. They ask him who he is and why he is baptizing. See map (page 15) for location of Bethany-beyond-the-Jordan.

Book of John: LIFE IN JESUS, THE SON OF GOD

P R O L O G U E	SIGNS WROUGHT			SELF REVEALED		E P I L O G U E 21: 25
	PUBLIC MINISTRY -3 YEARS-		(GREAT) (PAUSE) ▶	PRIVATE MINISTRY -FEW DAYS-		
	ERA OF INCARNATION BEGINS	YEARS OF CONFLICT	DAY OF PREPARATION	HOUR OF SACRIFICE	DAWN OF VICTORY	
1:1	1:19	5:1	12:36b	18:1	20:1	21:1

THE LAMB OF GOD

19 And this is the WITNESS of **John**,
    when the JEWS sent to him
  priests and **Levites** from JERUSALEM to ask him,
    "Who are you?"
20 And he confessed, and did not deny,
  and he confessed,
    "I am not the Christ."
21 And they asked him,
    "What then? Are you **Elijah**?"
  And he said, "I am **not**."
      "Are you **THE PROPHET**?"
  And he answered, "No."
22   They said then to him,
  "Who are you,
so that we may give an answer to those who sent us?
    What do you say about yourself?"
23 He said, "I am A VOICE
    of one crying in the wilderness,
    'Make straight the **WAY of THE LORD**,'
    as ISAIAH the prophet said."   [Isaiah 40:3]

24 Now they had been **sent** from the PHARISEES.
25 And they asked him, and said to him,
    "Why then are you **baptizing**,
    if you are not (1) THE CHRIST, nor (2) ELIJAH,
    nor (3) THE PROPHET?"
26   John answered them saying,
  "I **baptize** in water, but **among you** stands
    ONE whom YOU DO NOT KNOW.
27 "It is HE who comes after me,
the thong of whose sandal I am **not worthy** to untie."
28   These things took place
      in Bethany beyond the Jordan,
      where John was **baptizing**.

29 The next day
    he **SAW Jesus** coming to him, and said,
  "BEHOLD, THE LAMB OF GOD
    who takes away the **sin of the world**!
30 "This is He on behalf of whom I said,
    'After me comes A MAN
    who has a **higher rank** than I,
    for He existed before me.'
31 "And I **did not recognize** Him,
  but in order that He might be **manifested to Israel**,
    I came **baptizing** in water."
32 And John bore WITNESS saying,
    "I have BEHELD THE SPIRIT
  (1) **descending** as a **dove** out of HEAVEN, and
  (2) He **remained upon Him**.
33 "And I **did not recognize** Him,
  but He who sent me to **baptize** in water
  said to me,
  'He upon whom you see
  the SPIRIT **descending** and **remaining upon Him**,
    THIS IS THE ONE
      WHO BAPTIZES IN THE HOLY SPIRIT.'
34 "And I
    (1) have seen, and
    (2) have borne WITNESS
  that THIS IS THE SON OF GOD."

(margin labels: "WHO?", "WHY?", "BEHOLD!")

Key Words and Phrases

1:19 __ "Who are you?" _____
   20 _____
   21 _____
   23 _____
   25 _____
   29 _____
   33 _____
   34 _____
others: _____

OBSERVATIONS

Segment Survey

1. The intense action of this narrative is compressed into three solid paragraphs that exalt Jesus. Scan the paragraphs. Who magnifies Jesus?

_____

How does he do this? _____

_____

What is John's first introduction of Jesus?

_____

2. How does the segment outline (who-why-behold) represent the flow of the narrative?

_____

3. Compare the opening verse (1:19) and the closing verse (1:34). _____

_____

4. What phrase of the segment identifies the spiritual plight of the world?

_____

Paragraph Analysis

1:19-23
1. What is the repeated three-word question?

_____

2. Compare John's three answers in verses 20 and 21. _____

_____

3. How does his answer in verse 23 differ from the earlier ones? _____

_____

_____

_____

1:24-28

1. Why is it understandable that the emissaries asked the question in verse 25? As of that time, had John directly introduced Jesus to them (v. 26)? _____

_____

2. Does John answer the question in verse 25 directly? If not, how does he use the occasion of the question?_____

_____

1:29-34

1. By what names and titles does John identify Jesus? What does each reveal about Jesus?

_____

_____

_____

_____

2. Relate verse 30 to verse 27.

_____

_____

3. How does verse 31 answer the question in verse 25?_____

4. What experience led John to bear witness that Jesus was THE SON OF GOD?

_____

_____

Related Verses

Exodus 12:3_____

_____

Deuteronomy 18:15,18_____

_____

Isaiah 53:4-12_____

_____

Malachi 4:5 _____

_____

John 7:40,41_____

_____

Acts 3:22,23 _____

_____

1 John 2:2_____

_____

INTERPRETATIONS

1. "Christ" (1:20). Read 1:41 for the alternate translation. The literal meaning of the name "Christ" is "the anointed one."

2. "The Prophet" (1:21). That Prophet was Jesus, prophesied in Deuteronomy 18:15. (Cf. Acts 3:22-23.)

3. "Make straight" (1:23). Read Isaiah 40:3 for the meaning of "straight." How did John the Baptist fulfill that ministry?

_____

4. "Pharisees" (1:24). This "ultra" party of Jews claimed salvation on the basis of physical descent from Abraham and a strict adherence to the law.

5. "Baptize in water" (1:26). This was not Christian baptism, but a special temporary ordinance symbolizing the washing away of sins. Thus John preached "a baptism of repentance for forgiveness of sins" (Luke 3:3). How did John's ministry prepare the way for Jesus' coming?

_____

6. "Baptizes in the Holy Spirit" (1:33). John does not expand on the meaning of this, but he does contrast Spirit with water. What does that suggest?_____

Read Acts 1:5 and 2:1ff, concerning the historical occasion of the church's baptism with the Holy Spirit (Pentecost day).

APPLICATIONS

1. Record valuable lessons this passage teaches you about witnessing. (TBS#7).

_____

Where do you need to improve most in your own experience, and how can you do this?

_____

2. John's humility is prominent here. What is true humility? _____

What do you learn from John's magnifying Jesus?_____

_____

Summary of Passage

A deputation of Jewish leaders from Jerusalem challenges John's ministry of baptizing by asking for his credentials. John identifies his mission as that of preparing the way for Jesus' coming. The next day he sees Jesus coming toward him and calls out, "Look! There is the Lamb of God who takes away the world's sin!" John talks more about Him, and closes with the powerful declaration, "This is the Son of God."

Memory Verse   1:29

Looking Ahead

The apostle reports on Jesus' calling His first disciples to Himself.

SETTING On the two days following Jesus' first introduction to the people as the Lamb of God, He calls His first disciples to Himself. He is still in Bethany, and is making preparations for a journey to Galilee.

Book of John: LIFE IN JESUS, THE SON OF GOD

P R O L O G U E	SIGNS WROUGHT			SELF REVEALED		E P I L O G U E 21: 25
	PUBLIC MINISTRY -3 YEARS-		(GREAT) (PAUSE) ▶	PRIVATE MINISTRY -FEW DAYS-		
	ERA OF INCARNATION BEGINS	YEARS OF CONFLICT	DAY OF PREPARATION	HOUR OF SACRIFICE	DAWN OF VICTORY	
1:1	1:19	5:1	12:36b	18:1	20:1	21:1

GREAT DISCOVERIES

35 Again the next day JOHN was standing,
     with two of his disciples;
36 and he looked upon JESUS ◄
          as He walked, and said,
     "BEHOLD, THE LAMB OF GOD!"
37 And the two disciples **heard** him speak,
     and they followed JESUS. ◄
38 And JESUS turned, and **BEHELD** them **following**,
     and said to them, "What do you **seek**?"
     And they said to Him,
     "RABBI (which translated means TEACHER),
     where are you staying?"
39   He said to them, "**Come**, and you will **see**."
     They **came** therefore and **saw** where He was staying;
     and they STAYED WITH HIM that day,
        for it was about the tenth hour.

BAPTIZER JOHN & TWO DISCIPLES

40 One of the two who heard John speak,
       and followed Him,
     was ANDREW, SIMON PETER'S brother.
41 He found first his own brother SIMON,
     and said to him, "We have **found** THE MESSIAH"
        (which translated means CHRIST).
42 He brought him to JESUS.
       JESUS **looked** at him, and said,
     "You **are** SIMON the son of John;
     You **shall be called** CEPHAS"
        (which translated means PETER).

ANDREW & SIMON

43   The next day
       He **purposed** to **go forth** into GALILEE,
     and He **found** PHILIP,
     and JESUS **said** to him, "FOLLOW ME."
44 Now PHILIP was from BETHSAIDA,
     of the city of ANDREW and PETER.
45 PHILIP found NATHANAEL, and said to him,
     "We **have found** Him,
     of whom MOSES in the LAW,
     and the PROPHETS, **wrote**,
     JESUS OF NAZARETH, the son of JOSEPH."
46   And Nathanael said to him,
     "Can **any good thing** come out of NAZARETH?
     PHILIP said to him, "**Come** and see."

PHILIP & NATHANAEL

47   JESUS **saw** NATHANAEL coming to Him,
     and said of him,
     "BEHOLD, an Israelite indeed, in whom is **no guile**!"
48 NATHANAEL said to Him, "How do you know me?"
     JESUS answered and said to him,
     "Before PHILIP called you,
     when you were under the fig tree, I SAW YOU.
49 NATHANAEL answered Him,
     "RABBI, You are THE SON OF GOD;
       You are THE KING OF ISRAEL."
50   JESUS answered and said to him,
     "Because I said to you
     that I saw you under the fig tree, do you BELIEVE?
     You shall see greater things than these."
51 And He said to him,
     "**Truly, Truly,** I say to you, **you shall see**
     (1) the HEAVEN OPENED, and
     (2) the ANGELS OF GOD ascending
        and descending upon the SON OF MAN."

JESUS & NATHANAEL

Key Words and Phrases

1:37 _____ "followed Jesus"
  39 _____
  41 _____
  42 _____
  43 _____
  45 _____
  49 _____
  51 _____
others: _____

OBSERVATIONS

Segment Survey

This segment is the account of Jesus' contacts with His first followers. The four paragraphs may be identified in various ways (e.g. persons, discoveries). Record the kinds shown below.

	35-39	40-42	43-46	47-51
main persons				
titles of Jesus				
who are "found"				
whom Jesus calls				

Paragraph Analysis

1:35-39

1. Compare John's identification of Jesus with the way his two disciples identified Him.

_____

2. What was the good outcome of the disciples' request? _____

1:40-42

1. Compare Andrew's testimony about Jesus with John's (verse 36). _____

2. Jesus gave Simon a surname. What is significant about receiving a new name from *Jesus*?

_____

1:43-46

1. What are your observations about Jesus' call of Philip? _____

2. How does Philip relate Jesus to the Old Testament? _____

_____

Were John's and Andrew's testimonies of Jesus also geared to a Jewish hearing? If so, how?

_____

3. What do you learn about Nathanael?

_____

Related Verses

Genesis 28:10-19_____

Daniel 7:13,14_____

Matthew 16:17-19_____

John 4:24-26_____

John 7:40-43_____

John 7:52_____

John 12:13-15_____

INTERPRETATIONS

1. The names and titles of Jesus in this passage are significant. Spend time thinking about what each points to in the ministry of Christ. Record your conclusions._____

_____

2. "Jesus of Nazareth" (1:45). Sometimes Jesus was called a Nazarene, in answer to the prophecy of Isaiah 11:1 (*nezer* = "shoot"). His friends used the name in a friendly way (Acts 2:22; 3:6), but His enemies used it in scorn (Mark 14:67). Jesus' birthplace—Bethlehem of Judea—was humble, and so was His homeplace—Nazareth of Galilee. (See map.)

3. The name "Peter" ("Cephas" in Aramaic—1:42) means *stone*. Jesus gave the new name to prophesy that He would make Peter a strong and stable believer and disciple. (Cf. Matthew 16:17-19.)

4. "Tenth hour" (1:39). In Roman time, this was 10 A.M.

5. "No guile" (1:47). Jesus was not saying that Nathanael was sinless, just that deceit was not his life-style.

6. "Son of Man" (1:51). This was Jesus' favorite identification. Except for Stephen (Acts 7:56), He is the only one to use it of Himself.

APPLICATIONS

1. This is a passage of great discoveries (you have already observed the repeated word "found"). Should discoveries be part of the Christian's experience? If so, what kind? What should be the *follow-up* of such discoveries?

_____

2. What do you learn here about following Jesus and fellowshiping with Him? In a practical way, how can you fellowship with Jesus today?

_____

Summary of Passage

In the early days of His public ministry Jesus draws to Himself a number of followers. Among these are John the Baptist, who calls Him "the Lamb of God"; Andrew, who exclaims, "We have found the Messiah"; Philip, who sees Him as the fulfillment of Old Testament prophecies; and Nathanael, who acclaims Him as Son of God and King of Israel.

Memory Verses   1:35,36

Looking Ahead

Jesus performs the first of His miracles, in Cana of Galilee.

SETTING After a couple of days' journey from Bethany, Jesus arrives in Galilee. (Cf. 1:43 and 2:1.) He is invited to a wedding in Cana, north of Nazareth (see map). Among those attending are His mother and His disciples.

Book of John: LIFE IN JESUS, THE SON OF GOD

P R O L O G U E	SIGNS WROUGHT			SELF REVEALED		E P I L O G U E 21: 25
	PUBLIC MINISTRY -3 YEARS-	(GREAT) (PAUSE) ▶		PRIVATE MINISTRY -FEW DAYS-		
	ERA OF INCARNATION BEGINS	YEARS OF CONFLICT	DAY OF PREPARATION	HOUR OF SACRIFICE	DAWN OF VICTORY	
1:1	1:19	5:1	12:36b	18:1	20:1	21:1

BEGINNING OF SIGNS

1 And on the third day
　　　there was a WEDDING in CANA of GALILEE,
　　　and the **mother** of JESUS was there;
2 and **JESUS ALSO WAS INVITED**,
　　and **HIS DISCIPLES**,
　　　　　to the wedding.
3 And when the **wine gave out**,
　　　the mother of JESUS said to Him,
　　　"They **have no wine**."
4 And JESUS said to her,
　　　"Woman, what do I have **to do with you**?
　　　MY HOUR has NOT YET COME."
5 His mother said to the servants,
　　　"**Whatever He says** to you,
　　　　　　DO IT."

PREDICAMENT

6 Now there were six stone waterpots set there
　　　for the JEWISH CUSTOM of PURIFICATION,
　　　　containing twenty or thirty gallons each.
7 JESUS said to them,
　　　"**Fill** the waterpots **with water**."
　　And they **filled** them **up to the brim**.
8　And He said to them,
　　　　"**Draw some out** now, and
　　　　take it to the headwaiter."
　　And they took it to him.
9 And when the headwaiter **tasted**
　　　THE WATER which had become WINE,
　　and did not know where it came from
　　　(but the servants
　　　　who had drawn the water knew),
　　the headwaiter called the bridegroom,
10 and said to him,
　　　"Every man serves the **GOOD** WINE FIRST,
　　　and when the men have **drunk freely**,
　　　then　　　→　that which is **POORER**;
　　you have kept the GOOD WINE until now."

SOLUTION

11 This **BEGINNING** of **HIS SIGNS**
　　　JESUS DID in CANA of GALILEE,
　　and **MANIFESTED HIS GLORY**,
　　　and HIS DISCIPLES BELIEVED in HIM.

SUMMARY

Key Words and Phrases

2:2 ____ "invited" ____

3 _____

4 _____

5 _____

9 _____

10 _____

11 _____

11 _____

others: _____

_____

OBSERVATIONS
Segment Survey

1. Read the segment a few times, trying to visualize the setting and action as you read.
2. The narrative has two main parts. How are these indicated on the textual re-creation chart?

_____

_____

3. Compare the atmosphere of the opening and concluding verses, whether implied or stated explicitly. _____

_____

_____

4. What phrase or sentence of the segment stands out most prominently to you?

_____

_____

Paragraph Analysis
2:1-5
1. Compare the first statement made by Mary (Jesus' mother) with the last.

_____

_____

_____

_____

Account for the change.

_____

_____

_____

2. What do you think Jesus meant by the question, "What do I have to do with you?"

_____

(NIV paraphrases, "Why do you involve me?")
Was Jesus expecting an answer? _____
3. Why do you think Jesus added the words, "My hour has not yet come?" _____

_____

2:6-10
1. What are Jesus' two command verbs?

_____

_____

2. Where in the narrative is the moment of transformation from water to wine?

_____

_____

3. What do verses 9 and 10 add to the character of the miracle?_____
_____
_____

Related Verses

Isaiah 55:8,9_____
_____

Luke 2:51_____
_____

John 7:30_____
_____

John 11:40 _____
_____
_____

John 12:23,27 _____
_____

John 13:1_____
_____

John 17:1_____
_____

INTERPRETATIONS

1. "Woman" (2:4). In the oriental culture this mode of address was very respectful. Jesus even used it while on the cross. (See 19:26.)

2. "My hour" (2:4). Read the last three verses cited under *Related Verses*. What hour did Jesus mean by "My hour"?

_____
_____

What, then, was there about Mary's request that made Jesus correct her?

_____
_____
_____
_____

3. Did Mary therefore bypass Jesus when she advised the servants? What does this reveal about Mary's faith? _____
_____
_____

4. How do verses 9 and 10 amplify the authenticity of the miracle?_____
_____

5. "Signs" (2:11). What was Jesus' underlying purpose for these miracles? Recall 20:30 and 31. _____
_____
_____

APPLICATIONS

1. What effect should this account have on all Christians who read it?_____
_____
_____

2. Why is it so important for all Christians to grow deeper in their knowledge of who Jesus is?

_____
_____

What does the passage teach about Jesus' purposes and power?_____
_____
_____

3. Does Jesus still perform miracles? If so, what kind, how often, and with what objectives?

_____
_____
_____
_____

Summary of Passage

Jesus, His mother and His disciples are invited to a wedding in Cana of Galilee. When the wine gives out, Mary seeks Jesus' help. He reminds her that the objective of His mission is the forthcoming hour of sacrifice. Then He relieves the predicament of the bridegroom by changing water to good wine, and in so doing He manifests His glory to all who believe.

Memory Verse   2:11

Looking Ahead

Jesus drives the merchandisers out of the Temple because they are profaning it with their trades.

SETTING After a few days' visit at Capernaum with His disciples and with His family, Jesus travels to Jerusalem. It is the week of Passover, the most important Jewish annual feast.

Book of John: LIFE IN JESUS, THE SON OF GOD

P R O L O G U E	SIGNS WROUGHT			SELF REVEALED		E P I L O G U E 21:25
	PUBLIC MINISTRY -3 YEARS-		(GREAT) (PAUSE) ▶	PRIVATE MINISTRY -FEW DAYS-		
	ERA OF INCARNATION BEGINS	YEARS OF CONFLICT	DAY OF PREPARATION	HOUR OF SACRIFICE	DAWN OF VICTORY	
1:1	1:19	5:1	12:36b	18:1	20:1	21:1

MY FATHER'S HOUSE

—transition—

12 After this He went down to CAPERNAUM,
　　　He and His mother, and His BROTHERS,
　　　　　and His DISCIPLES;
　　　and there they stayed a few days.

TEMPLE: BUILDING

13 And the PASSOVER of the JEWS was at hand,
　　　and JESUS **went** up to JERUSALEM.
14 And He found in the TEMPLE
　　　　　those who were **SELLING**
　　　oxen and sheep and doves,
　　and the **MONEYCHANGERS** seated.
15 And He made a **SCOURGE** of **CORDS**,
　　　and **drove** them all **out** of the TEMPLE,
　　　　　　with the sheep and the oxen;
　　And He **poured out** the coins
　　　　of the **MONEYCHANGERS**,
　　　　　and **overturned** their tables;
16 and to those who were **SELLING** the doves He said,
　　　"**TAKE** these things **AWAY**;
　　　STOP making MY FATHER'S HOUSE
　　　　　a house of MERCHANDISE."
17 His DISCIPLES REMEMBERED
　　　　　that it was written,
　　"ZEAL for THY HOUSE will CONSUME ME."
　　　　　　　　　　[Psalm 69:9]

TEMPLE: BODY

18 The JEWS therefore answered and said to Him,
　　"What SIGN do You **show to us**,
　　　seeing that You **DO THESE THINGS**?"
19 JESUS answered and said to them,
　　　"**Destroy this** TEMPLE,
　　　and in **three days** I will **raise it up**."
20 The JEWS therefore said,
　　"It took forty-six years to **build this** TEMPLE,
　　　and will You **raise it up** in three days?"
21 BUT He was speaking
　　　　　of the TEMPLE of HIS BODY.
22 When therefore He was RAISED from the DEAD,
　　　HIS DISCIPLES **remembered**
　　　　　　that HE **said this**;
　　and they BELIEVED
　　　　(1) the SCRIPTURE, and
　　　　(2) the **word** which JESUS **had spoken**.

BELIEF

23 Now when HE was in JERUSALEM
　　　at the PASSOVER,
　　　　during the FEAST,
　　many BELIEVED in HIS NAME,
　　　beholding HIS SIGNS which HE was **doing**.
24 BUT JESUS, on HIS part,
　　was **not entrusting** HIMSELF **to them**, for
25 (1) HE KNEW ALL MEN, and because
　　(2) HE DID NOT NEED anyone
　　　　　to bear witness concerning man
　　for HE HIMSELF KNEW **what was in man**.

Key Words and Phrases

2:13 _"Passover"_____

　14 _____

　16 _____

　17 _____

　19 _____

21 _____

22 _____

25 _____

others: _____

OBSERVATIONS

Segment Survey

1. Note that this segment is divided into four paragraphs. The first short paragraph serves as a transition from the preceding one. Then the two main paragraphs follow. What subject is common to each?_____

_____

_____

2. How does the last paragraph conclude this segment?_____

_____

_____

Paragraph Analysis

2:12

What does this verse teach about Jesus?

_____

_____

2:13-17

1. The Temple was intended to be the place to worship God. How was the spirit of worship profaned by the moneychangers and merchants?

_____

_____

2. Can you think of one word which describes Jesus' action in the Temple? Compare this with how the disciples described it when they quoted Psalm 69:9. Compare the prediction "will consume me" with 2:19._____

_____

_____

2:18-22

1. What was the spirit of the Jews' reaction to Jesus' scourging? _____

_____

What specifically were they demanding (verse 18)?_____

_____

2. How did Jesus use their question to point to a key truth of His mission?

3. Compare the Jews' response (verse 20) and the disciples' later understanding (verse 22).

_____

_____

2:23-25
Whom did many trust in this paragraph?

_____

Whom did Jesus not trust in this paragraph?

_____

Related Verses
Exodus 12 _____

_____

Malachi 3:1-3 _____

_____

Matthew 27:39,40 _____

_____

John 6:30 _____

_____

John 9:4 _____

_____

Acts 6:14 _____

_____

1 Corinthians 6:19 _____

_____

INTERPRETATIONS
1. "Capernaum" (2:12). Matthew 9:1 says that this was Jesus' "own city." It served as His "headquarters" for His mission in Galilee. (See map.)
2. "Moneychangers" (2:15). These dealers exchanged other currency for the official Temple currency, charging exorbitant rates for the exchange. The doves (2:16) were sold for the rites of purification, making the place of worship a marketplace.
3. The Jews challenged Jesus' authority to cleanse the Temple. "What miraculous sign can you show us to prove your authority to do all this?" they asked (2:18, NIV). Why do you think Jesus answered that question with the reference to His forthcoming death and resurrection

(2:19,21)? _____

_____

_____

4. "Many believed...beholding His signs" (2:23). This was not genuine trust, but a miracle-faith.

How do verses 23-25 point to this deficiency?

_____

_____

_____

State in your own words what you believe these people were thinking about Jesus.

_____

_____

_____

_____

APPLICATIONS
1. Why does the Lord highly regard the *meeting-place* of believers for their worship of Him? How can the *place* and the *service* contribute to that worship? Read 1 Timothy 3:14-16.

_____

_____

_____

_____

_____

_____

2. Jesus knows all the thoughts and intentions of your heart. Even if they are good and acceptable, does His existence and glory depend on you?

_____

As one of His disciples, what does He entrust

to you? _____

_____

_____

_____

Summary of Passage
When it is almost time for the Jewish Passover, Jesus travels from Capernaum to Jerusalem. He goes to the Temple, and drives out all the merchandisers who are profaning it by making it a marketplace. The Jews challenge His authority, and He prophesies His resurrection—an even greater demonstration of power.

At this time many are believing in Him only because of the miracles, but He knows their hearts, and does not trust Himself to them.

Memory Verse   2:16
Looking Ahead
Jesus talks to Nicodemus about his need of being born again.

SETTING About the time of the cleansing of the Temple a ruler of the Jews comes to Jesus by night to talk with Him about who He is and what He came to do.

Book of John: LIFE IN JESUS, THE SON OF GOD

P R O L O G U E	SIGNS WROUGHT			SELF REVEALED		E P I L O G U E 21: 25
	PUBLIC MINISTRY -3 YEARS-		(GREAT) (PAUSE) ▶	PRIVATE MINISTRY -FEW DAYS-		
	ERA OF INCARNATION BEGINS	YEARS OF CONFLICT	DAY OF PREPARATION	HOUR OF SACRIFICE	DAWN OF VICTORY	
1:1	1:19	5:1	12:36b	18:1	20:1	21:1

YOU MUST BE BORN AGAIN

1 Now there was **a man of the PHARISEES,**
    (1) named **NICODEMUS,** (2) a ruler of the **JEWS;**
2 this man **came to Him** by **NIGHT,**
    and said to Him,
    "RABBI, we know that **You have come**
        (1) from **GOD**
        (2) as a teacher;
    for no one can **do these** SIGNS that You do
        unless GOD IS WITH HIM."
3 JESUS answered and said to him,
    "TRULY, TRULY, I say to you,
        unless one is **BORN AGAIN,**◀
    he **cannot see** the KINGDOM of GOD."
4   NICODEMUS said to Him,
    "How can a man be **born** when he is **old?**
    He **cannot enter** a second time
        into his mother's womb and be **born, can he?"**
5 JESUS answered,
    "TRULY, TRULY, I say to you,
        unless one is **BORN** of **water and the Spirit,**
    he **cannot enter into** the KINGDOM of GOD.
6 "**That which is born of the flesh** is flesh;
    and that which is **born of the Spirit** is **spirit.**

7 "Do not **marvel** that I said to you,
    'You **must be BORN AGAIN.'**
8 "The wind blows where it wishes
    and you hear the sound of it,
    but do not know
        (1) where it **comes from** and
        (2) where it is **going;**
          SO is
    everyone who is BORN of the SPIRIT."
9 NICODEMUS answered and said to him,
        "How can these things be?"
10 JESUS answered and said to him,
    "Are you the TEACHER of ISRAEL,
    and do not **understand** these things?
11 "TRULY, TRULY, I say to you,
    (1) we speak that which we **know,** and
    (2) bear witness of that which we have **seen;**
        and **YOU DO NOT RECEIVE** our witness.
12 "If I TOLD you earthly things
        and you do not BELIEVE,
    how shall you BELIEVE
    if I TELL you **heavenly** things?

13 "And no one has ascended into heaven
        but He who descended from heaven,
    even the SON OF MAN.
14 "And as MOSES **lifted up** the **serpent**
      in the wilderness,
    even so
        MUST the SON OF MAN be **LIFTED UP;**
15 that WHOEVER BELIEVES
        may IN HIM have eternal life."

(vertical labels: NEW BIRTH / UNBELIEF / CROSS)

Key Words and Phrases

3:2   "God is with him" _____

3 _____

3 _____

5 _____

6 _____

---

11 _____

12 _____

14 _____

others: _____

OBSERVATIONS

Segment Survey

1. Read the segment, and record in your own words the main subject of each paragraph:

3:1-6 _____

3:7-12 _____

3:13-15 _____

2. Observe that the first paragraph is about Nicodemus' need, and the second is about his stumbling-block.

3. What key event cited in the segment originates the glad tidings of the passage?

_____

_____

Paragraph Analysis

3:1-6

1. Who opens the conversation?

_____

Does he ask a question, or make some statements?

_____

What do you learn here about his spiritual perception? _____

2. How does Jesus respond (verse 3)?

_____

3. What question does this raise?

_____

How does Jesus answer the question?

_____

3:7-12

1. Record what the text reveals about Nicodemus' heart and mind:

verse 7 _____

verse 10 _____

verse 11 _____

verse 12 _____

2. Compare "you do not know" (verse 8) with "that which we know" (verse 11).

_____

_____

3. The key to believing is implied in verse 11. What is that? _____

_____

_____

3:13-15

1. Compare the words "heaven" (verse 13) and "heavenly" (3:12) with "kingdom of God" (3:3,5).

_____

_____

What was Nicodemus failing to perceive?

_____

2. Who is the central person of the paragraph, and what is His work?_____

_____

_____

Related Verses

Numbers 21:5-9 _____

_____

Ezekiel 11:19_____

_____

John 7:50,51_____

_____

John 12:32,33_____

_____

John 19:39,40_____

_____

Titus 3:5_____

_____

1 Peter 1:23_____

_____

INTERPRETATIONS

1. "Ruler of the Jews" (3:1). Nicodemus was one of the seventy-member Sanhedrin, the highest Jewish tribunal.
2. "Born again" (3:3). Another possible translation is "born from above." Both renderings teach a supernatural act of regeneration.
3. "Born of water" (3:5). This phrase has been interpreted in different ways: (a) symbolical of repentance, as John the Baptist's water baptism was; (b) cleansing by the Word (1 Peter 1:23); (c) natural birth, thus, "except a man be born the first time by water and the second time by the Spirit..."; (d) a synonym for the Holy Spirit, translating "by water, even the Spirit." Whatever the intended meaning, the phrase in its context teaches that the new birth is a supernatural work of God from above, through the Spirit.
4. What is the connection between "you do not receive our witness" (3:11) and "you do not believe" (3:12)? _____

_____

5. How did Jesus fulfill the type of the wilderness

setting of Numbers 21:5-9?

_____

_____

APPLICATIONS

1. What do you learn from Jesus about personal evangelism? (TBS#7) _____

_____

_____

_____

2. Nicodemus was a learned Jewish leader, and yet he was ignorant of eternal truths. How do you explain that there are biblically literate people who refuse to acknowledge and respond to the Bible's truth? How can such people be reached with the gospel?_____

_____

_____

_____

_____

Summary of Passage

Nicodemus, a ruler of the Jews, comes to Jesus by night and the two discuss the spiritual experience of the new birth. Jesus teaches that a person must be born again, from above, by the Holy Spirit, to enter the kingdom of God. Nicodemus does not understand this. He will not accept Jesus' testimony of these heavenly truths, and so he does not believe.

Jesus says more—that one day He must be lifted up, on the cross, and only those who believe in Him will be saved.

Memory Verse   3:3
Looking Ahead

Jesus continues to teach about how a person receives eternal life.

SETTING Jesus continues His teaching about how a person receives eternal life. In the discussion with Nicodemus, the last spoken words of the Jewish ruler are recorded in 3:9. Verses 11-21 comprise Jesus' discourse to Nicodemus. The passage of this unit concludes that discourse.

Book of John: LIFE IN JESUS, THE SON OF GOD

P R O L O G U E	SIGNS WROUGHT			SELF REVEALED		E P I L O G U E 21: 25
	PUBLIC MINISTRY -3 YEARS-		(GREAT) (PAUSE) ▶	PRIVATE MINISTRY -FEW DAYS-		
	ERA OF INCARNATION BEGINS	YEARS OF CONFLICT	DAY OF PREPARATION	HOUR OF SACRIFICE	DAWN OF VICTORY	
1:1	1:19	5:1	12:36b	18:1	20:1	21:1

GOD GAVE HIS SON

16 "For GOD
     so loved THE world
       THAT
HE GAVE
        HIS **only begotten** SON,
  that
      whoever BELIEVES IN HIM
  should
       ➤ not PERISH
       ➤ but HAVE ETERNAL LIFE.
17 "For GOD did not **send** THE SON
    into the world
  to judge the world
    but that the world
       should be SAVED through HIM.

(margin: GOD)

18 "He who BELIEVES IN HIM
    is **not judged**;
  he who does **not** BELIEVE
    has been **judged already,**
  because
    he has **not** BELIEVED in the name
    of the **only begotten** Son of God.
19 "And this is the **judgment,**
  that the LIGHT is come into the world,
  and men **loved the darkness**
    rather than the LIGHT;
      for their **deeds** were **evil.**
20 "For everyone who **does evil** hates the LIGHT,
    and does not come to the LIGHT,
  lest his **deeds** should be **exposed.**
21 "But he who **practices the truth**
    comes to the LIGHT,
  that his **deeds** may be **manifested**
    as having been WROUGHT IN GOD."

(margin: SINNERS)

Key Words and Phrases

3:16 _____ "so loved" _____
  16 _____
  17 _____
  18 _____
  19 _____
  20 _____
  21 _____
others: _____
_____

OBSERVATIONS

Segment Survey

1. This is John's amplification of the favorite verse, John 3:16. Read the two paragraphs, and observe how they differ as to main emphasis. Try to justify the reasons for the simple outline shown:

3:16,17	GOD
3:18-21	SINNERS

2. Observe on the chart the choice of (1) the key center, "He gave His only begotten Son"; and (2) the related master title, *God Gave His Son*. Try looking for a different key center, and assign a title to it.

Paragraph Analysis

3:16,17

Mark with a pencil on the textual re-creation chart the different parts of the paragraph that could be identified by the words WHAT, WHEREFORE, and WHY.

1. What does the word "For" (verse 16) refer to?

_____
_____

2. What four persons or groups appear in the paragraph? _____
_____
_____
_____

3. What truths of salvation are taught by verse 16? _____
_____
_____
_____

4. What words identify the destiny of unbelievers?
_____

Of believers? _____

3:18-21

1. How much of the paragraph is about unbelievers? _____
Record the references to them, such as names, activities and destiny. _____
_____
_____
_____

2. According to verse 20, who "does not come to the light"? _____

According to verse 21, who "comes to the light"?
_____
Compare your two answers.
_____
_____

3. How many times does the word "light" appear
in the paragraph? _____

Related Verses

Luke 19:10 _____
_____

John 6:40 _____
_____

John 12:44-48 _____
_____

Romans 5:8 _____
_____

Ephesians 5:11,13 _____
_____

2 Thessalonians 2:16 _____
_____

1 John 4:9,10,14 _____
_____

INTERPRETATIONS

1. "Only begotten Son" (3:16). The phrase "only
begotten" means unique, one of a kind. Jesus
was the Son from eternity, before His incarnation. And His Father gave Him unto death as an
offering for sin. (Cf. Genesis 22:2; 1 John 4:10).
2. "Judge the world" (3:17). This may also be
translated "condemn the world."
3. "Light is come into the world" (3:19). Review
your study of the prologue, 1:1-18. How many
times does the word "light" appear in the
prologue? _____
Compare John's words about the light with
Jesus' words in 3:19-21.
_____
_____
_____

What is the light, according to John (1:4)?
_____

4. Why does the one who practices evil hate the
light? _____
_____

5. Try to put 3:21 into your own words.
_____
_____
_____

APPLICATIONS

1. How would you describe "the world" in
John 3:16? _____
_____
_____
_____

2. What is the measure of God's love, according
to 3:16? _____
_____
_____

How would you answer someone who asked,
"Why does God love me, a sinner?"
_____
_____
_____

3. Why do people love darkness (3:19)?
_____
_____

What is the one solution to darkness?
_____
_____

Summary of Passage

God sent His only begotten Son into this
world to save sinners from their sins and to give
eternal life. The Son is the light given to dispel
the spiritual darkness, and those who believe in
Him come to the light and practice the truth.
Those who do not believe in the Son are condemned already.

Memory Verses   3:16,17
Looking Ahead

John the Baptist gives warm testimony and clear
teaching about Jesus.

SETTING Jesus and His disciples have left Jerusalem for other parts of Judea, probably along the Jordan River. John the Baptist is in Samaria, baptizing in Aenon, in the vicinity of the Jordan. (See map.)

Book of John: LIFE IN JESUS, THE SON OF GOD

P R O L O G U E	SIGNS WROUGHT			SELF REVEALED		E P I L O G U E
	PUBLIC MINISTRY -3 YEARS-		(GREAT) (PAUSE) ▶	PRIVATE MINISTRY -FEW DAYS-		21: 25
	ERA OF INCARNATION BEGINS	YEARS OF CONFLICT	DAY OF PREPARATION	HOUR OF SACRIFICE	DAWN OF VICTORY	
1:1	1:19	5:1	12:36b	18:1˙	20:1	21:1

JESUS MUST INCREASE

22 After these things
　　JESUS and **His DISCIPLES** CAME
　　　　into the land of JUDEA,
　　and there He was spending time **with them**
　　　　　　　　　and baptizing.
23 And JOHN also
　　　　was baptizing in AENON near SALIM,
　　　　because there was much water **there**;
　　　　and they were coming, and were being baptized.
24 For John had **not yet** been thrown into prison.

—setting—

25 There arose therefore
　　a discussion on the part of **John's disciples**
　　　with a Jew about **purification**.
26 And they came to John, and said to him,
　　"Rabbi,
　　　HE who was with you beyond the Jordan
　　　TO WHOM you have **borne witness**,
　　behold, HE is baptizing,
　　　　and ALL ARE COMING TO HIM."
27 John answered and said,
　　"**A man** can **receive nothing**,
　　　unless it has been given him from HEAVEN.
28 "You yourselves bear me witness,
　　that I said,
　　　'I am not THE CHRIST', but,
　　　'I have been **sent before HIM**.'
29 "He who has the **bride** is the **bridegroom**;
　　but the FRIEND of the bridegroom,
　　　who stands and hears him,
　　　REJOICES GREATLY
　　　　because of the BRIDEGROOM'S VOICE.
　　And so THIS JOY of mine **has been made full**.
30 "HE must **increase**, but I must decrease."

"I AM NOT THE CHRIST"

31 "He who **comes from** above is ABOVE ALL,
　　he who is of the **earth**
　　　　is from the **earth** and
　　　　speaks of the **earth**.
　　He who **comes** from heaven is ABOVE ALL.
32 　　"What he has seen and heard,
　　of that He bears witness;
　　　　and **no man** receives **His witness**.
33 "He who **has received** His witness
　　has set his **seal** to this,
　　　　that GOD IS TRUE.
34 "For He whom **GOD HAS SENT**
　　　speaks the **words of God**;
　　for He **gives** the SPIRIT **without measure**.
35 "The **FATHER LOVES THE SON**,
　　and has given **all things** into His hand.
36 "He who BELIEVES IN THE SON
　　　　has ETERNAL LIFE;
　　but he who **does not obey** the SON
　　　　shall **not see** LIFE,
　　but the WRATH OF GOD abides on him."

"IT IS HE"

Key Words and Phrases

3:22 ___ "baptizing" ___

　25 _____

　26 _____

　28 _____

　29 _____

　30 _____

　31 _____

　33 _____

others: _____

OBSERVATIONS

Segment Survey

1. The segment has three paragraphs, the first of which describes the setting. Who are the two main persons in the opening paragraph?

_____

_____

2. Read the second paragraph. With whom is John comparing himself?

_____

_____

3. Read the third paragraph. With whom does John associate Jesus in verses 31-35?

_____

Paragraph Analysis

3:22-24

What two baptizing ministries were being offered at the same time, in different places?

_____

_____

What natural question might arise from this?

_____

3:25-30

1. What question is implied in verse 26?

_____

2. In short, what was John's answer?

_____

_____

3. Actually, John answered the implied question in four ways. In your own words, record these:

　verse 27 _____

_____

　verse 28 _____

_____

　verse 29 _____

_____

　verse 30 _____

_____

3:31-36

1. In this paragraph John magnifies Jesus and shows His credentials. Study verses 31-35 and

record where and how each of those purposes is accomplished.

Jesus is magnified:_____

_____

_____

_____

Jesus' credentials: _____

_____

_____

2. How is verse 36 an echo of earlier words spoken by Jesus? _____

_____

_____

Related Verses

Matthew 4:12 _____

_____

Matthew 11:27 _____

_____

John 1:7 _____

_____

John 1:23 _____

_____

John 4:2 _____

_____

Acts 19:1-7 _____

_____

1 John 5:9-12 _____

_____

INTERPRETATIONS

1. "There He was...baptizing" (3:22). How is 4:2 more explicit as to the actual performing of the ceremony? _____

_____

2. Who was having a problem about a supposed "rivalry" between John and Jesus over baptizing? Why did John not have such a problem?

_____

_____

_____

3. Which of John's four responses in verses 27-30 sounds closest to his earlier testimony in 1:23? Explain your answer.

_____

_____

4. Record what the last paragraph (3:31-36) teaches about each person of the Trinity:

GOD THE FATHER _____

_____

GOD THE SON _____

_____

GOD THE SPIRIT _____

_____

APPLICATIONS

1. Pressures often bear down heavily on Christian workers. What pressures did John the Baptist deal with? How did he deal with them? Apply this to your own situation.

_____

_____

2. John the Baptist showed genuine humility in his relationship to Christ. Why is this so important in Christian living and serving?

_____

3. How can you use 3:31-36 in your witness to unsaved persons?

_____

_____

_____

Summary of Passage

John is baptizing people in Samaria while Jesus and His disciples are baptizing in Judea. Some of John's disciples and a certain Jew view this as a rivalry, and they ask John about it. John points them to Jesus as the Messiah and bridegroom sent from heaven, who is the one to be believed and followed. "He must increase, but I must decrease," insists Jesus' forerunner.

Memory Verses 3:30,31
Looking Ahead

Jesus talks with a woman of Samaria about the water of life.

SETTING Jesus and His disciples leave Judea for Galilee, and on the journey through Samaria they stop at Sychar. At noon, Jesus converses with a woman at Jacob's well.

Book of John: LIFE IN JESUS, THE SON OF GOD

P R O L O G U E	SIGNS WROUGHT			SELF REVEALED		E P I L O G U E 21: 25
	PUBLIC MINISTRY -3 YEARS-		(GREAT) (PAUSE) ▶	PRIVATE MINISTRY -FEW DAYS-		
	ERA OF INCARNATION BEGINS	YEARS OF CONFLICT	DAY OF PREPARATION	HOUR OF SACRIFICE	DAWN OF VICTORY	
1:1	1:19	5:1	12:36b	18:1	20:1	21:1

LIVING WATER

1 When therefore the LORD knew
    that the PHARISEES had **heard**
    that JESUS was **making** and **baptizing**
        more DISCIPLES than JOHN
2 (although JESUS **HIMSELF** was not baptizing,
    but **HIS DISCIPLES** were),
3 He left JUDEA,
    and **departed** again into GALILEE.
4 And **He had to go** through SAMARIA.
5 So He came to a city of SAMARIA, called SYCHAR,
    near the parcel of ground
    that JACOB gave to his son JOSEPH;
6   And JACOB'S WELL was there.
Jesus therefore,
    being **wearied** from His journey,
    was **sitting** thus **by the well**.
        It was about the sixth hour.

—setting—

7 There came a woman of SAMARIA
    to draw water.
JESUS said to her,
    "Give Me a drink."
8   For HIS DISCIPLES had gone away
        into the city
    to buy **food**.
9 The Samaritan woman therefore said to Him,
    "How is it that
    You, being a JEW,
    ask **me** for a drink
        since I am a SAMARITAN woman?"
(For JEWS have **no dealings** with SAMARITANS.)

WELL WATER

10 JESUS answered and said to her,
    "If you knew
    (1) the GIFT OF GOD, and
    (2) **who** it is that says to you,
        'Give Me a drink';
    you would have **asked Him**,
    and He would have given you LIVING WATER."
11   She said to Him,
    "Sir, you have nothing to draw with
    and the well is deep;
    where then
    do you get that LIVING WATER?
12 "You are not **greater**
    than our father JACOB, are You,
    who gave us the well,
        and drank of it himself,
        and his sons, and his cattle?"
13 JESUS answered and said to her,
    "Everyone who drinks of this water
        shall **thirst again**;
14 but whoever drinks
    of the water that I shall give him
        shall **never thirst**;
    but the water that I shall give him
        shall become **in him**
    a well of water springing up to ETERNAL LIFE."
15 The woman said to Him,
    "Sir, give me **this** water,
    so that I will not be thirsty,
    nor come all the way here to draw."

LIVING WATER

Key Words and Phrases

4:4 _____ "Samaria" _____

6 _____

7 _____

9 _____

10 _____

10 _____

14 _____

15 _____

others: _____

OBSERVATIONS

Segment Survey

1. The segment contains three paragraphs, each having a different purpose. Read each paragraph, and record what it is mainly about.

4:1-6 _____

4:7-9 _____

4:10-15 _____

2. Compare the beginning and end of the segment, regarding water. Before you finish analyzing the segment, you will want to compare the symbolic meanings of both kinds of water.

Paragraph Analysis

4:1-6

What three geographical provinces are mentioned in verses 3 and 4? (See map.) Most Jews traveling from Judea to Galilee would avoid Samaria. How?

_____

What did Jesus do?

_____

4:7-9

1. How intense was the antipathy between Samaritans and Jews?

_____

2. The Samaritan woman's question was basically a "why" question. What kind of an answer do you think she was expecting from Jesus?

_____

4:10-15

1. What two things did the woman need to know (verse 10)?

    (1) _____

(2)_____

2. Where in the conversation did the subject of "who" come up? _____

_____

What question was raised?_____

3. Where in the conversation did the subject of "gift" come up? _____

_____

What did Jesus say about this?
_____
_____

4. What response did He get from the woman (verse 15)?_____
_____
_____

Related Verses

Genesis 33:18-20_____
_____

Ezra 4:1-6_____
_____

Jeremiah 17:13_____
_____

Zechariah 14:8_____
_____

Matthew 10:5,6_____
_____

Matthew 25:46 _____
_____

John 7:37-39_____

INTERPRETATIONS

1. "Being wearied from His journey" (4:6). This is one of many statements in the gospel which teach the *humanity* of Jesus.

2. "No dealings with Samaritans" (4:9). The rivalry originated after the nation was divided and Israel, the northern kingdom (including Samaria), was taken captive to Assyria in 722 B.C. The captors allowed some Jews to remain in the land. These eventually intermarried with Gentiles. Jews returning to Jerusalem under Nehemiah around 445 B.C. refused the offer of these "half-Jew" Samaritans to help rebuild the holy city and its Temple (cf. Ezra 4:1-6). The Samaritans were offended, and started their own religion, changing the Pentateuch to fit their sect (e.g., their temple on Mt. Gerizim replaced the Temple on Mt. Zion).

3. Read John 7:37-39. What is the living water, according to this passage? Now interpret 4:10-15 in light of this. Record some of the vital truths Jesus is teaching:

_____
_____
_____
_____
_____

APPLICATIONS

1. What can Christians learn from Jesus' traveling in Samaria and speaking to a Samaritan woman? Apply this to your ministry of witnessing to lost souls. (TBS#7)

_____
_____
_____

2. Why is it good for a believer to be reminded of the truth of the humanity of Jesus?

_____
_____

3. The indwelling Spirit is living water to the Christian. List some ministries this metaphor suggests about the Spirit. Are you appropriating all of these? (TBS#3)

_____
_____
_____
_____
_____

Summary of Passage

Jesus and His disciples leave Judea for Galilee when Jesus learns that the Pharisees have heard of His popularity. On His way, He rests at a well in the city of Sychar of Samaria. In a long conversation with a Samaritan woman, He talks about the gift of living water which He came to give to all who ask. "Sir, give me this water," is her response.

Memory Verse   4:14

Looking Ahead

Jesus talks more with the Samaritan woman, especially about worship.

SETTING The setting is the same as that of the preceding segment. Jesus and the Samaritan woman are talking at the well, on the outskirts of Sychar.

Book of John: LIFE IN JESUS, THE SON OF GOD

P R O L O G U E	SIGNS WROUGHT			SELF REVEALED		E P I L O G U E 21: 25
	PUBLIC MINISTRY -3 YEARS-		(GREAT) (PAUSE) ▶	PRIVATE MINISTRY -FEW DAYS-		
	ERA OF INCARNATION BEGINS	YEARS OF CONFLICT	DAY OF PREPARATION	HOUR OF SACRIFICE	DAWN OF VICTORY	
1:1	1:19	5:1	12:36b	18:1	20:1	21:1

TRUE WORSHIP

16 He said to her,
    "**Go**, call your husband, and **come** here."
17 The woman answered and said,
    "I have no husband."
    JESUS said to her,
    "You have **well** said,
                    'I have no husband';
18 for you have had **five** husbands,
    and the one whom you **now** have
        is **not your husband**;
    this you have said **truly**."
19 The woman said to Him,
    "Sir, I **perceive** that YOU ARE A PROPHET.
20 "Our fathers WORSHIPED in this mountain,
and you people say
      that in **JERUSALEM**
  is THE PLACE where men ought to WORSHIP."

PROPHET

21 JESUS said to her,
    "Woman, **believe Me**,
      an hour is coming when
          (1) neither in this mountain,
          (2) nor in JERUSALEM,
      shall you WORSHIP THE FATHER.
22 "You **worship that** which you **do not know**;
  we **WORSHIP** that which we **KNOW**,
    for
        SALVATION is from the JEWS.
23 "But
    (1) an **hour is coming**, and
    (2) **now is**,
  when the TRUE WORSHIPERS
    shall WORSHIP THE FATHER in **spirit and truth**;
  for such people
    the FATHER **seeks** to be HIS WORSHIPERS.
24 "GOD IS SPIRIT,
    and those who WORSHIP HIM
        must WORSHIP in **spirit and truth**."

WORSHIP

25 The woman said to Him,
    "I know that **MESSIAH IS COMING**
          (He who is called CHRIST);
    when **THAT ONE** COMES,
      He will declare **all** things to us."
26 JESUS said to her,
    "I who speak to you
      AM HE."

MESSIAH

Key Words and Phrases

4:17 ___"no husband"_____
  19 _____
  20 _____
  21 _____
  22 _____
  23 _____
  24 _____
  25 _____
others: _____

OBSERVATIONS
Segment Survey
1. Which paragraphs are about Jesus?
_____
_____

What title does He have in each?
_____
_____

2. Who is the main person of the Trinity in the middle paragraph?
_____

What is the main subject of this paragraph?
_____

How is it related to each of the two surrounding paragraphs? _____
_____
_____

Paragraph Analysis
4:16-20
1. What do you learn about the woman in verses 16-18?_____
_____
_____

2. What do you learn about Jesus in those same verses, and also in verse 19?
_____
_____

3. What brought on the woman's recognition in verse 19?_____
_____

4. Verse 20 is an implied question. What did the woman want to know?
_____
_____

Why do you think she brought up this subject at this time? For example, do you think she was trying to change the subject of verses 16-18?
_____
_____

4:21-24
1. The woman had brought up the subject of *place* of worship (verse 20). What did Jesus teach about *where* to worship (verse 21)?
_____
_____
_____

2. What did Jesus teach about the how and what of worship?

HOW _____

_____

WHAT _____

_____

4:25,26

1. Earlier, the woman had called Jesus a prophet (that is, one of a number of prophets). What do you think moved her to mention the name Messiah (verse 25)?

_____

2. Jesus declared His Messiahship to the woman. The next time He would do that would be at one of His trials. Read Mark 14:60-62.

Related Verses

Genesis 12:6,7 _____

_____

Genesis 33:18-20 _____

_____

Deuteronomy 11:29 _____

_____

Deuteronomy 18:15-18 _____

_____

Matthew 21:11 _____

_____

Mark 14:60-62 _____

_____

Luke 7:39 _____

_____

Romans 9:5 _____

_____

INTERPRETATIONS

1. "You are a prophet" (4:19). What kind of powers did Old Testament prophets have which made the woman think Jesus was a prophet?

_____

2. "Our fathers worshiped in this mountain" (4:20). The woman probably pointed to Mt. Gerizim as she said this. And she was probably thinking of such patriarchs as Abraham and Jacob, who had erected altars at Shechem on or near Mt. Gerizim (Genesis 12:7; 33:18-20). Gerizim was to the Samaritans what Zion was to the Jews.

3. "Salvation is from the Jews" (4:22). Recall Jesus' earlier use of the word "saved" in 3:17. Salvation is the deliverance and rescue of the sinner from the guilt, pollution and punishment of his sin, on the basis of the redemptive work of Christ. The Jews, not the Samaritans, were the channels of this message of salvation, and the Savior Himself was a Jew. (Cf. Psalm 147:19,20; Isaiah 2:3; Romans 3:1,2; 9:3-5.)

4. "Worship in spirit and truth" (4:24). Genuine worship is "in spirit," for God is spirit; and it is "in truth," because God is absolute truth.

APPLICATIONS

1. Jesus knows everything about us, and He also wants to reveal to us whatever truth we need to know. When you think about this, what does it do to you, in your personal life, and in your desire to serve Him?

_____

_____

_____

2. What do you think Jesus meant by the words, "Worship in spirit and truth"? How do you worship God? When, and where? How can you improve this important activity of your life?

_____

_____

_____

Summary of Passage

The Samaritan woman thinks Jesus is a prophet, because He knows about her private life. In the conversation about this, she changes the subject to worship. Jesus tells her that what matters is not where you worship, but what and how. "God is spirit," He says, "and those who worship Him must worship in spirit and truth."

Memory Verse   4:24

Looking Ahead

The sequels to Jesus' conversation with the Samaritan woman are a teaching session with His disciples and the conversion of many Samaritans.

SETTING Jesus and His disciples are still in the vicinity of Sychar. At some Samaritans' request Jesus remains with them for two extra days. They talk with Him about His work and about their spiritual needs.

Book of John: LIFE IN JESUS, THE SON OF GOD

P R O L O G U E	SIGNS WROUGHT			SELF REVEALED		E P I L O G U E
	PUBLIC MINISTRY -3 YEARS-		(GREAT) (PAUSE) ▶	PRIVATE MINISTRY -FEW DAYS-		L 21 25
	ERA OF INCARNATION BEGINS	YEARS OF CONFLICT	DAY OF PREPARATION	HOUR OF SACRIFICE	DAWN OF VICTORY	
1:1	1:19	5:1	12:36b	18:1	20:1	21:1

SAVIOR OF THE WORLD

WOMAN'S TESTIMONY

27 And at this point HIS DISCIPLES came,
 and they marveled
  that He had been speaking with a **woman**;
 yet no one said,
  "**What** do You seek?"
 or, "**Why** do You speak with her?"
28 So the woman left her waterpot,
  and went into the city,
  and said to the men,
29 "Come, see a man,
 who told me **all** the things that I have done;
  this is **not** THE CHRIST,
    is it?
30 They went out of the city, and
   were **coming to Him**.

JESUS' TEACHING

31 In the meanwhile
 the DISCIPLES were requesting Him,
   saying, "RABBI, eat."
32 But He said to them,
 "I have FOOD TO EAT that **you do not know** about."
33 The DISCIPLES therefore
  were saying to one another,
 "No one brought Him anything to eat, did he?"
34 JESUS said to them,
 "**My food** is
 (1) to **do the WILL** of HIM WHO SENT ME, and
 (2) to accomplish HIS WORK.
35 "Do you not say,
  'There are **yet** four months,
  and **then** comes the HARVEST'?
  BEHOLD, I say to you,
  (1) **LIFT UP YOUR EYES**, and
  (2) **LOOK ON THE FIELDS**,
   that they are **white for HARVEST**.
36 "Already he who REAPS is
 (1) receiving WAGES, and is
 (2) gathering FRUIT for LIFE ETERNAL;
  that he who **SOWS** and he who **REAPS**
   may **rejoice together**.
37 "For in this case the saying is true,
 'One sows, and another reaps.' [Job 31:8; Micah 6:15]
38 "**I sent you** to REAP
  that for which you have **not labored**;
  others have labored,
  and **you** have entered into their labor."

SAMARITANS' CONVERSIONS

39 And from that city
 many of the SAMARITANS
 BELIEVED IN HIM
  because of the word of the woman,
 who testified,
  "He told me **all the things** that I have done."
40 So when the SAMARITANS came to Him,
 they were asking Him to stay with them;
   and He **stayed there** two days.
41 And **many more**
 BELIEVED
  because of HIS word;
42   And they were saying to the woman,
 "It is **no longer because** of what **you** said
  that we BELIEVE,
 for we have **heard for ourselves** and **know**
  that THIS ONE is **indeed**
 THE SAVIOR OF THE WORLD."

Key Words and Phrases

4:29 ___ "told me all" _____
 29 _____
 32 _____
 34 _____
 35 _____
 35 _____
 36 _____
 42 _____
others: _____

OBSERVATIONS

Segment Survey

1. How does the first paragraph connect this segment with the preceding one?

_____

2. Compare the context of the second and third paragraphs. Start with the outline words, SOWER; SAVIOR.

_____

3. What different names in the segment refer to Jesus? _____

_____

Paragraph Analysis

4:27-30

1. Compare the disciples, the woman, and the men of the city.

 disciples: _____
 woman: _____
 men of the city: _____

2. Compare the names:

 "a man" _____
 "the Christ" _____

4:31-38

1. How did Jesus and His disciples get into a discussion about the harvest?

_____

2. The metaphor in verses 34-38 is about a harvest. What words in these verses *explicitly* point to a spiritual harvest?

_____

_____

3. Is Jesus sower, reaper, or both?

_____

_____

Are the disciples sowers, reapers, or both?

_____

4:39-42

Compare "many...believed" (verse 39) and "many more believed" (verse 41). Account for the increase. _____

_____

_____

Related Verses

Luke 10:2_____

_____

John 5:30-36_____

_____

John 6:38_____

_____

John 7:26-31_____

_____

John 17:4_____

_____

1 Corinthians 9:17ff._____

_____

1 John 4:14_____

_____

INTERPRETATIONS

1. Does John's gospel report the conversion of the Samaritan woman? Compare her responses in these verses: 4:15,25,29.

_____

_____

_____

How effective was the woman's testimony in the conversion of the Samaritans?

_____

_____

_____

Discuss this in your group.

2. In the harvest field there are sowers and reapers. Did Jesus sow seed in the woman's heart? Explain.

_____

_____

3. "White for harvest" (4:35). If fields in the world are now white for harvest, what needs to be done?

---

4. "Fruit for life eternal" (4:36). What is this fruit, and whose is it? _____

_____

_____

APPLICATIONS

1. Jesus said He came to accomplish His Father's work. What kind of service is your goal?

_____

_____

2. In the Lord's work there are all kinds of needs. These are met by different kinds of workers. Of these, some are sowers, and some are reapers. Record some specific examples of each.

_____

_____

_____

3. Both sower and reaper are to rejoice together (4:36). Apply this to your own place in the harvest field.

_____

_____

4. What do you learn from Jesus about how to start a conversation as you witness to an unsaved person? Discuss this with your group. (TBS#7)

_____

_____

_____

_____

_____

_____

_____

_____

Summary of Passage

The Samaritan woman hurries into the city and tells everyone about Jesus. "This may be the Messiah!" While this is going on, Jesus talks with His disciples about sowing and reaping in His Father's harvest field. "Look on the fields," He says, "for they are waiting to be harvested."

Many Samaritans believe in Jesus because of the woman's testimony. After Jesus extends His visit by two days, many more believe Him to be the world's Savior, because of the words *He* speaks to them.

Memory Verse   4:35

Looking Ahead

Jesus performs His second miracle in Galilee.

SETTING This passage marks the beginning of Jesus' second year of public ministry. Jesus arrives at Cana of Galilee. A royal official from Capernaum asks Him to heal his critically ill son. Locate Cana and Capernaum on the map.

Book of John: LIFE IN JESUS, THE SON OF GOD

P R O L O G U E	SIGNS WROUGHT			SELF REVEALED			E P I L O G U E 21: 25
	PUBLIC MINISTRY -3 YEARS-		(GREAT) (PAUSE) ▶	PRIVATE MINISTRY -FEW DAYS-			
	ERA OF INCARNATION BEGINS	YEARS OF CONFLICT	DAY OF PREPARATION	HOUR OF SACRIFICE	DAWN OF VICTORY		
1:1	1:19	5:1	12:36b	18:1	20:1	21:1	

YOUR SON LIVES

43 And after the two days
    He went forth from there into GALILEE.
44   For JESUS HIMSELF testified,
    that A PROPHET has no honor
      in his own country.
45 So when He came to GALILEE,
    the GALILEANS received Him,
  having seen all the things that He did
    in JERUSALEM at THE FEAST;
  for they themselves also went to THE FEAST.

46 He came therefore again to CANA of GALILEE
    where He had made the water wine.
  And there was a certain royal official,
    whose son was sick at CAPERNAUM.
47 When he heard
  that JESUS had come out of JUDEA into GALILEE
  he
    (1) went to Him, and
    (2) was requesting Him to come down
        and HEAL HIS SON;
      for he was at the point of death.
48 JESUS therefore said to him,
  "Unless YOU PEOPLE
    see signs and wonders,
    you simply WILL NOT BELIEVE."
49 The royal official said to Him,
  "Sir, COME DOWN
    before my child dies."
50 JESUS said unto him,
  "Go your way;   ▷ YOUR SON LIVES."
  The man BELIEVED THE WORD
    that JESUS spoke to him,
  and he started off.

51 And as he was now going down,
    his slaves met him,
    saying that HIS SON WAS LIVING.
52 So he inquired of them
    the hour when he began to get better.
    They said therefore to him,
  "Yesterday at the seventh hour the fever left him."
53 So the father knew
    that it was at that hour
    in which JESUS said to him,
      ▷ "YOUR SON LIVES";
  and he himself BELIEVED,
  and his whole household.

54 This is again a SECOND SIGN
    that JESUS performed,
  when He had come out of JUDEA into GALILEE.

(margin labels: GALILEE · CANA · CAPERNAUM)

Key Words and Phrases

4:44 "no honor" _____

   45 _____

   47 _____

   48 _____

   50 _____

   52 _____

   53 _____

   54 _____

others: _____

OBSERVATIONS

Segment Survey

1. The segment contains four paragraphs, determined by the action in them. How does the last verse identify what the segment is about?

_____

2. Observe the geographical movement in the first three paragraphs.

3. Where is a direct reference to the water-wine miracle of Cana? Where is an indirect reference?

_____

4. Try making your own outline of the general content of these three paragraphs:

    4:43-45 _____

    4:46-50 _____

    4:51-53 _____

Paragraph Analysis

4:43-45

1. Before studying the paragraph, make the following revisions (see INTERPRETATIONS):

    "Now" in place of "For" (verse 44); also regard all of verse 44 as a parenthesis (NIV).

    Omit "So" in verse 45, and begin the verse with "When" (NIV).

2. What was the normal pattern of Galilean reaction to Jesus, according to verse 44?

_____

Do you think such honoring (verse 44) is the same as *receiving* (verse 45)? If so, what problem arises about interpreting this paragraph?

_____

_____

4:46-50

1. Relate verse 48 to verse 45.

_____

_____

2. Jesus has in mind two kinds of believing. One is believing *after* seeing. What is the other kind?

_____

_____

What kind did the father have, according to the text?_____

3. How did the father demonstrate his faith after Jesus spoke the words, "Your son lives"?

_____

_____

4:51-53
1. Why did the father inquire about the *time* the son began to get better?

2. Compare "he himself believed" (verse 53) with the earlier "the man believed" (verse 50).

_____

_____

_____

_____

Related Verses

Daniel 6:27 _____

_____

Matthew 13:53-58 _____

_____

Mark 9:22-24_____

_____

John 2:1-9_____

_____

John 2:1-9_____

_____

Acts 2:22-24 _____

_____

Acts 2:39_____

_____

Acts 11:14_____

_____

INTERPRETATIONS

1. "No honor in his own country" (4:44). Some interpret "his own country" as Judea, because that was the land of His birth. This author chooses the interpretation of Galilee, based on Matthew 13:53-58. Jesus went to Galilee without having a concern for premature confrontation with His opponents (Pharisees) over His popular program. The Galileans would *receive* Him, but they would not hail Him as Messiah (cf. 4:48; 6:41; 6:66).
2. What kind of faith is this: "I will believe in Jesus if I see signs and wonders performed by Jesus" (cf. 4:48)?

_____

Did the father have faith *before* he had any

indication from Jesus of a healing?

If so, what kind of faith was that, compared to Jesus' words of verse 48?

_____

_____

3. "His whole household" (4:53). This would include the mother, servants, the healed son, and any other children. What does this tell you about how much the father spread the news of this wonderful miracle?_____

_____

_____

_____

APPLICATIONS

1. What does this passage teach you about different kinds of belief?

_____

In thinking about this, review the key verse of John 20:31, observing why John was inspired to include miraculous signs in his gospel account.

_____

_____

_____

_____

2. When you approach an unbeliever about the message of salvation, what do you identify as the object of belief for salvation? Discuss this with your group. (TBS#7)

_____

_____

_____

_____

Summary of Passage

When Jesus arrives in Galilee, He is warmly received by all who have seen His works in Jerusalem. A royal official from Capernaum finds Jesus at Cana, and pleads with him to come and heal his son, who is at the point of death. Jesus sees in the man's heart genuine faith, and says, "Your son lives." The man hastens home, and finds that his son had been healed at the very hour when Jesus had said those dramatic words.

Memory Verse   4:50

Looking Ahead

Jesus is back in Jerusalem. He begins a new period of His ministry in which He faces conflicts and false charges.

YEARS of CONFLICT
5:1–12:36a

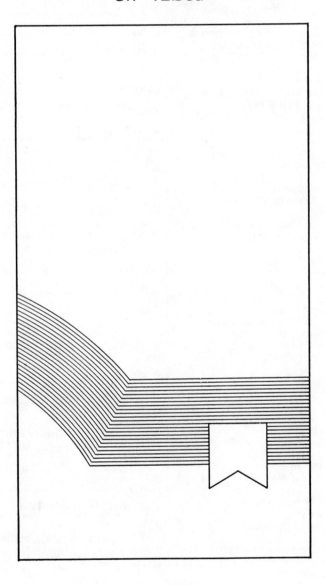

SETTING John skips over some of the ministry of Jesus in Galilee, and picks up the story at Jerusalem, with an unnamed feast of the Jews —possibly the annual Passover (April, A.D. 28). Observe on the survey chart that 5:1 begins the YEARS OF CONFLICT (about two years).

Book of John: LIFE IN JESUS, THE SON OF GOD

P R O L O G U E	SIGNS WROUGHT			SELF REVEALED		E P I L O G U E 21: 25
	PUBLIC MINISTRY -3 YEARS-		(GREAT) (PAUSE) ▶	PRIVATE MINISTRY -FEW DAYS-		
	ERA OF INCARNATION BEGINS	YEARS OF CONFLICT	DAY OF PREPARATION	HOUR OF SACRIFICE	DAWN OF VICTORY	
1:1	1:19	5:1	12:36b	18:1	20:1	21:1

ARISE AND WALK

1 After these things there was a FEAST of the JEWS,
       and JESUS went up to JERUSALEM.
2 Now there is in JERUSALEM
    by the sheep gate a **pool**,
      which is called in Hebrew BETHESDA,
           having five porticoes.
3 In these lay a **multitude**
    of those who were **sick**, **blind**, **lame**, and **withered**,
      waiting for the **moving** of the **waters**;
4 for an **angel** of the **LORD** went down
    at **certain** seasons into the **pool**,
    and **stirred up** the water;
whoever then **first**, after the **stirring up** of the water,
      stepped in was MADE WELL
    from **whatever disease** with which he was afflicted.

WAITING

5 And a **certain man** was there,
    who had been thirty-eight years **in his sickness**.
6 When JESUS saw him lying there,
    and knew that he had already been
      a **long time** in **that condition**,
He said to him, "Do you **wish** to GET WELL?"
7 The sick man answered Him,
    "Sir, I have no man to put me into the **pool**
      when the water is **stirred up**,
    but while I am coming,
       another steps down **before** me."
8 JESUS said to him,
    "ARISE, TAKE UP your pallet, and WALK."
9a And **immediately** the man became well,
    and TOOK UP his pallet and began to WALK.

WALKING

9b Now it was the SABBATH on that day.
10   Therefore the JEWS were saying
       to him who was CURED,
    "It is the SABBATH,
    and it is **not permissible**
         for you to carry your pallet."
11 But he answered them,
    "He who **made me well**
      was the one who said to me,
       'TAKE UP your pallet, and WALK.'"
12 They asked him,
    "Who is **the man** who said to you,
      'TAKE UP your pallet, and WALK'?"
13 But he who was **healed**
       DID NOT KNOW who it was;
    for JESUS had slipped away
      while there was a crowd in that place.

WONDERING

14 Afterward **JESUS found him** in the TEMPLE,
    and said to him,
    "BEHOLD, you have **become well**;
    do not SIN anymore,
      so that **nothing worse** may befall you."
15 The man went away,
    and told the JEWS
      that IT WAS JESUS
        who had **made him well**.

WITNESSING

Key Words and Phrases

5:3 _____ "waiting" _____

4 _____

5 _____

6 _____

7 _____

8 _____

9b _____

12 _____

others: _____

OBSERVATIONS

Segment Survey

1. Who is the key character of the narrative, other than Jesus?_____
How much does the segment reveal about him?
_____
_____

2. What is the main point of each of the four paragraphs?
    5:1-4_____
    5:5-9a_____
    5:9b-13 _____
    5:14,15_____

3. How is Jesus the central person in each of these paragraphs?
    5:5-9a_____
    5:9b-13 _____
    5:14,15_____

4. Justify the outline shown: WAITING, WALKING, WONDERING, WITNESSING.
_____
_____

Paragraph Analysis

5:1-4

1. This paragraph describes the setting of the story. Record what John writes about each of these.
    time and place: _____
_____
    characters: _____
_____
    action: _____
_____

2. How does the word "waiting" (verse 3) represent an atmosphere of the paragraph?

_____

5:5-9a
1. Compare the time references of verse 5 and verse 9a._____

2. Did the man know who Jesus was? (Cf. verse 13.)_____
What kind of an answer did he give Jesus?

_____

How would the previous 38 years explain why he answered that way?

_____

3. Does the text say that the man had faith?

_____

4. What *two* miracles are involved in verse 9a?

_____

5:9b-13
1. How did the man defend carrying his pallet on the Sabbath?_____

2. Why do you think Jesus "had slipped away" (verse 13)?_____

5:14,15
Jesus revealed Himself to the man, and left a command with him. What was the man's response? _____

Related Verses

Nehemiah 3:1_____

_____

Nehemiah 13:15-19 _____

_____

Jeremiah 17:19-27_____

_____

Matthew 9:6_____

_____

Matthew 12:1-8_____

_____

Mark 2:5-12 _____

_____

John 8:11_____

_____

John 9:13ff. _____

_____

INTERPRETATIONS

1. "Pallet" (5:8). This was a thin mattress, like a camp-bed.
2. "Immediately the man became well" (5:9a).

John emphasizes that the miracle happened all at once, by using the word "immediately." The word seldom appears in the gospel. (See 6:21 and 18:27.) What does this teach about Jesus' miracle power?_____

3. "The Jews" (5:10). These were religious leaders of the Jews (cf. 1:19).
4. "Not permissible for you to carry your pallet" (5:10). The prohibition of such passages as Exodus 20:10 and Jeremiah 17:19-27 applied to situations involving labor for gain, such as trading and marketing. According to the Jews' extra-canonical Mishnah, a pallet could be carried only if it had a person on it. Do you think these Jewish objectors were faulting the man, or Jesus? Explain.

_____

_____

5. Was faith involved in this healing? If so, discuss with your group why the word "faith" or "believe" does not appear in the account.
6. "So that nothing worse may befall you" (5:14). Jesus did not say what this recompense was—the worst recompense for anyone is eternal hell. Jesus did indicate that the man's spiritual well-being was more important than his physical wholeness.
7. John records just one verse (verse 14) of spiritual instruction by Jesus. Do you think Jesus spoke more to the man? _____

APPLICATIONS

1. Everyone has needs, including physical, material, spiritual, and social needs. When you are witnessing to an unsaved person, how can you lead the conversation from lesser needs to eternal needs? Discuss this in your group. (TBS#7)
2. Who should be the central person in all our Christian witnessing? Observe how John concludes this segment: "The man went away, and told the Jews that IT WAS JESUS WHO HAD MADE HIM WELL" (5:15).

Summary of Passage

At the pool of Bethesda in Jerusalem Jesus instantly heals a man with a 38-year affliction. The man takes up his pallet and walks. This happens on a Sabbath, and Jewish opponents of Jesus object that the law does not allow the man to carry his pallet on the Sabbath. The man replies that his healer told him to do this. He does not know it was Jesus, but some time after, Jesus identifies Himself and talks with the man about his soul. Then the man tells the Jews that it was Jesus who had healed him.

Memory Verse   5:15

Looking Ahead

The Jewish leaders try to kill Jesus for breaking the Sabbath and claiming equality with God.

SETTING Jesus is still in Jerusalem, and the Jewish leaders are trying to kill Him. He uses the confrontation as an opportunity to teach them about Himself and His mission.

Book of John: LIFE IN JESUS, THE SON OF GOD

P R O L O G U E	SIGNS WROUGHT		SELF REVEALED		E P I L O G U E 21: 25
	PUBLIC MINISTRY -3 YEARS-	(GREAT) (PAUSE) ▶	PRIVATE MINISTRY -FEW DAYS-		
	ERA OF INCARNATION BEGINS	YEARS OF CONFLICT	DAY OF PREPARATION	HOUR OF SACRIFICE	DAWN OF VICTORY
1:1	1:19	5:1	12:36b	18:1	20:1	21:1

THE GIFT OF LIFE

16 And for this reason
　the JEWS were **persecuting** JESUS,
　　because He was doing these things on the SABBATH.
17 But He answered them,
　　　"MY FATHER is **working** until now, ◀
　　and I MYSELF am **working**."
18 For this cause therefore
　the JEWS were **seeking all the more** to KILL HIM,
　because He
　　not only was **breaking the SABBATH**,
　　but also was calling GOD HIS OWN FATHER,
　　　making Himself **equal with God**.

JEWS & JESUS

19 JESUS therefore answered and was saying to them,
　　"**Truly, truly**, I say to you,
　　the SON can do **nothing of Himself**,
　unless it is something He sees the FATHER doing;
　　for **whatever** the FATHER does,
　　these things the SON also does in like manner.
20 "For THE FATHER LOVES THE SON,
　　and shows Him all things
　　　that He Himself is doing;
　and **greater works** than these will He show Him,
　　　　that you may **marvel**.
21 "For just as the FATHER **raises the dead**
　　　　　　and **gives them LIFE**,
　even so the SON also gives LIFE
　　　　　　to whom He wishes.
22 "For not even the FATHER **judges** anyone,
　but He has given **all judgment** to the SON,
23 in order that **all** may HONOR THE SON,
　　　even as they HONOR THE FATHER.
　He who does not **honor** the SON
　　does not **honor** the FATHER who **sent** Him.
24 "**Truly, truly**, I say to you,
　he who
　　(1) **hears My word**, and
　　(2) BELIEVES HIM who sent ME,
　HAS ETERNAL LIFE,
　　and does not come into **judgment**,
　　but has passed **out** of DEATH **into** LIFE.

FATHER & SON

25 "**Truly, truly**, I say to you,
　an hour is coming and **now is**,
　when the dead shall hear the **voice**
　　　　　　of THE SON OF GOD;
　and those who hear shall LIVE.
26 "For just as the FATHER has LIFE in HIMSELF,
　　even so He gave to the SON also
　　　to have LIFE in HIMSELF;
27 and He gave Him **authority** to **execute judgment**,
　　because He is THE SON OF MAN.
28 "**Do not marvel** at this;
　for an hour is coming,
　　in which all who are in the tombs
　　　(1) shall **hear His voice**, and
29　　(2) shall **come forth**;
　those who did the **good deeds**,
　　　to a RESURRECTION OF LIFE,
　　　those who committed the **evil deeds**
　　　to a RESURRECTION OF JUDGMENT."

THE EVIL & THE GOOD

Key Words and Phrases

5:16 ___ "persecuting"

17 _____

18 _____

19 _____

20 _____

21 _____

24 _____

27 _____

others: _____

OBSERVATIONS

Segment Survey

1. How does the first paragraph relate to the preceding passage? _____

How does the first paragraph lead into Jesus' discourse that follows, beginning at verse 19? _____

2. Note the outline that shows three groups of two. Which paragraph contains mainly doctrine? _____

Which are the prophetic passages? _____

3. Mark with a pencil on the textual re-creation every reference to life.

Paragraph Analysis

5:16-18

1. Why were the Jews persecuting Jesus? _____

2. Why did they try all the harder to kill Him? _____

3. How did He claim equality with God? _____

5:19-24

1. List the ways the Son is shown to be equal to the Father:

verse 19 _____

verse 20 _____

verse 21 _____

verse 22 _____

verse 23 _____

verse 24 _____

2. How is verse 24 an invitation?

_____

_____

What are the invitation's main ingredients?

_____

_____

_____

5:25-27

1. Who shall hear Jesus' voice: the righteous dead or the unrighteous dead?

_____

2. Jesus is "the Son of God" in verse 25 and "the Son of Man" in verse 27. What work is associated with Him in each reference?

_____

_____

5:28,29

How does this paragraph differ from the preceding one?_____

_____

Related Verses

Genesis 2:2_____

_____

Daniel 7:13,14 _____

_____

Matthew 25:31ff._____

_____

John 3:18,19_____

_____

John 7:30_____

_____

Acts 24:15_____

_____

Revelation 20:4-6_____

_____

INTERPRETATIONS

1. Note the repeated word "working" in 5:17. Do you think Jesus introduced this truth because of what had transpired earlier? _____

Explain._____

_____

2. Did Jesus use the pronouns "I" and "me" in the discourse of verses 19b-23 and 25-29?_____ Why do you think He spoke this way?

_____

_____

How does verse 24 stand out in the middle of the discourse? _____

3. "Not even the Father judges" (5:22). That is, the Father never acts alone in pronouncing judgment. He always works through the Son. See verse 23a for the reason.

4. "Hour...now is" (5:25). Verse 25 describes Jesus' present work in the spiritual realm. Verses 28 and 29 announce the future physical resurrections, "a time is coming" (5:28, NIV).

5. What is the intended contrast between "life" and "judgment" (5:29)?

_____

_____

APPLICATIONS

1. Jesus could not do what He did unless He was who He was. His works depended on His Person. That is why He especially wanted to show that He was the Son of God (cf. 20:31). In your personal witness to an unsaved soul, how do you teach the deity of Jesus? How much importance do you attach to this doctrine? Why?

_____

_____

_____

2. There are only two ultimate destinies: eternal life and eternal death. Discuss with your group how to bring this crucial doctrine into your witness to an unsaved person. (TBS#7).

Summary of Passage

The Jews are persecuting Jesus for healing on the Sabbath, and they try all the harder to kill Him when He claims equality with God. Jesus uses this opportunity to teach His enemies that His Father has given Him the authority and power to do the works the Father does.

Jesus prophesies times of reckoning to come— life for the righteous believer, and death for the unrighteous unbeliever.

Memory Verse   5:25

Looking Ahead

Jesus continues His discourse to the Jewish leaders at Jerusalem.

SETTING This passage concludes Jesus' discourse to the Jewish leaders at Jerusalem who are trying to kill Him because He claims equality with God.

Book of John: LIFE IN JESUS, THE SON OF GOD

P R O L O G U E	SIGNS WROUGHT			SELF REVEALED		E P I L O G U E 21: 25
	PUBLIC MINISTRY -3 YEARS-		(GREAT) (PAUSE) ▶	PRIVATE MINISTRY -FEW DAYS-		
	ERA OF INCARNATION BEGINS	YEARS OF CONFLICT	DAY OF PREPARATION	HOUR OF SACRIFICE	DAWN OF VICTORY	
1:1	1:19	5:1	12:36b	18:1	20:1	21:1

UNWILLING TO COME TO JESUS

30 "I can do nothing on My own initiative.
　　As I **hear**, ⟶ I **judge**;
　　and My judgment is just
　　　　because I do not seek **My own will,**
　　　　but the **will of Him** who sent Me.
31 "If I **ALONE** bear witness of Myself,
　　My testimony is **NOT TRUE.** ◄
32 "There is another who bears witness of Me;
　　and I know that
　　　　the testimony which He bears of Me is **TRUE.** ◄

33 "You have sent to John,
　　and he has borne witness to **the TRUTH.**
34 "But the witness which I receive
　　　　　　　　　is not from man,
　　　but I say these things, that YOU MAY BE SAVED.
35 "He was **the lamp**
　　　that was burning and was **shining**
　　and you were willing
　　　　to REJOICE for awhile **in his light.**

36 "But the witness which I have
　　　is **greater** than that of John;
　　for the **works** which the FATHER has given Me
　　　to **accomplish,**
　　　the **very works** that I do,
　　　　bear witness of ME,
　　　　that the FATHER HAS SENT ME.
37 "And the **FATHER** who **sent Me,**
　　HE has borne witness of Me.
　　You have neither **heard** HIS VOICE at any time,
　　　　nor **seen** HIS FORM.
38 "And you do not have
　　　　HIS WORD **abiding in you,**
　　for you do not BELIEVE HIM
　　　　　whom He sent.
39 "You search THE SCRIPTURES,
　　　because you **think**
　　　that in **them** YOU HAVE ETERNAL LIFE;
　　and it is **these** that bear witness of ME;
40　　and you are **unwilling to come to Me,**
　　　　　that you may HAVE LIFE.

41 "I do not receive **glory from men;**
42　　BUT I KNOW YOU
　　　　that you do not have THE LOVE OF GOD
　　　　　　in yourselves.
43 "I have come in MY FATHER'S NAME,
　　　and you **do not receive** Me;
　　if **another** shall come in his own name,
　　　you will receive **him.**
44 "How can you BELIEVE,
　　　when you receive **glory** from one another,
　　and **you do not seek the glory**
　　　　that is from the ONE AND ONLY GOD?

45 "Do not think
　　　that I will **accuse** you before the FATHER;
　　the one who **accuses** you
　　　is MOSES,
　　　　in whom you have set your HOPE.
46 "For if you BELIEVED MOSES,
　　　you would BELIEVE ME;
　　　for **he wrote of ME.**
47 "But if you do **not** BELIEVE **his** writings,
　　　how will you BELIEVE **My** words?"

(side labels: WITNESSES, GLORY, MOSES)

Key Words and Phrases

5:30 ___ "will of Him"

31 _____

34 _____

36 _____

39 _____

41 _____

44 _____

45 _____

others: _____

OBSERVATIONS

Segment Survey

1. Read the segment a few times, noting the paragraph divisions as you read. Compare the endings of paragraphs 2, 3, 4 and 5.

2. Do you observe in the segment that Jesus gets more intense in His exposure of the Jews, as He moves from point to point? _____
Compare the first paragraph and the last.

_____

_____

3. What is the key word repeated in the first three paragraphs? Underline each appearance of it.

4. For the first three paragraphs, record in the margin what the witness of Jesus is. For example, the witness of verse 36 is Jesus' *works*.

5. The outline shows that the segment has three parts:

　WITNESSES (5:30-40)—The Jews reject the witnesses of Jesus.

　GLORY (5:41-44)—The Jews reject the glory of God.

　MOSES (5:45-47)—The Jews reject the words of Moses and Jesus.

Paragraph Analysis

5:30-32

1. What was Jesus careful not to do (verses 30 and 31)? _____

_____

2. Who is the witness of verse 32?

_____

_____

5:33-35

1. How did Jesus commend John's witness?

_____

_____

How did He qualify that commendation?

_____

_____

2. What is crucial about the phrase "for awhile" (verse 35)?_____

_____

5:36-40
1. What three witnesses did Jesus cite, according to this paragraph?_____

_____

2. Compare the Jews' relationship to the Word:

verse 38_____

verse 39_____

5:41-44
1. Note the appearances of the word "glory" ("praise"—NIV).
2. What was Jesus' diagnosis of why the Jews could not believe in Him?

_____

_____

5:45-47
1. How did Jesus use logic here?

_____

2. Why would a Jew not want to be accused by Moses of anything?

_____

Related Verses

Deuteronomy 18:15-18_____

_____

John 1:35,36_____

_____

John 8:14_____

_____

John 8:19_____

_____

John 12:42,43_____

_____

INTERPRETATIONS
1. "My testimony is not true" (5:31). That is, Jesus' testimony "alone" would not be admissible as legal evidence in the people's court. Corroborating testimony would make a difference. What was the very next supporting witness which Jesus cited (5:32)?

_____

2. John's witness of Jesus (cf. 1:35,36) was true and good. What kinds of witness were even "greater" (5:36) than John the Baptist's?

_____

_____

What did Jesus mean by "greater"? Was He recognizing different degrees of truth?

_____

If not, what?_____

_____

3. "You search the Scriptures" (5:39). The Jews studied their Scriptures, knowing that God speaks about salvation in His Word. But they did not see Jesus in the Book, even though the Scriptures "bear witness of" Him. How does verse 40 explain this darkness of mind and heart?

_____

_____

APPLICATIONS
1. There have always been many voices in the world pointing people to false gods and saviors. The key to finding the one God and Savior is to locate the *true* witness. Truth is the key. When you are talking with a seeking unbeliever, what do you say about true witness, and what true witnesses do you point to as dependable?

_____

_____

_____

2. Jesus wholly knew the hearts and minds of His opponents. That is why He could say the things He said about them (e.g., 5:42-44). Jesus knows all your thoughts, including the innermost ones. How does this affect your living? How *should* it affect your living?

_____

_____

_____

Summary of Passage

Jesus continues His response to the Jewish leaders who have challenged His claim to being God's Son. He cites the witnesses that support that claim: the Father, John the Baptist, His own works, and the Scriptures.

The Jews do not believe Jesus because they reject His witnesses, prefer man's glory to God's, and do not believe Moses' writings.

Memory Verse   5:44

Looking Ahead

John skips over many of Jesus' activities in Galilee (Matthew 12:1–14:12; Mark 2:23–6:30; Luke 6:1—9:10a), and reports a miraculous feeding of thousands of people.

SETTING Jesus and His disciples have withdrawn to a mountain near Bethsaida (Luke 9:10), northeast of the Sea of Galilee. A multitude surrounds them, numbering 5,000 men plus women and children (Matthew 14:21). It is around the end of Jesus' second year of public ministry (cf. John 5:1 and 6:4).

Book of John: LIFE IN JESUS, THE SON OF GOD

P R O L O G U E	SIGNS WROUGHT			SELF REVEALED		E P I 21: L 25 O G U E
	PUBLIC MINISTRY -3 YEARS-		(GREAT) (PAUSE) ▶	PRIVATE MINISTRY -FEW DAYS-		
	ERA OF INCARNATION BEGINS	YEARS OF CONFLICT	DAY OF PREPARATION	HOUR OF SACRIFICE	DAWN OF VICTORY	
1:1	1:19	5:1	12:36b	18:1	20:1	21:1

"THIS IS THE PROPHET!"

1 After these things JESUS **went away**
   to the other side of the Sea of Galilee (or Tiberias).
2 And a GREAT MULTITUDE was following Him,
   because they were **seeing** the SIGNS
     which He was performing on those who were **sick.**
3 And JESUS **went up** on the **mountain,**
   and there He SAT WITH HIS DISCIPLES.
4 Now the PASSOVER,
   the FEAST of the JEWS,
     was at hand.

CURIOUS

5 JESUS therefore **lifting up His eyes,**
   and seeing that
     a GREAT MULTITUDE was coming to Him,
   said to PHILIP,
   "Where are we to buy bread, that these may eat?"
6 And this He was saying to **test** him;
   for He Himself knew what he was intending to do.
7 PHILIP answered Him,
   "Two hundred denarii worth of bread
     is **not sufficient** for them,
   for **every one** to receive a **little.**"
8 One of His disciples,
   ANDREW, Simon Peter's brother,
     said to Him,
9 "There is a lad here,
   who has
     (1) five barley loaves, and
     (2) two fish;
   but what are these for **so many people**?
10 JESUS said,
   "Have the people **sit down.**"
   Now there was **much grass** in the place.
   So the men sat down, in number about five thousand.

HUNGRY

11 JESUS therefore took the **loaves;**
   and having given THANKS,
   He distributed to those who were seated;
     likewise also of the fish as much as they wanted.
12 And when they were FILLED,
   He said to HIS DISCIPLES,
   "Gather up the **left-over fragments**
     that **nothing** may be **lost.**"
13 And so they gathered them up,
   and filled twelve baskets
     with fragments from the five barley loaves,
   which were **left over** by those who had eaten.

FULL

14 When therefore THE PEOPLE saw the SIGN
   which He had performed,
   they said, "This is **of a truth**
     THE PROPHET
      who is to **come into the world.**"
15 JESUS therefore perceiving
   that they were intending
     to come and **take Him by force,**
     to MAKE HIM KING,
   withdrew again to the mountain
      BY HIMSELF ALONE.

AMAZED

Key Words and Phrases

6:2 _____ "seeing the signs" _____
  4 _____
  5 _____
  7 _____
  9 _____
 13 _____
 14 _____
 15 _____
others: _____

OBSERVATIONS

Segment Survey

1. The segment contains four paragraphs, reporting general setting, immediate setting, miracle, and reaction. How would you describe the multitudes in each paragraph?

_____

Compare your answer with the outline shown.

_____

2. What are the last three words of the segment?

_____

Compare this with the remainder of the passage.

_____

Paragraph Analysis

6:1-4

1. Where did Jesus go with His disciples? (See map.)
2. Where did the Jews observe the annual Passover (verse 4; see John 2:13)?

_____

Why do you think John included verse 4 in his reporting? _____

_____

6:5-10

1. Compare the responses of Philip and Andrew.

_____

2. How would you describe the tone of Jesus' question (verse 5) and instruction (verse 10)?

What does this tell you about Jesus?

_____

_____

6:11-13
1. What miracles do you see in this paragraph?

_____

2. Compare Jesus' part and the disciples' part.

_____

_____

6:14,15
1. Note the people's identification of Jesus: "The Prophet." What does this reveal about their

perception?_____

_____

2. Jesus knew their intentions. What was He

trying to avoid? _____

Why?_____

Related Verses

Deuteronomy 18:15,18_____

_____

Matthew 20:2 _____

_____

Mark 6:31-34_____

_____

Mark 6:39,40_____

_____

John 1:20,21_____

_____

John 1:43,44_____

_____

John 6:51_____

_____

John 12:21 _____

_____

John 18:36 _____

_____

INTERPRETATIONS

1. "The Passover was at hand" (6:4). The key event of Passover was the slaying of the lamb (Exodus 12:1-14). In John 6:51, Jesus, the Lamb of God, identifies His flesh—given for the life of the world—as bread. How then may John have been connecting the Passover with this miracle involving bread?

_____

_____

2. "Two hundred denarii" (6:7). One denarius was one day's wage for a laborer. Two hundred denarii could purchase lunch for 5000-6000 people. How many people needed lunch?

_____

3. "Five barley loaves" (6:9). These were small barley-cakes, wholesome food of the masses.
4. "He distributed" (6:11). Read Mark 6:41 to see how Jesus used the disciples for the distribution. Identify the moment of the miracle of

multiplication._____

_____

5. "Intending...to make Him king" (6:15). If the people were beginning to view Jesus as their Messiah, it was a political messiah of Phariseeism. John reports that Jesus perceived their intentions (6:15).

APPLICATIONS

1. The withdrawal of Jesus and the disciples to the mountain, at the beginning of this passage, was for rest. (See Mark 6:31.) What was the purpose of Jesus' withdrawal at the end of the

passage? _____

_____

What did Jesus do in these rest periods (cf.

Matthew 14:23)? _____

_____

2. Why do Christian workers need periods of rest

and prayer?_____

_____

Does it help to plan such periods? _____

If so, why?_____

_____

3. What do you do for spiritual rest and invigoration? How can you improve on this? Discuss this subject with your group.

Summary of Passage

Jesus withdraws with His disciples to a mountain on the other side of the Sea of Galilee to escape the pressure of the mobs. The multitudes want to see more miracles, and they refuse to go home. It is meal time, and they are without food. Jesus has them sit down (5,000 men plus women and children!), and He multiplies a lad's five barley loaves and two fish, distributing more than enough food to everyone. The people are amazed, and want to make Jesus their king. He withdraws to the nearby mountain to be alone.

Memory Verse   6:15

Looking Ahead

Jesus walks on water in the presence of His frightened disciples.

SETTING The disciples are sailing at night to Capernaum when a storm arises. Jesus appears to them, walking on the water, and they immediately reach the shore.

The multitudes who had witnessed the miracle of bread and fish search for Jesus, but cannot find Him.

Book of John: LIFE IN JESUS, THE SON OF GOD

P R O L O G U E	SIGNS WROUGHT			SELF REVEALED		E P I L O G U E 21: 25
	PUBLIC MINISTRY -3 YEARS-		(GREAT) (PAUSE) ▶	PRIVATE MINISTRY -FEW DAYS-		
	ERA OF INCARNATION BEGINS	YEARS OF CONFLICT	DAY OF PREPARATION	HOUR OF SACRIFICE	DAWN OF VICTORY	
1:1	1:19	5:1	12:36b	18:1	20:1	21:1

NO NEED TO FEAR

16 Now when **evening** came,
     HIS DISCIPLES went down to the sea,
17 and after getting into a boat,
     they started to cross the sea to CAPERNAUM.
          And it had already become **DARK**,
          and JESUS had **not yet come to them.**
18 And the sea began to be **STIRRED UP**
     because a **strong wind was blowing.**
19 When therefore they had rowed
          about three or four miles,
     they BEHELD JESUS
          (1) walking on the sea and
          (2) drawing near to the boat;
          and they were **FRIGHTENED.**
20 But He said to them,
     "IT IS I;
     DO NOT BE AFRAID."
21 They were willing therefore
          to **receive Him** into the boat;
     and **immediately** the boat was at the land
          to which they were going.

BEHOLDING JESUS

22 The next day
     the MULTITUDE that stood on the other side of the sea
          saw that there was no other **small boat** there,
               except one,
     and that JESUS had **not** entered
          with HIS DISCIPLES
               into the boat,
     but that HIS DISCIPLES had **gone away alone.**
23 There came other small boats
               from Tiberias
          near to the place where they ate the bread
               after the LORD **had given thanks.**
24 When the MULTITUDE therefore
     saw that JESUS WAS NOT THERE,
          nor HIS DISCIPLES,
     they themselves got into the small boats,
          and came to CAPERNAUM,
          seeking JESUS.

SEEKING JESUS

Key Words and Phrases

6:17 ____ "dark" ____
  18 _____
  19 _____
  19 _____
  20 _____
  21 _____
  24 _____
  24 _____
others: _____
_____

OBSERVATIONS
Segment Survey

1. Read this short segment a few times, observing the differences in its two paragraphs. Record some of those differences.

6:16-21	6:22-24

2. What would you say is the prominent *tone* of the first paragraph? _____
_____

Of the second paragraph? _____
_____

Paragraph Analysis
6:16-21

1. What was the disciples' destination? (See map.)
_____
_____

2. What words describe the fearful setting?
_____
_____

3. How many miracles do you see in the paragraph? _____
_____
_____

4. Why does John insert this statement in verse 17: "and Jesus had not yet come to them"?
_____
_____

5. Was the disciples' fright understandable?
_____

Explain. _____
_____

What was Jesus' formula for allaying their fear?
_____
_____

How did the disciples respond to this?
_____
_____
_____

6:22-24

1. In verse 22, change the phrase "saw that there was" to "realized that there had been."
2. Read the paragraph again, and answer the following questions about the action:

   a. As of this paragraph, when had the feeding of the 5,000 taken place?

   _____

   b. How many boats had brought Jesus and His disciples here?

   _____

   c. When had this boat left for Capernaum?

   _____

   d. Did Jesus go with His disciples?

   _____

   e. What was the "mystery" about Jesus? Where did the people think He was?

   _____

   f. Why does John include verse 23 (see verse 24)?_____

Related Verses

Isaiah 43:1-7 _____

_____

Matthew 14:24_____

_____

Matthew 14:26-32 _____

_____

Matthew 14:33_____

_____

Mark 6:48_____

_____

Mark 6:52_____

_____

INTERPRETATIONS

1. "The sea began to be stirred up" (6:18). The northern part of the Sea of Galilee is exposed to quick weather changes. When a storm comes into the general area, strong winds funnel down the many valleys northwest of the sea, and violently batter the sea. Boating and shipping suddenly become hazardous.
2. "They were frightened (6:19). The disciples saw the Person of God, their Master, and they also witnessed a miracle—Jesus' walking on the water—but they were still frightened. How is this explained by what the disciples did *not* learn from the miracle of the loaves and fish? (See Mark's comments, Mark 6:51,52.)

_____

_____

3. The presence of Jesus should cast out all fear. What verse in our passage in John teaches this?

4. "Seeking Jesus" (6:24). What one thing were the multitudes after?

_____

APPLICATIONS

1. In the first paragraph, Jesus sees the need of the disciples, and He comes to them. Write a list of the spiritual applications you derive from this paragraph. _____

_____

_____

_____

2. In the second paragraph, the people keep looking for Jesus. How can you apply this to personal evangelism? (TBS#7)

_____

_____

_____

_____

_____

_____

_____

_____

_____

_____

Summary of Passage

In the evening the disciples get into a boat to row to Capernaum. A violent storm suddenly comes upon them, stirring up the sea. They see Jesus walking on the water and are terrified. He assures them with the words, "It is I; don't be afraid." Immediately they reach the shore of their destination.

In the meantime the multitudes who had seen the miracle of the loaves keep looking for Jesus, traveling as far as Capernaum in their search.

Memory Verses   6:19,20

Looking Ahead

Jesus teaches the multitudes at Capernaum about the true bread of life.

SETTING The multitudes whom Jesus had fed on the mountain near Bethsaida have now found Him in Capernaum. Jesus uses the opportunity to teach them about the true bread of life.

Book of John: LIFE IN JESUS, THE SON OF GOD

P R O L O G U E	SIGNS WROUGHT		SELF REVEALED			E P I L O G U E
	PUBLIC MINISTRY -3 YEARS-	(GREAT) (PAUSE) ▶	PRIVATE MINISTRY -FEW DAYS-			
	ERA OF INCARNATION BEGINS	YEARS OF CONFLICT	DAY OF PREPARATION	HOUR OF SACRIFICE	DAWN OF VICTORY	21: 25
1:1	1:19	5:1	12:36b	18:1	20:1	21:1

THE BREAD OF LIFE

25 And when they **found Him**
         on the other side of the sea,
     they said to Him,
         "RABBI, when did you get **here?"**
26 JESUS answered them and said,
     "Truly, truly, I say to you,
YOU SEEK ME,
         not **because** you saw SIGNS,
     but **BECAUSE YOU** ATE of the loaves,
         and WERE FILLED.
27 "Do **not** work for the **food which perishes,**
     but for the food which ENDURES
                         TO ETERNAL LIFE,
     which the SON OF MAN shall give to you,
     for on HIM the FATHER, even GOD,
                         HAS SET HIS SEAL."

IMPERISHABLE FOOD

28 They said therefore to Him,
     "What shall we **do,**
         that we may **work** the **works of God?"**
29 JESUS answered and said to them,
     "This is the **work of God,**
         that you **BELIEVE IN HIM**
                 whom **He has sent."**
30 They said therefore to Him,
     "What then do YOU do for a SIGN,
         that we may SEE, and BELIEVE You?
     What **work** do you **perform?**
31 "Our fathers ate the **manna in the wilderness;**
     as it is written,
     'He gave them bread OUT OF HEAVEN to eat.'"
                         [Exodus 16:4; Psalm 78:24]
32 JESUS therefore said to them,
     "**Truly, truly,** I say to you,
         it is not Moses
     who has given you the bread out of HEAVEN,
         but it is MY FATHER
     who gives you the TRUE BREAD out of HEAVEN.
33 "For the BREAD OF GOD
         is that which comes down out of HEAVEN,
         and gives LIFE TO THE WORLD."
34 They said therefore to Him,
     "LORD, evermore **give us** THIS BREAD."

BREAD FROM HEAVEN

35 JESUS said to them,
     "I AM THE BREAD OF LIFE;
     he who **comes to Me** shall **not hunger,**
     and he who **believes in Me** shall **never thirst.**
36 "But I said to you,
     that you **have** seen Me, and **yet** do **not believe.**
37 "All that the FATHER gives Me shall come to Me;
     and the one who **comes to Me**
                 I will **certainly** not cast out.
38 "For I have come down from HEAVEN,
         not to do **My own will**
         but the will of Him who **sent Me.**
39 "And this is the will of Him who **sent Me,**
     that of all that He has given Me
     I lose nothing, but RAISE IT UP **on the last day.**
40 "For this is the will of My FATHER,
     that everyone who
         (1) **beholds** the SON and
         (2) **believes** in HIM,
     may have ETERNAL LIFE;
     and I Myself will RAISE HIM UP **on the last day."**

JESUS IS THE BREAD

Key Words and Phrases

6:26 _____ "you seek Me" _____

27 _____

27 _____

28 _____

29 _____

33 _____

35 _____

40 _____

others: _____

OBSERVATIONS

Segment Survey

1. How is the first paragraph the setting for the remainder of the segment?

_____

_____

2. Compare the second and third paragraphs. For example, in which paragraph does Jesus appear in the first person pronouns (I, Me)?

_____

_____

3. Compare the last verse (6:40) with the last verse of the first paragraph (6:27).

_____

_____

Paragraph Analysis

6:25-27

1. Compare the people's question (verse 25) and Jesus' response (verses 26 and 27).

_____

_____

2. How did Jesus move the conversation from the immediate setting to spiritual truth?

_____

_____

3. How did Jesus relate Himself to the Father?

_____

_____

6:28-34

1. In your own words, write down the following:

(1) the people's question _____

(2) Jesus' answer _____

(3) the people's second question _____

_____

(4) Jesus' answer _____

2. What request did the people then make?

_____

Do you think they were thinking of something higher than material provision?

_____

_____

6:35-40

1. What is the will of the Father?

_____

2. What responses are necessary for a person to receive eternal life?

_____

_____

Related Verses

Exodus 16:12-15 _____

_____

Numbers 11:7-9 _____

_____

Nehemiah 9:15 _____

_____

Isaiah 55:1,2 _____

_____

John 5:19ff. _____

_____

1 John 3:23 _____

_____

INTERPRETATIONS

1. "On Him the Father...has set His seal" (6:27). This was the seal of authentication. The Father gave the Son the power and authority to do His works. Read the Father's words at Jesus' baptism, recorded in Mark 1:9-11.

2. "I am the bread of life" (6:35). This is the first of seven great "I AM's" in John. Jesus is the *true* bread which gives true, eternal life. The people were talking about material food for physical life. Jesus was talking about spiritual food for spiritual life.

3. "All that the Father gives Me shall come to Me" (6:37). How does this teach the sovereignty of God in the salvation of a soul?

_____

_____

_____

_____

Read the next phrase, "the one who comes to Me." How does this teach human response and free will?

_____

_____

How are both of these truths brought together in verses 39 and 40?

_____

_____

_____

APPLICATIONS

1. This is a clear passage on the sin of materialism. Observe how Jesus rebuked the people: "You seek Me

NOT because you **saw** signs
BUT because you *ate...and were filled*."

Eating the food meant more than watching Jesus work. Can you identify parts of your life where materialism keeps creeping in, disturbing the priority of Christ above all? Where can you find help in such times of temptation?

_____

_____

_____

_____

_____

2. Discuss with your group the place of the sovereignty of God (e.g., 6:39) and free will of man (e.g., 6:35) in the soul's salvation. Avoid arguments; build on the Bible statements, and thank God for all His truth, whether understood fully or not.

Summary of Passage

The multitudes finally find Jesus at Capernaum, and ask Him when He got there. Jesus rebukes them because their interest in Him is over what material things they can get from Him, not over who He is or what miracles He has performed. He uses the opportunity to preach the evangel to them. "I am the true bread sent by my Father from heaven, to give eternal life to all who believe in Me. He whom the Father gives Me shall come to Me, and whoever comes to Me I will never drive away."

Memory Verse   6:27

Looking Ahead

The Jews react to Jesus' teaching about the bread of life, and He expands on the subject.

SETTING The Jewish leaders murmur and argue about what Jesus has already spoken. He expands on the subject in the synagogue at Capernaum.

Book of John: LIFE IN JESUS, THE SON OF GOD

P R O L O G U E	SIGNS WROUGHT			SELF REVEALED		E P I L O G U E 21: 25
	PUBLIC MINISTRY -3 YEARS-		(GREAT) (PAUSE) ▶	PRIVATE MINISTRY -FEW DAYS-		
	ERA OF INCARNATION BEGINS	YEARS OF CONFLICT	DAY OF PREPARATION	HOUR OF SACRIFICE	DAWN OF VICTORY	
1:1	1:19	5:1	12:36b	18:1	20:1	21:1

COME TO ME

41 The JEWS therefore were **grumbling** about Him,
    because He said,
        "I AM THE BREAD that came down out of
HEAVEN."
42 And they were saying,
    "Is not this JESUS, the son of JOSEPH,
        whose father and mother we know?
    How does He now say,
        'I have come down out of HEAVEN'?"
43 JESUS answered and said to them,
    "Do not **grumble** among yourselves.
44 "No one can **come to Me,**
    unless the FATHER who sent Me DRAWS him;
    and I will RAISE HIM UP on the **last day.**
45 "It is written in the prophets,
    'And they shall all be TAUGHT OF GOD.'
                       [Isaiah 54:13]
    Everyone who has **heard** and **learned**
        from the FATHER,
            COMES TO ME.
46 "Not that **any man** has **seen** the FATHER,
    except the ONE who is from GOD;
        HE has seen the FATHER.

COME

47 "**Truly, truly,** I say to you,
    he who BELIEVES has ETERNAL LIFE.
48 "I AM THE BREAD OF LIFE.
49 "Your fathers ate the MANNA
        in the wilderness,
        and they DIED.
50 "This is the BREAD
    which comes down out of HEAVEN;
    so that one may **eat of it** and not die.
51 "I AM THE LIVING BREAD
    that came down out of HEAVEN;
    if any one eats of this bread, he shall LIVE FOREVER;
    and the **bread** also which I **shall give**
        for the **life of the world**
        is MY FLESH."

BELIEVE

52 THE JEWS therefore began to **argue**
                with one another,
    saying, "How can THIS MAN give us HIS FLESH
                  to eat?"
53 JESUS therefore said to them,
    "**Truly, truly,** I say to you,
    unless you
        (1) **eat the flesh** of the SON OF MAN and
        (2) **drink His blood,**
    you have **no** LIFE in yourselves.
54 "He who **eats My flesh** and **drinks My blood**
        (1) has ETERNAL LIFE, and
        (2) I will RAISE HIM UP **on the last day.**
55 "For
        (1) My flesh is **true** food, and
        (2) My blood is **true** drink.
56 "He who **eats My flesh** and **drinks My blood**
        (1) **abides in Me,** and
        (2) **I in him.**
57 "As the LIVING FATHER **sent** Me,
        and I **live** because of the FATHER;
    so he who eats Me,
        he also shall **live** because of Me.
58 "This is the BREAD
    which came down out of HEAVEN;
    not as the fathers ate, and died;

EAT

    he who eats this BREAD shall live FOREVER."
59 These things He said in the SYNAGOGUE,
    as He taught in CAPERNAUM.

Key Words and Phrases

6:41   "grumbling" _____

  42 _____

  44 _____

  46 _____

  48 _____

  51 _____

  53 _____

  57 _____

others: _____

OBSERVATIONS

Segment Survey

1. The first two paragraphs report the outcome of the Jews' grumbling (6:41). What outcome does the last paragraph report?

_____

_____

2. Observe in the Bible text how "come" and "eat" are key repeated words of the first and last paragraphs.

3. The segment opens with a reference to Jesus' claim, "I am the bread." How does the segment conclude with an invitation concerning this bread? _____

_____

_____

Paragraph Analysis

6:41-46

1. Note again the various appearances in the paragraph of the word "come" (and its corollaries). What two comings are involved?

_____

_____

2. How many fathers are mentioned? _____

Compare the two with reference to Jesus.

_____

_____

3. How did Jesus turn attention from Himself and direct it to the prophets and to the Father (verses 44-46)? _____

Why did He do this? _____

_____

_____

_____

6:47-51

1. Note that every verse has a reference to life or death, or both. How does this identify the main theme of the paragraph?

_____

_____

2. This is the only place in the entire segment where the word "believes" appears. Why is it a key word at this location in view of the surrounding verses? _____

_____

_____

6:52-58,59

1. What word of the preceding paragraph leads into this paragraph?

_____

2. What are repeated key words of the paragraph?

_____

_____

3. What did Jesus intend by the phrases, "eat My flesh" and "drink My blood"?

_____

_____

4. How does verse 59 explain the extended length of Jesus' discourse?

_____

_____

Related Verses

Leviticus 17:10-14 _____

_____

Mark 6:2,3 _____

_____

Luke 22:14-23 _____

_____

John 1:18 _____

_____

1 Corinthians 11:23-26 _____

_____

Galatians 2:20 _____

_____

Ephesians 5:2 _____

_____

INTERPRETATIONS

1. "'They shall all be taught of God'" (6:45). The taught ones are those who listen to the Father and learn from Him, and, responding in faith, come to Jesus. Why do you think Jesus added the

words of verse 46 after verse 45? In answering this, compare the words "heard," "learned," and "seen." _____

_____

2. "My flesh" (6:51). Jesus is prophesying that He would be giving His life as a sacrifice "for the life of the world."

3. "Eats My flesh and drinks My blood" (6:54). This is intended as symbolic participation in the sacrificial death and sustaining life of Jesus. This signifies eternal life and a day-by-day, abiding life. Compare John 6:56 with Galatians 2:20.

APPLICATIONS

1. What does this passage teach about Jesus' authority? Why is this an important truth in presenting a Christian witness to an unbeliever? (TBS#7) _____

_____

_____

_____

_____

2. What is the abiding life (6:56)? What does Jesus say about it in this passage, directly or indirectly? _____

_____

_____

_____

_____

_____

Discuss this with your group. (TBS#2)

Summary of Passage

In the synagogue at Capernaum the Jews charge the Galilean, Jesus, with falsehood for claiming to have come from heaven. Jesus says He is the true bread from heaven, sent here by the Father, with the invitation to true seekers to come to Him and believe. His last words of the discourse are, "he who eats this bread shall live forever."

Memory Verse   6:56

Looking Ahead

Some of the larger group of Jesus' disciples withdraw from Him.

SETTING Jesus has finished His discourse to the Jews in the synagogue at Capernaum. Some of His disciples share their reactions with Him.

Book of John: LIFE IN JESUS, THE SON OF GOD

P R O L O G U E	SIGNS WROUGHT		SELF REVEALED			E P I L O G U E
	PUBLIC MINISTRY -3 YEARS-		(GREAT) (PAUSE) ▶	PRIVATE MINISTRY -FEW DAYS-		21 25
	ERA OF INCARNATION BEGINS	YEARS OF CONFLICT	DAY OF PREPARATION	HOUR OF SACRIFICE	DAWN OF VICTORY	
1:1	1:19	5:1	12:36b	18:1	20:1	21:1

WALKING WITH JESUS

60 Many therefore of HIS DISCIPLES,
　　　　when they heard this,
　said, "This is a **difficult statement**;
　　who can **listen** to it?"
61 BUT JESUS,
　conscious that HIS DISCIPLES **grumbled** at this,
　said to them,
　　"Does this cause you to **stumble**?
62 "What then if you should BEHOLD
　　THE SON OF MAN
　　　ascending where He was before?
63 "It is THE SPIRIT who gives LIFE;
　　the flesh profits **nothing**;
　　the words that I have spoken to you
　　　(1) are spirit and
　　　(2) are life.
64　"But there are some of you who do **not** BELIEVE."
　　For JESUS knew from the beginning
　　　(1) who they were who did **not** BELIEVE, and
　　　(2) who it was that would **betray** Him.
65　　And He was saying,
　　"For this reason I have said to you,
　　　that no one can come to Me,
　　　unless it has been **granted him** from the
FATHER."
66 As a result of this,
　　　MANY OF HIS DISCIPLES **withdrew**,
　　and were **not walking with Him**
　　　　　　　　anymore.

DEFECTORS

67 JESUS said therefore to THE TWELVE,
　　"You do not want to go away **also**,
　　　　DO YOU?"
68 SIMON PETER answered Him,
　　"LORD, to whom shall we go?
　　　You have the words of ETERNAL LIFE.
69 "And we
　　(1) have BELIEVED and
　　(2) have come to KNOW
　　that You are THE HOLY ONE OF GOD."

FOLLOWERS

70 JESUS answered them,
　　"Did I Myself not **choose** you, THE TWELVE,
　　　and yet **one** of you is a **devil**?"
71 Now He meant
　　　JUDAS the son of Simon Iscariot,
　　for he,
　　　one of THE TWELVE,
　　　was going to **betray Him**.

BETRAYER

Key Words and Phrases

6:60　"difficult" _____

61 _____

62 _____

63 _____

64 _____

66 _____

69 _____

71 _____

others: _____

OBSERVATIONS

Segment Survey

1. Read the three paragraphs. How many disciples (followers) are in view in each paragraph?
_____

2. Compare the defectors and the betrayer.
_____
_____
_____
_____

Paragraph Analysis

6:60-66

1. Who are the disciples in verse 60, compared with "the twelve" in verse 67?
_____
_____

2. What were the disciples referring to by the words, "This is a difficult statement" (verse 60)?
_____
_____

3. What is the force of verse 62? Read it aloud the way you think Jesus spoke it. (NIV punctuates the sentence with an exclamation point.)

4. How is verse 63 Jesus' commentary on the discourse which He just delivered?
_____
_____

5. How do verses 61-63 lead into 64ff. by the connective "But"? _____
_____
_____

6. Observe the progression in the remainder of the paragraph, noticing how it is built around the connectives, "For," "For this reason," and "As a result of this."

6:67-69

1. What is the key word of Jesus' question (verse 67)? _____

2. Peter spoke for the twelve disciples. What do you learn about them, from verses 68 and 69?
_____
_____
_____
_____

6:70,71

Why do you think Jesus shared this truth about Judas at this time?_____
Relate it to what Peter had just said.

_____

_____

Related Verses

Psalm 71:22 _____

_____

Isaiah 1:4_____

_____

Matthew 14:33_____

_____

Matthew 16:16_____

_____

Mark 1:24_____

_____

John 1:13_____

_____

John 13:2_____

_____

INTERPRETATIONS

1. Read the passage again and observe the statements that indicate Jesus' supernatural knowledge of the hearts of men.

_____

_____

2. What did Jesus mean when He said that His words were spirit and life (6:63)?

_____

_____

3. What do verses 64 and 65 teach about God's foreknowledge?_____

_____

_____

4. "The twelve" (6:67). In most instances hereafter, John's references to "disciples" are to this chosen group of twelve. (Cf. 7:3 and 8:31.)
5. "One of you is a devil" (6:70). The word translated "devil" means literally *slanderer, false accuser*. Judas would be an instrument of Satan to deliver up Jesus to the enemy. When Jesus chose the twelve, was Judas already planning betrayal?_____
What does this tell you about Satan's power?

_____

_____

APPLICATIONS

1. This passage teaches much about what's involved in being a true disciple of Jesus (for example, disciples *walk with* Jesus). Make a list of the things you learn about being a disciple from the passage. Also measure your own spiritual condition as a disciple, and determine ways to improve.

_____

_____

_____

_____

_____

_____

_____

_____

_____

2. Where does the word "know" appear in the passage? _____
How important are assurance and conviction in the Christian life? Why?

_____

_____

_____

_____

_____

_____

_____

Summary of Passage

Many of those who have been following Jesus murmur over what He has taught about eating His flesh and drinking His blood. They cannot understand it because they do not believe. And so they withdraw, and do not walk with Jesus anymore.

Jesus asks the twelve chosen disciples if they will also go away. Peter, their spokesman, declares loyalty, saying that they believe and know Him to be the Holy One of God. Jesus responds with the shocking words, "Yet one of you is a devil."

Memory Verse   6:66

Looking Ahead

John skips over more ministries of Jesus in Galilee, and picks up the story in Jerusalem, at the Feast of Tabernacles.

SETTING John uses one verse (7:1) to summarize further ministries Jesus performed in Galilee (cf. Matthew 15:1—18:35; Mark 7:1—9:50; Luke 9:18-50). Then John picks up the story when Jesus makes a secret visit to Jerusalem during the Feast of Tabernacles.

Book of John: LIFE IN JESUS, THE SON OF GOD

P R O L O G U E	SIGNS WROUGHT			SELF REVEALED		E P I L O G U E 21: 25
	PUBLIC MINISTRY -3 YEARS-		(GREAT) (PAUSE) ▶	PRIVATE MINISTRY -FEW DAYS-		
	ERA OF INCARNATION BEGINS	YEARS OF CONFLICT	DAY OF PREPARATION	HOUR OF SACRIFICE	DAWN OF VICTORY	
1:1	1:19	5:1	12:36b	18:1	20:1	21:1

12 _____

others: _____

MY TIME IS STILL FUTURE

—transition—

1 And after these things
      JESUS was **walking** in GALILEE;
    for He was unwilling to **walk** in JUDEA,
      because the JEWS were seeking to KILL HIM.

2 Now the FEAST of the JEWS,
      the FEAST of BOOTHS,
        was **at hand.**
3 HIS BROTHERS therefore said to Him,
      "Depart from here,
        and go into JUDEA,
    that YOUR DISCIPLES also
      may BEHOLD Your **WORKS** which You are doing.

SHOW YOURSELF

4 "For no one does anything in **secret,**
    when he himself seeks to be known **publicly.**
  If You do these things,
      show Yourself to THE WORLD."
5   For not even His brothers
        were BELIEVING IN HIM.

6 JESUS therefore said to them,
    "My time is **not yet** at hand;
  but **your time** is **always opportune.**
7 "The WORLD cannot hate you;
  but it hates Me
    because I testify of it,
      that its **DEEDS are evil.**
8 "Go up to the FEAST yourselves;
  I do not go up to this FEAST [yet—NIV],
  because
  My time has **not yet fully** come."

NOT YET

9   And having said these things to them,
    He stayed in GALILEE.

10 But when HIS BROTHERS had gone up
        to the FEAST,
      then HE HIMSELF also went up,
        not publicly
    but as it were, in **secret.**
11 The JEWS therefore
    were **seeking Him** at the FEAST,
    and were saying, "WHERE IS HE?"
12 And there was **much grumbling**
    among the MULTITUDES concerning Him;
    some were saying, "He is A GOOD MAN";
    others were saying, "No, on the contrary,
        He **leads** the MULTITUDE astray."
13   Yet no one was speaking **openly** of Him
      for **fear** of the JEWS.

NOW, IN SECRET

Key Words and Phrases

7:1 _____ "kill Him" _____

2 _____

3 _____

4 _____

5 _____

7 _____

11 _____

OBSERVATIONS
Segment Survey

1. The opening short paragraph summarizes the remainder of Jesus' Galilean ministry, which had begun at John 4:45. At chapter 7, verse 2, John begins to focus on Judea, which is the introduction to the later Judean ministry of Christ (7:10—10:39).
2. Read the three main paragraphs, observing prominent things in each.

Record your observations.

	outline	main persons	places
7:2-5	Show yourself.		
7:6-9	Not yet.		
7:10-13	Now, in secret.		

Paragraph Analysis
7:1
Compare the last half of this verse with verse 3. What are your reactions?

_____

_____

7:2-5
1. What do you learn about Jesus' brothers?

_____

_____

_____

2. Jesus' brothers wanted a certain group to see the works which He had been doing. Identify the group. _____
Why does this request seem strange in view of what the disciples had already seen?

_____

_____

7:6-9
1. Why did Jesus delay His trip to Jerusalem? (Cf. 7:1.) _____

_____

_____

2. Jesus knew the future. So He scheduled His every move according to the divine time table. He told His brothers He was not going up to the Tabernacles Feast *yet* (verse 8). What happened first, before He went up (verse 10)?

Can you think of a reason for this pattern?

_____

_____

7:10-13

1. What are the secretive, hidden aspects of this account? _____

_____

_____

_____

2. Compare the Jews in verse 13 with the Jews in verse 1. _____

_____

Related Verses

Leviticus 23:34-36 _____

_____

Deuteronomy 16:16 _____

_____

Matthew 12:46-49 _____

_____

John 2:3,4 _____

_____

John 7:30 _____

_____

John 9:22 _____

_____

John 20:19 _____

_____

INTERPRETATIONS

1. "Feast of Booths" (7:2). Another name for this annual feast was Feast of Tabernacles. Held in the autumn, after the harvest, it commemorated the wilderness journeys. It lasted for eight days, and was a very joyous time for the people.

2. "Not even His brothers were believing in Him" (7:5). What was John's reaction, in view of his words, "not even"?

_____

_____

_____

3. "My time is not yet at hand" (7:6). Jesus was referring to the time of His sacrifice. He knew what must transpire before His death, and anything that hastened (or delayed) that date was not allowable. He would be going up to the feast (7:8), but not in the way and time suggested by His brothers.

4. "The Jews...were seeking Him" (7:11). These were the Jewish leaders who were mentioned in John 7:1 as having murderous intent. For the time being, Jesus would stay hidden from every-

body (7:10). But, at the right time, He would appear in public again. (Read 7:14.)

APPLICATIONS

Record some spiritual lessons which you learn from this passage on these subjects:

1. Being persecuted for your Christian faith:

_____

_____

2. Being falsely accused regarding your Christian position:

_____

_____

_____

3. Being slighted or rejected by close friends or relatives:

_____

_____

_____

Summary of Passage

At the end of His ministry in Galilee, Jesus is approached by His brothers, who want Him to attend the Feast of Tabernacles at Jerusalem and show everybody what He is doing. Jesus objects, affirming it is not the time to make such a move. To go early would be to hasten His death.

When the right time comes, Jesus travels to Jerusalem, secretly. He hides Himself from the mobs, for everyone wants to see Him.

Memory Verse   7:12

Looking Ahead

Jesus goes up into the Temple and begins to teach the people, unhindered.

SETTING Halfway through the Feast of Tabernacles Jesus goes up to the Temple court and begins to teach the people, including the Jewish leaders. He answers their challenges.

Book of John: LIFE IN JESUS, THE SON OF GOD

P R O L O G U E	SIGNS WROUGHT			SELF REVEALED		E P I L 21: O 25 G U E
	PUBLIC MINISTRY -3 YEARS-		(GREAT) (PAUSE) ▶	PRIVATE MINISTRY -FEW DAYS-		
	ERA OF INCARNATION BEGINS	YEARS OF CONFLICT	DAY OF PREPARATION	HOUR OF SACRIFICE	DAWN OF VICTORY	
1:1	1:19	5:1	12:36b	18:1	20:1	21:1

"WHY KILL ME?"

14 But when it was now the **midst** of the FEAST
    JESUS WENT UP
        INTO THE TEMPLE
           and began to **teach.**
15 The JEWS therefore were **marveling,** saying,
    "How has THIS MAN become **learned,**
        having never been **educated?**"
16 JESUS therefore answered them, and said,
    "**My teaching** is not Mine,
        but His who sent Me.
17 "If ANY MAN is **willing** to do His will,
    he shall **know** of the teaching,
      whether it is OF GOD,
    or whether I speak from Myself.
18 "He who speaks from himself
          seeks **his own glory;**
  but **He** who is seeking
      the **glory** of the one who sent Him,
  He is true,
      and there is no unrighteousness in Him.
19 "Did not MOSES give you the LAW,
  and yet
        none of you **carries out** the LAW?
  Why do you seek to kill Me?"

20 The MULTITUDE answered,
    "You have a **demon!**
    Who seeks to **kill** You?"
21 JESUS answered and said to them,
    "I did one deed,
    and you all **marvel.**
22 "On this account
  MOSES has given you CIRCUMCISION
      (not because it is from MOSES,
      but from the FATHERS);
  and on the SABBATH YOU circumcise a man.
23 "If a man receives circumcision
        on the SABBATH
    that the LAW of MOSES may not be broken,
    are you angry with Me
    because I **made** an **entire** man **well**
        on the SABBATH?
24 "Do not judge according to **appearance,**
    but judge with righteous judgment."

(margin: ONE TRUE SOURCE / ONE GOOD DEED)

Key Words and Phrases

7:14   "began to teach"

15 _____

17 _____

18 _____

19 _____

20 _____

22 _____

24 _____

others: _____

_____

OBSERVATIONS

Segment Survey

1. There are just two paragraphs in this segment. What question concludes the first paragraph?

_____

What question is implied in the last verse of the second paragraph? _____

_____

2. Who challenges Jesus in the first paragraph?

_____

Who challenges Him in the second paragraph?

_____

Distinguish between the two.

_____

_____

Paragraph Analysis

7:14-19

1. Earlier (verse 10), Jesus had hidden Himself from the crowds. Now He appears openly. How can you explain the difference?

_____

_____

2. What impressed the Jewish leaders? What is the tone of their question (verse 15)?

_____

_____

3. What was Jesus quick to do?

_____

What was the reason for this strategy?

_____

_____

4. Jesus offered two tests for the people to apply, to determine if He was teaching the truth. In your own words, what were they?

    verse 17 _____

_____

    verse 18 _____

7:20-24

1. Jesus did one deed, and the crowd marveled (v. 21). *But,* what was the other reaction of the people? _____

2. How did Jesus show the people that their accusation was inconsistent at the least?

_____

_____

_____

3. Compare verses 22 and 19.

_____

_____

Related Verses

Leviticus 12:3 _____

_____

Leviticus 19:15 _____

_____

Isaiah 11:3 _____

_____

Mark 3:22 _____

_____

John 3:10-12 _____

_____

John 5:18 _____

_____

John 5:41 _____

INTERPRETATIONS

1. "Having never been educated" (7:15). Jesus had never been trained in a rabbinical school. The Jews equated formal education with learning. Jesus impressed the Jewish leaders that He *was* learned. How do you think He left that impression?

_____

_____

2. "No unrighteousness in Him" (7:18). Jesus was stressing the absence of *falsehood* in His life. NIV reads, "There is nothing false about Him."
3. "None of you carries out the law" (7:19). How did Jesus take the offensive at this point?

_____

_____

He could do this because He knew their hearts. What commandment were they guilty of breaking in their heart (verse 19)?

_____

_____

4. "Who seeks to kill You?" (7:20). If this was an honest question, those who asked it were not aware of the Jewish leaders' intentions.
5. "From the fathers" (7:22). The rite of circumcision was practiced long before the time of Moses (Genesis 17:9-14,23-27; 21:4).

APPLICATIONS

1. What do you learn from Jesus about doing all things for the glory of God?

_____

Why is such living the best testimony a Christian can give to the world?

_____

_____

_____

2. Make these two appraisals of yourself:

  a. your education _____

_____

  b. your learning _____

What did you learn yesterday?

_____

_____

_____

What do you want to learn today?

_____

_____

_____

_____

_____

_____

Summary of Passage

Halfway through the Feast of Tabernacles Jesus goes up to the Temple and begins to teach the people. The Jewish leaders are amazed at His learning, but they indirectly challenge His authority. Jesus claims that all His teaching is from God, and therefore is true. He rebukes the leaders and the crowds for their hostility and murderous intentions.

Memory Verse   7:17

Looking Ahead

Attempts are made to seize Jesus.

SETTING The setting portrays confusion, mainly in the outer court of the Temple. Jesus' opponents want to seize Him, and various groups express their feelings about Him.

Book of John: LIFE IN JESUS, THE SON OF GOD

P R O L O G U E	SIGNS WROUGHT			SELF REVEALED		E P I L O G U E 21: 25
	PUBLIC MINISTRY -3 YEARS-		(GREAT) (PAUSE) ▶	PRIVATE MINISTRY -FEW DAYS-		
	ERA OF INCARNATION BEGINS	YEARS OF CONFLICT	DAY OF PREPARATION	HOUR OF SACRIFICE	DAWN OF VICTORY	
1:1	1:19	5:1	12:36b	18:1	20:1	21:1

HOUR NOT YET COME

25 Therefore **some** of the PEOPLE OF JERUSALEM
        were saying,
    "Is this not THE MAN
        whom they are seeking to kill?
26 "And look,
        He is speaking **publicly**,
        and they are **saying nothing** to Him.
    The RULERS do not **really know**
        that this is the CHRIST,
            do they?
27 "However, **we** know where THIS MAN is from;
    but whenever THE CHRIST may come,
        no one knows where He is from."
28 JESUS therefore cried out in the TEMPLE,
        teaching and **saying**,
    "You both
        (1) know Me, and
        (2) know where I am from;
    and I have **not come** of Myself,
    but He who **sent** Me is TRUE,
        whom you do not know.
29   "I know Him; because
    I am from Him,
        and He sent Me."

30 They were seeking therefore
                to **seize Him**;
    and NO MAN **laid his hand on Him**,
    because
            HIS HOUR had NOT YET COME.
31 But Many of the MULTITUDE BELIEVED in HIM;
        and they were saying,
    "When the CHRIST shall come,
    He will not perform more SIGNS
        than those which **THIS** MAN has,
    WILL HE?"

32 The PHARISEES heard the MULTITUDE
        muttering these things about Him;
    and the CHIEF PRIESTS
    and the PHARISEES
                sent OFFICERS to seize Him.
33 JESUS therefore said,
    "For a **little while longer**
            I AM WITH YOU,
    then I go to Him who sent Me.
34 "You shall **seek** Me,
    and shall **not find** Me;
        and where I am,
            you cannot come."
35 The JEWS therefore said to one another,
    "Where does **THIS MAN** intend to go
        that we shall **not find** Him?
    He is not intending to go
        to the Dispersion among the GREEKS,
        and **teach** the GREEKS,
    is He?
36 "What is this statement that He said,
    'You will **seek** Me,
    and will **not find** Me;
    and where I am
        you cannot come'?"

(sidebar markings: WHERE I AM FROM / WHAT I AM DOING / WHERE I AM GOING)

Key Words and Phrases

7:25 ___ "seeking to kill" ___

    26 _____

    27 _____

    28 _____

    30 _____

    31 _____

    32 _____

    33 _____

    35 _____

others: _____

OBSERVATIONS

Segment Survey

1. Read the segment, and observe how the middle
   paragraph is different from the surrounding
   ones.
2. Who are the groups mentioned in each
   paragraph? _____
   _____
   _____
   _____

3. Note the outline: WHERE I AM FROM;
   WHERE I AM GOING. Read the paragraphs
   involved, to justify the outline.

Paragraph Analysis

7:25-29

1. What conflicting situation was confusing some
   of the people?

    verse 25b _____

    verse 26a _____

2. Everyone knew that Jesus was from Nazareth
of Galilee (6:42; 7:41). This is probably what the
people meant by the words, "We know where this
man is from" (verse 27; cf. 7:41,42,52). If this is
so, was Jesus' response ("cried out") one of irony:
"So, you [think you] know Me, and know where
I am from!" (7:28)? List the truths He clearly
taught after that response:

_____
_____
_____
_____
_____
_____
_____

7:30,31

1. Compare the two groups in this paragraph.

_____

2. Observe in the paragraph (1) a hindered arrest and (2) a tentative faith. Compare these as to time and divine activity.

_____
_____
_____

3. What kind of faith do you think these people had?_____

7:32-36

1. How did Jesus show the Jewish leaders that He and the Father were in total control of things?

_____

2. Why did the Jews suggest an explanation about a ministry that involved Greeks?

_____
_____

Related Verses

Matthew 11:27_____

_____

Matthew 12:14_____

_____

John 2:4_____

_____

John 8:24_____

_____

John 16:16ff. _____

_____

Acts 1:6,7_____

_____

INTERPRETATIONS

1. "We know where this man is from" (7:27). If the people were talking about the place of Jesus' birth, they meant Bethlehem. See John 7:42.
2. Observe the prominence Jesus gave to His origin—from His Father God. Why did Jesus want everyone to know truly *who* He was?

_____
_____

3. "Many of the multitude believed in Him" (7:31). They probably saw in Jesus no more than a *political* messiah, who would give them things. How is this suggested by what they said, quoted in 7:31?_____

4. "Chief priests and the Pharisees" (7:32). Most of the chief priests were Sadducees, so these rival groups got together on this plot.
5. "A little while longer" (7:33). Jesus knew that in half a year the hour of His death would arrive.

APPLICATIONS

1. What do you learn about Jesus and His Father that can help you in your Christian walk? For example, what does Jesus' intimate fellowship with His Father reveal about His praying to the Father? Read John 17 as you think about this.

_____
_____
_____
_____
_____
_____

2. Jesus knew He was going away soon. And when that time came, He went. Now we await His return to this earth. At the time foreordained by the Father, He shall return. Are you awaiting His coming? How should this expectation affect your Christian living?

_____
_____
_____
_____
_____
_____

Summary of Passage

People are confused over Christ's identity. Most think He is not the true Messiah, but many believe in Him as a political messiah. The Jewish leaders keep trying to kill Him, but no one is able to lay a hand on Him because His hour of sacrifice has not yet come.

Jesus keeps teaching the crowds where He came from and where He is going. "When I'm gone," he says, "you'll seek Me and not find Me."

Memory Verse 7:30

Looking Ahead

On the last day of the Feast, Jesus gives an invitation to the people to follow Him.

SETTING The time is the last day of the feast. John reports Jesus' invitation to the people, various reactions to Him, and conversations of the scribes and Pharisees with the officers and with Nicodemus.

Book of John: LIFE IN JESUS, THE SON OF GOD

P R O L O G U E	SIGNS WROUGHT		SELF REVEALED		E P I L O G U E
	PUBLIC MINISTRY -3 YEARS-	(GREAT) (PAUSE) ►	PRIVATE MINISTRY -FEW DAYS-		
	ERA OF INCARNATION BEGINS	YEARS OF CONFLICT	DAY OF PREPARATION	HOUR OF SACRIFICE	DAWN OF VICTORY	21: 25
1:1	1:19	5:1	12:36b	18:1	20:1	21:1

"COME TO ME"

37 Now on the **last day**,
    the **great day** of the FEAST,
    JESUS stood and **cried out**, saying,
    "If ANY MAN is **thirsty**,
        let him come to Me and drink.
38 "He who BELIEVES IN ME,
    as the Scripture said,
    'From his innermost being
        shall flow **rivers of living water**.'"
                    [Ezekiel 47:1-12; cf. Isaiah 53:1]
39 But this He spoke
    of THE SPIRIT
            whom those who BELIEVED IN HIM
                were to **receive**;
    for THE SPIRIT was not yet **given**,
    because JESUS was not yet **glorified**.

JESUS INVITES

40 Some of the MULTITUDE therefore,
    when they heard these words,
        were saying, "This certainly is THE PROPHET."
41 Others were saying, "This is THE CHRIST."
    Still others were saying, "Surely THE CHRIST is
            not going to come from GALILEE,
                is He?
42 "Has not the Scripture said that
    THE CHRIST COMES
        (1) from the offspring of DAVID, and
        (2) from BETHLEHEM,
            the village where DAVID was?" [Micah 5:2]
43 So there arose a **division** in the MULTITUDE
        because of Him.
44 And **some** of them wanted to seize Him,
    but **no one** laid hands on Him.

CROWD IS DIVIDED

45 The OFFICERS therefore came
        to the CHIEF PRIESTS and PHARISEES,
    and they said to them,
        "Why did you not bring Him?" [See John 7:32.]
46 The OFFICERS answered,
    "Never did a man speak the way THIS MAN speaks."
47 The PHARISEES therefore answered them,
    "You have not also been **led astray**,
        have you?
48 "No one of the RULERS or PHARISEES
    has BELIEVED IN HIM, has he?
49 "But THIS MULTITUDE
        which does **not know** the LAW is **accursed**."
50 NICODEMUS said to them
    (he who came to Him before, being one of **them**),
51 "OUR LAW does not **judge a man**,
    unless
        (1) it first hears from him and
        (2) knows what he is doing, does it?"
52 They answered and said to him,
    "You are not also from GALILEE, are you?
    Search, and
        see that **no** PROPHET arises out of GALILEE."

LEADERS MOCK

Key Words and Phrases

7:37 ___ "come to me and drink"

38 _____

39 _____

40 _____

41 _____

42 _____

46 _____

49 _____

others: _____

OBSERVATIONS

Segment Survey

1. Which is the brightest paragraph of this

segment?_____

Why?_____

_____

2. Compare the second and third paragraphs for likenesses and differences.

_____

_____

_____

_____

Paragraph Analysis

7:37-39

1. What three phrases in verse 37a call attention to the setting's crucial character?

_____

_____

_____

2. How did Jesus speak to these (verses 37b-39):

(a) the soul's need _____

_____

(b) three required responses _____

_____

(c) the blessed outcome _____

7:40-44

1. Compare the three reactions to Jesus' invitation.

_____

_____

_____

_____

2. Of what were some in the crowd ignorant (verse 42)?_____

3. Compare verse 44 and verse 30.

_____

7:45-52

1. What does this paragraph reveal about these:

(a) the officers _____

(b) the Pharisees_____

(c) Nicodemus_____

2. How did the Pharisees indict the multitude?

_____

Related Verses

Deuteronomy 28:15 _____

Isaiah 44:3,4_____

Isaiah 58:11 _____

Micah 5:2_____

Zechariah 14:8_____

John 4:14_____

John 16:7_____

INTERPRETATIONS

1. "If any man is thirsty" (7:37). On each day of the feast, except the last, pouring of water commemorated the Jews' supply of water in the wilderness journeys. Compare John 7:37 with John 4:14. How well does the figure of drinking water for thirst represent the sinner's experience of salvation?_____

Compare the drinking of this water (7:37b) with the flowing of rivers (verse 38). Are other people reached by the latter? If so, how?

_____

When was the Holy Spirit given for this? See Acts 1:8; 2:1ff.

2. "The way this man speaks" (7:46). What kind of speaking do you think impressed the officers?

_____

3. "Our law does not judge a man, unless..." (7:51). What two things about Jesus did Nicodemus say should be examined before judgment is made? _____

APPLICATIONS

1. Read again Jesus' invitation to salvation (7:37,38). If you are not a believer, this invitation is to you, now. If you are a believer, think of some unsaved person to whom you can relay this invitation today.

2. What do you learn about the Holy Spirit from the first paragraph? Discuss this with your group. (TBS#3)

_____

3. False teaching destroys souls. What do you learn about this from this passage?

_____

Summary of Passage

On the last day of the feast, Jesus stands before the crowd and invites them to come to Him and drink of the spiritual water that He offers. The reactions of those in the crowd vary. Some say He is The Prophet; others, that He is the Christ; still others, that He is not the Christ.

The Pharisees rebuke the officers for not arresting Jesus, and one of their number, Nicodemus, reproves them for not giving Jesus a fair hearing.

Memory Verses   7:38,39

Looking Ahead

The scribes and Pharisees bring to Jesus a woman caught in adultery.

SETTING Jesus is in the Temple, teaching the people. The scribes (teachers of the law) and Pharisees (strict legalists) bring to Him a woman caught in adultery, and they inquire about His judgment regarding the matter.

Book of John: LIFE IN JESUS, THE SON OF GOD

P R O L O G U E	SIGNS WROUGHT			SELF REVEALED		E P I L O G U E 21 28
	PUBLIC MINISTRY -3 YEARS-		(GREAT) (PAUSE) ▶	PRIVATE MINISTRY -FEW DAYS-		
	ERA OF INCARNATION BEGINS	YEARS OF CONFLICT	DAY OF PREPARATION	HOUR OF SACRIFICE	DAWN OF VICTORY	
1:1	1:19	5:1	12:36b	18:1	20:1	21:1

"SIN NO MORE"

7:53 And EVERYONE went to his home;
8:1 BUT JESUS went to the **Mount of Olives.**
2 And **early** in the **morning**
    He came again into the TEMPLE,
    and ALL THE PEOPLE were coming to Him;
    and He sat down and began to **teach them.**

—setting—

3 And the SCRIBES and the PHARISEES
    brought a woman caught in **adultery,**
    and having set her in the midst,
4 they said to Him,
    "TEACHER, THIS WOMAN has been **caught
        in adultery,** in the **very** act.
5 "Now in the LAW
    MOSES commanded us to stone such women;
        [Leviticus 20:10; Deuteronomy 22:22-24]
      what then do You say?"
6a And they were saying this,
      testing Him,
  in order that they might have grounds
      for **accusing Him.**

ONE SIN

6b BUT JESUS stooped down,
    and with His finger wrote on the ground.
7 But when they persisted in asking Him,
    He straightened up,
      and said to them,
    "He who is without sin among you,
     let him be the **first**
    to **throw a stone** at her."
8 And **again** He stooped down,
        and wrote on the ground.
9   And when they heard it,
  they began to go out, ONE BY ONE,
        beginning with the older ones,
    and He was **left alone,**
    and the WOMAN,
        where she had been, in the midst.

MANY SINNERS

10 And straightening up, JESUS said to her,
    "WOMAN, where are they?
    Did **no one condemn you?**"
11 And she said,
    "No one, LORD."
  And JESUS said,
    "Neither do **I** condemn you;
    go your way;
      from now on,
        SIN NO MORE."

NO CONDEMNATION

Key Words and Phrases

8:3 _____ "caught in adultery" _____

5 _____

6a _____

6b _____

7 _____

9 _____

10 _____

11 _____

others: _____

OBSERVATIONS

Segment Survey

1. Note how the first paragraph serves as the setting. Then read the four paragraphs, and record the part Jesus plays in each:

    7:53—8:2 _____

    8:3-6a _____

    8:6b-9 _____

    8:10,11 _____

2. What words does the woman speak in the entire segment? _____

_____

_____

Paragraph Analysis

7:53—8:2

1. What activities of Jesus do you observe in the paragraph? _____

_____

_____

2. What do you think He was doing on the Mount of Olives? _____

_____

8:3-6a

1. What was the real motive of the leaders in bringing the woman to Jesus?

_____

_____

2. How did they try to force a confrontation between Moses' teaching and Jesus' teaching (verse 5)? _____

_____

_____

8:6b-9

1. Where do you think John learned of the Pharisees' motives recorded in verse 6a?

_____

_____

Was Jesus aware of those motives? If so, does this suggest what He may have written on the ground? _____
What do _you_ think He wrote?

_____

_____

_____

2. What made Jesus say the words of verse 7?

_____

_____

Then He wrote more on the ground. What might He have written?

_____

_____

3. The accusers exited one by one. Why?

_____

_____

8:10,11
How would these statements have helped the woman?

"Neither do I condemn you" _____

_____

"Sin no more" _____

_____

Related Verses

Leviticus 20:10 _____

_____

Deuteronomy 17:7 _____

_____

Deuteronomy 22:22-24 _____

_____

Luke 7:47 _____

_____

Luke 21:37 _____

_____

Luke 22:39,40 _____

_____

INTERPRETATIONS
(The event reported in this passage is recognized as genuine, even though many ancient manuscripts omit the reporting.)
1. "He sat down" (8:2). Compare John 7:37. What does the difference suggest?

_____

_____

2. "What then do you say?" (8:5). The true Messiah would have the correct interpretation of all Scripture. But were these religious leaders interested in knowing such truth? Earlier you observed that they wanted to test Jesus, to have grounds for accusing Him. Of what do you think they wanted to accuse Him?

_____

_____

_____

3. "Let him be the first to throw a stone" (8:7). Jesus was not rejecting the Law's teaching about judgment. Rather, He was pointing out that condemnation is in the hands of God, not sinful man. (Cf. 8:10-11).
4. "No one, Lord" (8:11). The woman may have used the Greek word *kurios* (Lord) as "Sir."

APPLICATIONS

1. This is one of the most tender stories of the gospels, showing Jesus' compassionate ways with a sinner. Observe how Jesus acted *in behalf of* the woman. Compare this with His subsitutionary work on the cross, dying for the sinner. Discuss this with your group. Jesus may be depended upon wholly to forgive sins that are confessed to Him. Read 1 John 1:9. To whom is this promise given, the believer or non-believer?

_____

Do you claim this promise? _____
2. Forgiveness is an act of the present over something of the past. But it also affects the future. In what ways? Observe the last few words of Jesus to the woman.

_____

_____

_____

_____

_____

_____

_____

Summary of Passage
While Jesus is teaching the people in the Temple, the scribes and Pharisees bring to Him a woman who has been caught in adultery. They remind Jesus that the Law says the woman must be stoned, and they want Jesus' view on this. Their ulterior motive is to accuse Him. Jesus does not verbally answer them. He writes on the ground, and tells the sinless person to cast the first stone. They all leave, and Jesus sends the woman on her way with the consolation and challenge: "I don't condemn you; sin no more."

Memory Verse   8:7b
Looking Ahead

Jesus and the Pharisees debate His claim to be the light of the world.

SETTING Jesus is teaching in the Temple area called the treasury, near the place where the offerings were placed. The Pharisees challenge His claim to be the light of the world.

Book of John: LIFE IN JESUS, THE SON OF GOD

P R O L O G U E	SIGNS WROUGHT		SELF REVEALED			E P I L O G U E 21: 25
	PUBLIC MINISTRY -3 YEARS-		(GREAT) (PAUSE) ▶	PRIVATE MINISTRY -FEW DAYS-		
	ERA OF INCARNATION BEGINS	YEARS OF CONFLICT	DAY OF PREPARATION	HOUR OF SACRIFICE	DAWN OF VICTORY	
1:1	1:19	5:1	12:36b	18:1	20:1	21:1

THE LIGHT OF THE WORLD

12 **Again** therefore JESUS spoke to them, saying,
    "I am the LIGHT OF THE WORLD;
  he who **follows Me**
      shall not walk in the **darkness**,
  but shall have the **light** of **LIFE**."
13 The PHARISEES therefore said to Him,
    "You are bearing **witness of Yourself**;
    Your **witness is not true**."
14 JESUS answered and said to them,
    "Even if I bear **witness of Myself**,
  My witness is true;
  for I know
      (1) where I came from, and
      (2) where I am going;
  but **you** do not know
    where I come from,
    or where I am going.
15 "YOU PEOPLE **judge** according to the **flesh;**
    I am **not judging** anyone.
16 "But even if I do **judge,**
  My judgment is true;
  for I am not alone in it,
  but **I and He** who **sent** Me.

17 "Even in your LAW it has been written,
    that the **testimony** of two men
      is TRUE.   [Deuteronomy 17:6]
18 "I am He
    who bears **witness** of Myself,
  and the FATHER
    who sent Me bears **witness** of Me."
19 And so they were saying to Him,
    "Where is Your FATHER?"
  JESUS answered,
    "You know neither Me,
      nor My FATHER;
  if you knew **Me**,
      you would know My FATHER also."

20 These words
    He spoke in the TREASURY,
    as He taught in the TEMPLE;
  and no one seized Him,
  because **HIS HOUR** had **not yet come**.

JESUS' WITNESS OF HIMSELF

FATHER'S WITNESS OF JESUS

conclusion

Key Words and Phrases

8:12 "light of the world" _____

  12 _____

  13 _____

  14 _____

  15 _____

  17 _____

  18 _____

  20 _____

others: _____

_____

OBSERVATIONS
Segment Survey

1. Read the segment. How does the last verse serve as a conclusion?

_____

2. Compare the first and second paragraphs as to their main content. (See the outline.)

3. How much of the segment is the spoken word of Jesus? _____

_____

How much is that of the Pharisees?

_____

_____

Paragraph Analysis
8:12-16

1. How did Jesus identify the world's problems?

_____

_____

2. What solution did He offer?

_____

_____

3. What do you think He meant by "light of life"?

_____

_____

_____

4. What is the key word of verses 13 and 14?

_____

5. On what did Jesus base the truth of His witness (verse 14)?

_____

_____

_____

Why is that a sound basis?

_____

_____

6. What was Jesus referring back to when He said, "You people judge..." (verse 15)?

_____

_____

7. Compare the two statements: "My witness is true" (verse 14); "My judgment is true" (verse 16). _____

_____

_____

_____

8:17-19

1. Then Jesus strengthened His claim of teaching the truth by citing another witness. Who was that?_____
How did Jesus identify Him (verse 18)?

2. What had Jesus said earlier that the Pharisees were ignorant of (verse 14)?

What did He *now* say they do not know (verse 19)?_____

8:20

1. How tense must this "teaching" session have been, in light of the concluding statement, "and no one seized Him"?

2. Compare verse 20 and John 7:30.

Related Verses

Deuteronomy 17:6_____

Mark 12:41-43_____

Luke 21:1_____

John 1:4,5,9,10_____

John 3:17_____

John 9:4,5_____

John 11:9,10_____

John 14:7,9_____

INTERPRETATIONS

1. "I am the light of the world" (8:12). This is the second of the seven "I Am's" of John. (Cf. 6:35.) The lighting of candelabra in the Court of the Women (where the treasury was located) was part of the ritual of the Feast of Tabernacles. This may have been the background for Jesus' talking about light.
2. "Light of life" (8:12). What is the scientific connection between light and physical life? Apply this to the spiritual realm.

_____

3. "Judge according to the flesh" (8:15). This is arriving at opinions and conclusions simply on the natural level. See 1 Corinthians 2:14.
4. "The Father bears witness of Me" (8:18). Two such witnesses were given at Jesus' baptism and transfiguration. Read the passages: Mark 1:9-13; 9:2-8.
5. "You would know My Father also" (8:19). Read also John 14:7,9 and Matthew 11:27. Jesus is the revelation of the Father: "He who has seen Me has seen the Father" (14:9). Why was it important that the Father was revealed by the incarnate (in-human-flesh) Son?

_____

APPLICATIONS

1. Write five to ten statements which describe the unbeliever's life as being one of darkness.

_____

2. Now write five to ten statements describing the believer's life as being one of light.

_____

How brightly is your light shining as a beacon in this dark world?

Summary of Passage

In the treasury area of the Temple Jesus continues teaching the people, saying that He is the light of the world. The Pharisees contest His claim, saying His witness is not true. Jesus counters, explaining why His witness and judgment are true, and that His Father bears witness of Him.

No one seizes Jesus because His hour has not yet come.

Memory Verse   8:12

Looking Ahead

Jesus identifies more fully who He is.

SETTING Jesus is still in the Temple, teaching the people. He and the Jews further discuss who He is.

Book of John: LIFE IN JESUS, THE SON OF GOD

P R O L O G U E	SIGNS WROUGHT			SELF REVEALED			E P I L O G U E 21: 25
	PUBLIC MINISTRY -3 YEARS-		(GREAT) (PAUSE) ▶	PRIVATE MINISTRY -FEW DAYS-			
	ERA OF INCARNATION BEGINS	YEARS OF CONFLICT	DAY OF PREPARATION	HOUR OF SACRIFICE	DAWN OF VICTORY		
1:1	1:19	5:1	12:36b	18:1	20:1	21:1	

"WHO ARE YOU?"

21 He said therefore again to them,
  "**I go away**,
    and you
    (1) shall **seek** Me, and
    (2) shall **DIE in your SIN**;
  where I am **going**, you **cannot come**."

22 Therefore the JEWS were saying,
  "**Surely** He will **not KILL HIMSELF**,
    will He, since He says,
  '**Where** I am **going**, you **cannot come**.'"

23 And He was saying to them,
        "You are from below,
                              I am from above;
  you are of this world;
                    I am not of this world.

24 "I said therefore to you,
    that you shall **DIE** in your **SINS**;
  for **unless**
      you BELIEVE THAT I AM HE,
      you shall **DIE** in your **SINS**."

25 And so they were saying to Him,
    "WHO ARE YOU?"
  JESUS said to them,
      "What have I been saying to you
          from the beginning?

26 "I have many things
      to **speak** and to **judge** concerning you,
    but HE who **sent** Me IS TRUE;
  and the things which I heard from HIM,
        these I speak to the WORLD."

27 They did not realize
        that He had been speaking to them
            about THE FATHER.

28 JESUS therefore said,
    "When you **LIFT UP** the SON OF MAN,
    then you will **know** that I AM HE,
    and I do nothing on My own initiative,
    but I speak these things as THE FATHER
                              taught Me.

29 "And He who **sent** Me
        is **with** Me;
      He has **not** left Me **alone**,
    for I always do the things
        that are pleasing to Him."

30 As He spoke these things,
        MANY came to BELIEVE IN HIM.

HEAVENLY HOME

EARTHLY MINISTRY

Key Words and Phrases

8:21 ___"I go away"___

  21 _____

  22 _____

  23 _____

  24 _____

  25 _____

  28 _____

  30 _____

others: _____

OBSERVATIONS

Segment Survey

1. How does the opening verse relate this passage to the preceding one?

_____

2. Who are conversing with Jesus?

_____

3. What verses of the segment quote these people?

_____

What is common to these verses, as to the people's knowledge of who Jesus is?

_____

4. Compare the concluding verse of each paragraph. _____

_____

_____

Paragraph Analysis

8:21-24

1. This is a paragraph about two worlds. Record in your own words the different references to those worlds.

_____

_____

2. Compare "I go away" (verse 21) and "You shall die" (verse 24). _____

_____

_____

3. Compare verse 21 and verse 24. What is the brightest note of the two verses?

_____

_____

4. What does "I am He" refer to?

_____

8:25-30

1. What is the Jews' key opening question?

_____

2. How did Jesus answer the question (verse 25b)? _____

_____

_____

_____

How did He expand on that answer in verse 26?

_____

_____

3. When would the Jews know who Jesus was?

_____

_____

4. Jesus' earthly ministry involved words and deeds. Mark in the Bible text every reference to *speaking* and *doing*. The climactic atoning work was His crucifixion. How did Jesus refer to that at this time?

_____

_____

5. What was the spiritual outcome of this conversation (verse 30)?_____

_____

_____

Related Verses

Exodus 3:14_____

_____

Deuteronomy 32:39 _____

_____

John 3:14,15_____

_____

John 5:36,37_____

_____

John 7:34,35_____

_____

John 13:33 _____

_____

Acts 6:7 _____

_____

INTERPRETATIONS

1. "The Jews" (8:22). It is difficult to determine whether John means the Jewish leaders, Jewish laity, or both. Some Bible students conclude that the discussion here points to Jewish laity.

2. "I am He" (8:24). "Believe that I am He" (8:24) and "know that I am He" (8:28) are key statements in Jesus' discussion with the Jews. Read Exodus 3:14. Most Bible students connect Jesus' words "I am He" with God's "I AM WHO I AM" (Exodus 3:14). God revealed Himself to Moses as Jehovah, the Maker and Keeper of the Covenant. Throughout Scripture Jesus is this Lord-Jehovah.

In the reference of John 8:24, if Jesus referred back to what He had just said, it was "I am He—the one from heaven." And in the John 8:28 reference, it was "I am He—the one from the Father."

3. "Many came to believe in Him" (8:30). The next passage (8:31ff.) discloses more about those who believed.

APPLICATIONS

1. What did Jesus teach about

sin?_____

judgment for sin?_____

who He is? _____

salvation? _____

hope?_____

Are these the subjects you talk about when you witness to an unsaved person? What do you learn from Jesus' methods of witnessing?

_____

_____

_____

_____

_____

_____

_____

2. Apply these words of Jesus to your own life: "I always do the things that are pleasing to Him" (8:29)._____

_____

_____

_____

_____

Summary of Passage

Jesus keeps talking with the Jews gathered around Him. He tells them that He is going away, and that unless they believe that He is truly who He claims to be, they will die in their sins. They press the blunt question, "Who are You?" and He gives the answer He has given all along, that He is the Son of the Father who sent Him to this world to do His will.

Many come to put their faith in Jesus.

Memory Verse   8:29

Looking Ahead

Jesus tells the people who a true disciple is.

SETTING Jesus is talking to Jews who had believed Him in a qualified way. The believers of 8:30 had put their faith in Jesus—that was genuine trust. They believed "*in* Him." (Note the wording of John's report: "many came to *believe in Him*"—8:30.) The believers (8:31) probably acknowledged Jesus' Messianic claims, but were not willing to give their lives to Him.

Book of John: LIFE IN JESUS, THE SON OF GOD

P R O L O G U E	SIGNS WROUGHT			SELF REVEALED		E P I L O G U E 21: 25
	PUBLIC MINISTRY -3 YEARS-		(GREAT) (PAUSE) ▶	PRIVATE MINISTRY -FEW DAYS-		
	ERA OF INCARNATION BEGINS	YEARS OF CONFLICT	DAY OF PREPARATION	HOUR OF SACRIFICE	DAWN OF VICTORY	
1:1	1:19	5:1	12:36b	18:1	20:1	21:1

FREE INDEED

31 JESUS **therefore** was saying
    to THOSE JEWS who had BELIEVED HIM,
    "If you **abide** in MY WORD,
    then you are **truly** DISCIPLES OF MINE;
32 and
    (1) you shall KNOW THE TRUTH, and
    (2) THE TRUTH shall MAKE YOU FREE."
33 They answered Him,
    "We are ABRAHAM'S offspring,
    and have never yet been ENSLAVED to anyone;
    how is it that You say,
    'You shall become FREE'?"

34 JESUS answered them,
    "**Truly, truly,** I say to you,
    everyone who **commits sin**
    is THE SLAVE OF SIN.
35 "And the SLAVE does not remain
    in the house **forever**;
    the SON **does** remain **forever.**
36 "If therefore
    THE SON SHALL MAKE YOU FREE,
    you shall be **free indeed.**
37 "I know that you are ABRAHAM'S offspring;
    yet you seek to KILL ME,
    because MY WORD
    has **no place in you.**
38 "**I speak** the things
    which I have seen
    with MY FATHER;
    therefore you also **do** the things
    which you heard
    from **your father.**"

FREEDOM

SLAVERY

Key Words and Phrases

8:31 _____ "abide" _____

31 _____

32 _____

33 _____

34 _____

36 _____

37 _____

38 _____

others: _____

_____

OBSERVATIONS
Segment Survey

1. Read the passage. To whom is Jesus speaking, according to verse 31?

_____

How does He identify His listeners in verse 37? (Cf. 8:45.) _____

_____

Among the possible explanations of the different listeners are these:

    a. The profession of faith in verse 31 was not a genuine, saving faith.

    b. After John 8:31,32, the larger group of unbelieving Jews came into the conversation, and Jesus directed His words to them.

2. What are the two contrasted subjects of the segment? _____

_____

_____

Paragraph Analysis
8:31-33

1. What makes a *true* disciple of Jesus?

_____

_____

2. Is it possible that Jesus spoke the words of verse 31b because the Jews who had just come to believe Him were not *true* believers? If so, may this explain His later indictment, such as that of verse 37? _____

_____

3. What does abiding in Jesus' word bring about ultimately? _____

4. How did the Jews react to Jesus' words in verse 32? _____

_____

What does this reveal about their heart-relationship to Him? _____

8:34-38

1. Who are slaves? _____

2. How does a son compare with a slave in a household? _____

How does this illustrate the truth of verse 36?

_____

_____

3. Compare what Jesus said about Abraham, His word, and His Father (verses 37 and 38).

_____

_____

_____

_____

4. Did Jesus identify "your father" (verse 38)?

_____

(See John 8:44, where this father is identified.) The next passage will show the Jews' reaction to the words "your father" (verses 39ff.).

Related Verses

Genesis 17:7_____

_____

Exodus 19:6_____

_____

Deuteronomy 7:6_____

_____

John 14:6_____

_____

Romans 9:4,5_____

_____

2 Corinthians 3:17 _____

_____

Galatians 3:7,29_____

_____

INTERPRETATIONS

1. "Abide in My word" (8:31). The Christian abides in Christ's word by obeying it, making it the practice of his life, and drawing from it all the power and strength needed to fulfill His desires. (Cf. John 15:1-11.) A disciple (8:31) is a learner. How does this relationship to Christ describe the life of abiding in His word?

_____

_____

2. "You shall know the truth" (8:32). This knowledge is recognition and perception. Compare John 8:28, where Jesus used the same Greek word translated "know."

3. "Everyone...is the slave of sin" (8:34). Compare Romans 3:9-18.

4. "The Son shall make you free" (8:36). The indwelling Christ inspires (does not compel) the believer to do what he should do, and empowers him to do it. This is true freedom.

5. "You are Abraham's offspring" (8:37). These Jews were physical descendants of Abraham, but they were not spiritual descendants of Abraham's family, because they did not have faith.

6. "Your father" (8:38). Who was the unbelieving Jews' father, according to John 8:44?

_____

APPLICATIONS

"To abide in Christ is to live in conscious dependence upon Him, recognizing that it is His life, His power, His wisdom, His resources, His strength and His ability, operating through you, which enable you to live according to His will." (TBS#2, p. 10) Read John 15:1-11, and relate the passage to the above definition. Then recall experiences you have had when Christ gave you the blessed fruits of abiding in Him. Record some of these.

_____

_____

_____

_____

_____

_____

_____

_____

Summary of Passage

Jesus continues to teach the people, saying that His true disciples abide in His word and obey His teaching. This is how they learn the truth which sets them free. Everyone is a slave of sin, and He, the Son, is their emancipator.

Jesus cites two reasons why the Jews are seeking to kill Him: (1) they have no room for His word; and (2) they do what they hear from their father [Satan].

Memory Verses   8:31b,32

Looking Ahead

Jesus tells His opponents that their father is not God but the devil.

SETTING Jesus continues talking with the Jews about who their father is.

ONE FATHER

39 They answered and said to Him,
      "**ABRAHAM** is our father."
   JESUS said to them,
      "If you are ABRAHAM'S **CHILDREN**,
         do the **deeds** of ABRAHAM.
40 "But as it is,
      you are seeking to KILL ME,
      a MAN who has told you THE TRUTH,
         which I heard from GOD;
         this ABRAHAM did not do.
41 "You are doing the deeds of your father."
      They said to Him,
         "We were not born of fornication;
         we have **one father**,
            even GOD."
42 JESUS said to them,
      "If GOD were your **FATHER**,
         you would **LOVE ME**;
      for
         (1) I proceed forth and
         (2) have come from GOD,
      for I have **not even** come on My own initiative,
         but **HE SENT ME**.

43 "**Why** do you **not understand**
            what I am saying?
      It is because you cannot **hear** MY WORD.
44 "You are of your father the DEVIL,
      and you want to **do**
            the desires of your father.
      He
         (1) was a MURDERER from the **beginning**, and
         (2) does not stand in the TRUTH,
            because there is **no truth in him**.
      Whenever he speaks a lie,
         he speaks from his own nature;
      for
         (1) he is a liar, and
         (2) the father of lies.
45   "But because I speak the TRUTH,
            you do **not** BELIEVE ME.
46 "Which one of you convicts Me of SIN?
      if I speak TRUTH,
      why do you **not** BELIEVE ME?
47 "He who is OF GOD
            hears the WORDS OF GOD;
      for this reason you do not hear them,
      because YOU ARE NOT OF GOD."

(margin labels: GOD? DEVIL!)

Key Words and Phrases

8:39 ___ "deeds of Abraham"

40 _____

41 _____

42 _____

43 _____

44 _____

46 _____

47 _____

others: _____

_____

Book of John: LIFE IN JESUS, THE SON OF GOD

P R O L O G U E	SIGNS WROUGHT			SELF REVEALED		E P I L O G U E 21:25
	PUBLIC MINISTRY -3 YEARS-	(GREAT) (PAUSE) ▶		PRIVATE MINISTRY -FEW DAYS-		
	ERA OF INCARNATION BEGINS	YEARS OF CONFLICT	DAY OF PREPARATION	HOUR OF SACRIFICE	DAWN OF VICTORY	
1:1	1:19	5:1	12:36b	18:1	20:1	21:1

OBSERVATIONS

Segment Survey

1. There are two paragraphs in the segment. What is the main subject of the segment?

_____

How is this introduced in the opening verse?

_____

2. Compare the two paragraphs. (Note the outline: GOD?; DEVIL!).

_____

_____

3. Compare the endings of the two paragraphs:

   8:42b—testimony—"I"_____

_____

   8:47—indictment—"you" _____

_____

Paragraph Analysis

8:39-42

1. The Jews claimed *two* fathers. Who were these?

   verse 39_____

   verse 41_____

2. How did Jesus throw down each claim?

   *Children of Abraham:*_____

_____

   Children of God: _____

_____

3. Jesus cited a third father in the middle of the conversation (verse 41a). Did He identify him yet?_____

4. Earlier (verse 38) Jesus had claimed God as His Father. Did He say this *explicitly* here (verses 39-42)? Did He teach it? If so, how?

_____

_____

8:43-47

1. Compare verse 43 with verse 47. Why couldn't the Jews understand Jesus?

_____

_____

Why couldn't they hear Jesus?

_____

_____

2. Compare verse 44a with verse 41a.

_____

_____

3. What did Jesus teach about the devil?

_____
_____
_____

4. How did He compare Himself with the devil?

_____
_____

5. What is the closing indictment of the passage (five words)? _____

Related Verses

Genesis 12:1-4 _____

_____

Deuteronomy 3:5,6 _____

_____

Matthew 3:8,9 _____

_____

John 13:3 _____

_____

John 18:37 _____

_____

1 John 3:8-12 _____

_____

1 John 5:1 _____

_____

INTERPRETATIONS

1. "This Abraham did not do" (8:40). Jesus was referring to the Jews' intent to kill Him (8:40a). Other renderings: "Abraham did not do such things" (NIV). "Abraham wouldn't do a thing like that!" (LB), that is, murder the Messiah.

2. "Not born of fornication" (8:41). This was probably not an indirect allusion to slanders about Jesus' birth. The Jews were claiming a heritage of faithfulness, not spiritual apostasy. (Cf. Malachi 2:10.) How did Jesus put their claim to the test (8:42a)?

_____
_____

3. "Because you cannot hear My word" (8:43). The Jews could not *bear* to hear Jesus' word. The Living Bible paraphrases "you are prevented from doing so!" Why could they not bear to hear Him? _____

_____

4. "No truth in him" (8:44). In what two ways did Jesus identify Satan?

_____

Why is falsehood a primary trait of Satan?

_____
_____

APPLICATIONS

1. Which one of Jesus' statements in this passage teaches that your actions reveal the true state of your heart? _____

Why are actions so important in the Christian life? For example, how do they affect your witness to lost souls?

_____
_____
_____

2. Why is truth a basic trait in the Christian life? Give five reasons.

_____
_____
_____
_____

Summary of Passage

The Jews claim that Abraham is their father and also that God is their Father. Jesus responds that Abraham did not do the things they are guilty of; and, if God is their Father, they would love the Son whom the Father sent to the world. No, their father is the devil, who was a murderer and is the father of lies. That explains why they do not want to believe in Jesus.

Memory Verse   8:44

Looking Ahead

The opposition to Jesus intensifies with charges that He has a demon and with attempts to stone Him.

SETTING Jesus is still in the Temple, answering the charges of His Jewish opponents. At the end of the passage John reports Him secretly fleeing from the Temple.

Book of John: LIFE IN JESUS, THE SON OF GOD

P R O L O G U E	SIGNS WROUGHT			SELF REVEALED			E P I L O G U E
	PUBLIC MINISTRY -3 YEARS-		(GREAT) (PAUSE) ▶	PRIVATE MINISTRY -FEW DAYS-			21 25
	ERA OF INCARNATION BEGINS	YEARS OF CONFLICT	DAY OF PREPARATION	HOUR OF SACRIFICE	DAWN OF VICTORY		
1:1	1:19	5:1	12:36b	18:1	20:1	21:1	

"GREATER THAN ABRAHAM?"

48 The JEWS answered and said to Him,
"Do we not say rightly
that
  (1) You are a SAMARITAN and
  (2) have a **demon**?"
49 JESUS answered,
"I do not have a **demon**;
  but I honor MY FATHER,
  and you dishonor ME.
50 "But I do not seek **My glory**;
  there is One who seeks and judges.
51 "Truly, truly, I say to you,
  if anyone KEEPS MY WORD
    he shall NEVER SEE DEATH."

DEMON IN JESUS?

52 The JEWS said to Him,
"Now we **know** that You have a **demon**.
  ABRAHAM **died**, and
  THE PROPHETS **also**;
and You say,
 'If anyone KEEPS MY WORD,
  he shall NEVER TASTE OF DEATH.'
53 "Surely You are **not greater**
than our father ABRAHAM, who **died**?
        THE PROPHETS **died too**;
whom do You make YOURSELF out TO BE?"
54 JESUS answered,
"If **I glorify** Myself, My **glory** is nothing;
it is MY FATHER who **glorifies** Me,
    of whom you say,
      'He is our God';
55   and you have not come to KNOW Him,
  but I KNOW HIM;
and if I say that I do not KNOW HIM,
  I shall be a **liar** like you,
but I do KNOW HIM, and KEEP HIS WORD.
56 "Your father ABRAHAM
    rejoiced to see MY DAY;
    and he saw it, and was **glad**."
57 The JEWS therefore said to Him,
"You are not yet fifty years old,
  and have You seen ABRAHAM?"
58 JESUS said to them,
"Truly, truly, I say to you,
    BEFORE ABRAHAM WAS BORN,
    I AM."

JESUS BEFORE ABRAHAM

59 Therefore they picked up STONES to throw at Him;
  but JESUS HID HIMSELF,
    and went out of the TEMPLE.

—reaction—

Key Words and Phrases

8:48 ___"demon"_____

49 _____

50 _____

51 _____

52 _____

54 _____

58 _____

59 _____

others: _____

OBSERVATIONS

Segment Survey

1. Observe how the segment is divided into three paragraphs. The last short paragraph reports the reaction to the heated discussion. The other two paragraphs report the confrontation itself.
2. Observe in the text the first accusation and the reply. Where does the new, second accusation appear?

_____

_____

3. How much of the remainder of the paragraph is Jesus' reply?

_____

_____

Paragraph Analysis

8:48-51

1. What two accusations did the Jews make?

_____

_____

Which one did Jesus answer?

_____

_____

2. In what three ways did He answer it?

  verse 49 _____

_____

  verse 50 _____

_____

  verse 51 _____

_____

8:52-58

1. What words of the previous paragraph brought on the repeated charge of demon-possession?

_____

_____

_____

How did the Jews try to discredit Jesus' promise to give eternal life to believers?

_____

_____

_____

2. What was the Jews' second accusation?

_____

_____

Record in your own words how Jesus answered the second charge.

verses 54,55 _____

_____

verse 56_____

_____

verses 57,58 _____

_____

8:59
Do you see a miracle here? If so, what was it?

_____

_____

Related Verses

Leviticus 24:16_____

_____

Matthew 25:46_____

_____

John 1:1,2_____

_____

John 5:24_____

_____

Colossians 1:17_____

_____

2 Timothy 1:9,10_____

_____

Hebrews 11:17-19_____

_____

INTERPRETATIONS
1. "You are a Samaritan" (8:48). Review what you studied at John 4:9. Then explain why this was a disparaging charge against Jesus.

_____

_____

2. "You...have a demon" (8:48). What may have brought on this charge at this time, in view of what Jesus had spoken in the preceding segment (8:39-47)? _____

_____

3. "If anyone keeps My word" (8:51). To keep Christ's word is to accept it by faith and obey it. See John 14:23,24; 1 John 2:4-6.
4. "Shall never see death" (8:51). The strong words "never" and "death" suggest "eternal life." Relate John 3:16 to this.

_____

_____

5. "Abraham rejoiced to see My day" (8:56). Abraham rejoiced in the promise of God that in the line of his son, Isaac, the Messiah would arrive to bless all people. (Cf. Genesis 15:4-6; 17:1-8; Hebrews 11:13.)
6. "Before Abraham was born, I am" (8:58). What attribute of Jesus does this teach? (Cf. 1:1,2.)

APPLICATIONS
1. Motives are crucial. The highest motive which you can have in any action is the glory of God. What do you learn about this from Jesus?

_____

_____

_____

2. Obedience to Christ is mandatory for successful and fruitful living. Write some practical ways you can keep Christ's word. (TBS#6)

_____

_____

_____

_____

_____

_____

_____

_____

_____

_____

Summary of Passage
The Jews charge Jesus with being a Samaritan and having a demon. Jesus denies having a demon, and indicts His opponents for dishonoring Him and judging Him. He says that only those who accept His word and obey it will never see death.

The Jews repeat their charge, and Jesus responds by claiming glorious acceptance by God, recognition by Abraham, and eternal being. They want to stone Him, but He secretly flees the Temple.

Memory Verse   8:51

Looking Ahead
Jesus heals a man who was blind from birth.

SETTING The day is Sabbath (9:14), possibly the day after Jesus fled the Temple (8:59). The disciples are with Jesus. As they are walking along, Jesus sees a man blind from birth.

Book of John: LIFE IN JESUS, THE SON OF GOD

P R O L O G U E	SIGNS WROUGHT			SELF REVEALED		E P I L O G U E 21: 25
	PUBLIC MINISTRY -3 YEARS-		(GREAT) (PAUSE) ▶	PRIVATE MINISTRY -FEW DAYS-		
	ERA OF INCARNATION BEGINS	YEARS OF CONFLICT	DAY OF PREPARATION	HOUR OF SACRIFICE	DAWN OF VICTORY	
1:1	1:19	5:1	12:36b	18:1	20:1	21:1

GOD'S WORKS DISPLAYED

1 And as He passed by,
    He saw a man **blind from birth.**
2 And HIS DISCIPLES asked Him, saying,
    "RABBI, **who sinned,**
        this man,
        or his parents,
        that he should be **born blind?**"
3 JESUS answered,
    "It was neither that this man sinned,
        nor his parents;
    but it was in order that
        THE WORKS OF GOD might be **displayed in him.**
4 "We must work
    the works of Him who **sent** Me,
        as long as it is DAY;
        NIGHT IS COMING, when no man **can work.**
5 "While I am in the world,
        I AM THE LIGHT OF THE WORLD."

DISPLAY

6 When He had said this,
    (1) He spat on the ground, and
    (2) made **clay** of the spittle, and
    (3) applied the **clay to his eyes,** and
7   (4) said to him,
    "**Go, wash** in the pool of SILOAM"
        (which is translated, SENT).
    And so he **went away** and **washed,**
        and CAME BACK SEEING.

MIRACLE

8   The NEIGHBORS therefore,
    and those who previously saw him as a BEGGAR,
      were saying, "Is not this
        the one who used to **sit** and **beg?**"
9 Others were saying, "This is he,"
    still others were saying, "No, but he is **like** him."
    HE kept saying,
                "I am the one."
10   Therefore they were saying to him,
    "How then were **your eyes opened?**"
11 He answered,
    "THE MAN who is called JESUS
        (1) made clay, and
        (2) anointed my eyes, and
        (3) said to me,
        'Go to SILOAM, and **wash**';
    so I **went away** and **washed,**
        and I RECEIVED SIGHT."
12 And they said to him,
    "WHERE IS HE?"
    He said,
    "I do not know."

TESTIMONY

Key Words and Phrases

9:2 _____ "who sinned" _____

3 _____

4 _____

5 _____

6 _____

7 _____

10 _____

---

12 _____

others: _____

OBSERVATIONS

Segment Survey

1. Read the three paragraphs, referring to the survey outline as you read (DISPLAY; MIRACLE; TESTIMONY).
2. Observe the questions asked, and how each one is answered.
3. Compare the closing lines of each paragraph:

    9:5b_____

    9:7b_____

    9:12b_____

4. How is Jesus identified, namewise

    (1) by the disciples?_____

    (2) by the blind man? _____

Paragraph Analysis

9:1-5
1. What one thing did the disciples think of when they saw the blind man?

_____

What did Jesus think of?

_____

_____

2. What word is repeated four times in verses 3 and 4? _____
3. Did Jesus say directly that He was about to heal the man?_____
Did He hint at it? If so, how?

_____

_____

4. How do verses 4 and 5 fit into what He was about to do?

    verse 4_____

    verse 5_____

9:6-7
1. Did the blind man say anything?

_____

Why is this significant? _____

_____

2. What did the man do?_____

What does this reveal about his heart?

_____

_____

3. Relate the last line of verse 7 to the last line of verse 3. _____

_____

9:8-12

Observe the three basic questions asked. In your own words, write out the questions and answers.

	QUESTION	ANSWER
Who?		
How?		
Where?		

Related Verses

Genesis 3:17-19 _____

_____

Exodus 20:5 _____

_____

Mark 7:33,34 _____

_____

John 1:14 _____

_____

John 14:12 _____

_____

Romans 8:20-23 _____

_____

1 Corinthians 15:21,22 _____

_____

INTERPRETATIONS

1. "Who sinned?" (9:2). All curses, judgment, sickness and death are traceable back to

what, ultimately? _____

_____

Why do you think the disciples interpreted the man's blindness as they did?

_____

_____

What did they overlook? _____

2. "Works of God might be displayed in him" (9:3). Read the continuation of this story in 9:13-41. How were God's works displayed in the life of this man, through the miracle?

_____

_____

_____

_____

3. "Came back seeing" (9:7). How do the actions of verses 6 and 7 point to the supernatural character of the healing?

_____

_____

4. Why do you think Jesus involved the man himself in the procedure?

_____

_____

APPLICATIONS

1. This world is in black darkness, in every way. Its spiritual darkness is crucial. God is working through His children, reaching and touching lost souls with the message of salvation before the end comes. List some practical truths about witnessing taught by John 9:4 and 5.

_____

_____

_____

2. Think back to when you saw an unsaved person for the first time. Can you recall what your **first** thoughts were? Were they about the person's sinful state, or about God and His love and His power? Whatever the pattern, were you overwhelmed afresh by the glory of God and His love for sinners? Share testimonies about this in your group. (TBS#7)

Summary of Passage

Jesus and His disciples see a beggar who was born blind. The disciples ask about the cause of the blindness. Jesus answers that the works of God will be displayed in the man's life. Jesus performs the first of these works by healing the man. People wonder how the man received his sight, and he gives credit to "the man who is called Jesus."

Memory Verse   9:4

Looking Ahead

The healing of the blind man stirs up the people: the Pharisees deny that the healer is from God, and many of the Jews challenge the fact of a genuine healing.

SETTING The healed man is brought to an informal meeting of Jesus' opponents, the Pharisees, who interrogate him about his healing. They also question his parents about the event.

Book of John: LIFE IN JESUS, THE SON OF GOD

P R O L O G U E	SIGNS WROUGHT			SELF REVEALED		E P I L 21: O 25 G U E
	PUBLIC MINISTRY -3 YEARS-		(GREAT) (PAUSE) ▶	PRIVATE MINISTRY -FEW DAYS-		
	ERA OF INCARNATION BEGINS	YEARS OF CONFLICT	DAY OF PREPARATION	HOUR OF SACRIFICE	DAWN OF VICTORY	
1:1	1:19	5:1	12:36b	18:1	20:1	21:1

"WHO HEALED THE MAN?"

13 They brought to the PHARISEES
     him who was formerly **blind.**
14 Now it was a SABBATH
     on the day when JESUS
       (1) *made* the clay, and
       (2) **opened** his eyes.
15 Again therefore
     the PHARISEES also were asking him
       how he received his sight.
     And he said to them,
       (1) "He applied clay to my eyes, and
       (2) I washed, and
       (3) I SEE."
16 Therefore some of the PHARISEES were saying,
     "THIS MAN
       is **not from God,**
     because He does not keep the Sabbath."
     But others were saying,
       "How can a **man who is a sinner**
         perform SUCH SIGNS?"
     And there was a **division** among them.
17 They said therefore
            to the **blind man** again,
     "What do you say about Him,
       since He OPENED YOUR EYES?"
     And he said,
     "HE IS A PROPHET."

"WHO IS THE HEALER?"

18 The JEWS therefore
          did NOT BELIEVE it of him,
     that he
       (1) had been **blind,** and
       (2) had received SIGHT,
     until they called the PARENTS
     of the very one who had received his SIGHT,
19 and questioned them, saying,
     "Is this YOUR SON,
     whom you **say** was **born blind?**
     Then HOW does he NOW SEE?"
20 His PARENTS answered them, and said,
       "We know
       (1) that this is OUR SON, and
       (2) that he was **born blind;**
21   but **HOW** he now SEES,
       we do not know;
       or **WHO** opened **his eyes,**
       we do not know.
         Ask **him;** he is of age,
           he shall speak for himself."
22 His PARENTS said this
       because they were afraid of the JEWS;
     for the JEWS had already agreed,
     that if **any one** should CONFESS HIM TO BE CHRIST,
       he should be **put out** of the SYNAGOGUE.
23 For this reason his parents said,
         "He is of age; ask **him.**"

"HOW DOES YOUR SON SEE?"

Key Words and Phrases

9:14 ___ "Sabbath" _____

16 _____

16 _____

17 _____

18 _____

19 _____

21 _____

22 _____

others: _____

OBSERVATIONS

Segment Survey

1. The segment has two paragraphs. Who are the main characters in each?

_____
_____

Compare the paragraphs as to the main thrust of the conversations.

_____
_____

Note the two-point outline shown on the chart.
2. What are the last two words of the segment? Relate this to the last sentence of the first paragraph.

_____
_____
_____

Paragraph Analysis

9:13-17

1. Verse 13 gives the setting of the paragraph. In a few words, write down the main content of each of the next verses. (Example shown.)

verse 14 _____
verse 15 _____
verse 16 ___ DIVISION _____
verse 17 _____

2. Compare the three identifications of Jesus in these verses:

verse 16a _____
verse 16b _____
verse 17b _____

3. What do you learn about the healed man from this paragraph?

_____
_____
_____
_____

9:18-23

1. What convinced the Jews that the man born blind could see?

_____

_____

2. After accepting that as fact, what was their question (verse 9b)?

_____

_____

What was the parents' answer to that question?

_____

_____

3. What else did the parents plead ignorance about? _____

Were they truthful about that? _____

Account for their holding back the information.

_____

4. The opponents of Jesus were trying to kill Him for claiming to be the Son of God. What was the lot of those who confessed Jesus to be the Messiah? _____

_____

Relate this to verse 3b. _____

_____

Related Verses

Mark 8:27-30 _____

_____

Luke 6:22 _____

_____

Luke 24:18-20 _____

_____

John 1:24 _____

_____

John 3:2 _____

_____

John 4:19 _____

_____

John 7:10-13 _____

_____

INTERPRETATIONS

1. "They brought to the Pharisees" (9:13). The Sanhedrin was the highest Jewish civil and criminal court. It was comprised of seventy members, and was presided over by the high priest. Its membership included chief priests, scribes and elders, most of whom were of the sect of Pharisees (cf. 11:47). The Pharisees were ultralegalist opponents of Christ. It is possible that the group of Pharisees in 9:13 was one of two mini-Sanhedrins which are said to have been in Jerusalem.

2. "He does not keep the Sabbath (9:16). How did the Pharisees conclude that Jesus had broken the Sabbath? _____

_____

3. "Who opened his eyes, we do not know" (9:21). Was this true, in view of verse 22? Does the last part of verse 22 indicate how far the parents had come in recognizing who Jesus was? Explain.

_____

_____

_____

4. "The synagogue" (9:22). Why would a Jewish family avoid being excommunicated from their synagogue? _____

_____

APPLICATIONS

1. "What do you say about Him?" (9:17). The man had a wonderful opportunity to give his personal testimony for Christ. If you were asked by an anti-Christian group what you thought of Christ, how would you answer that group?

_____

_____

_____

_____

_____

_____

2. What are you willing to give up for confessing Jesus as Christ? Discuss with your group this subject of persecution for the faith.

Summary of Passage

The man who had been blind is brought to the Pharisees. They ask questions about the healing, and are divided over who the healer can be. Some reject the healing outright, but have to change their minds after talking with the man's parents. The Jews want to know how it happened. The parents don't know, and they say they don't know who did it.

Memory Verses   9:20,21

Looking Ahead

The healed blind man has more opportunities to witness, and Jesus leads him to a saving faith.

SETTING The Pharisees call back the healed man for a second barrage of questioning. After he is thrown out of the meeting-place, Jesus finds him and talks with him. He believes in Christ, and Jesus then talks to the Pharisees.

Book of John: LIFE IN JESUS, THE SON OF GOD

P R O L O G U E	SIGNS WROUGHT			SELF REVEALED			E P I L O G U E
	PUBLIC MINISTRY -3 YEARS-		(GREAT) (PAUSE) ▶	PRIVATE MINISTRY -FEW DAYS-			21 25
	ERA OF INCARNATION BEGINS	YEARS OF CONFLICT	DAY OF PREPARATION	HOUR OF SACRIFICE	DAWN OF VICTORY		
1:1	1:19	5:1	12:36b	18:1	20:1		21:1

"DO YOU BELIEVE?"

24 So a second time they called the MAN
    who had been **blind**, and said to him,
    "Give GLORY to GOD;
      we know that this man is a SINNER."
25 He therefore answered,
    "Whether He is a SINNER, I do not know;
    one thing I do know,
    that, whereas I was blind,
    NOW I SEE."
26 They said therefore to him,
    "What did He do to you?
    How did He **open your eyes**?"
27 He answered them,
    "I told you already, and you **did not listen**;
    why do you want to hear it again?
    You do not want to become
    HIS DISCIPLES TOO, do you?"
28 And they reviled him, and said,
    "You are HIS DISCIPLE;
    but we are DISCIPLES of MOSES.
29 "We know that GOD **has spoken** to MOSES;
    but as for THIS MAN,
    we do not know where He is from."
30 The MAN answered and said to them,
    "Well, here is an amazing thing,
    that you do not know **where** He is from,
    and **yet** He **opened my eyes**.
31 "We know that GOD does not hear SINNERS;
    but if anyone
      (1) is GOD-FEARING, and
      (2) does HIS WILL,
         He hears him.
32 "Since the beginning of time
      it has never been heard
    that anyone **opened the eyes**
        of a person **born blind**.
33 "If this man were **not from God**,
      He could **do nothing**."
34 They answered and said to him,
    "You were **born entirely in sins**,
    and are YOU TEACHING US?"
      ➤ And they put him out. [John 9:22]

EXPULSION

35 JESUS heard that they had put him out;
    and finding him, He said,
    "Do you BELIEVE in the SON OF MAN?"
36 He answered and said,
    "And who is He, LORD,
    that I may BELIEVE IN HIM?"
37 JESUS said to him,
    (1) "You have both SEEN HIM, and
    (2) He is the one
        who is talking with you."
38 And he said,
    "LORD, I BELIEVE."
      ➤ And he worshiped Him.

CONVERSION

39 And JESUS said,
    "For judgment I CAME INTO THIS WORLD,
    that those who do not see may **see**;
    and that those who see may **become blind**."
40 Those of the PHARISEES who were with Him
    heard these things, and said to Him,
    "We are not BLIND too, are we?"

JUDGMENT

41 JESUS said to them,
    "If you were BLIND, you would have NO SIN;
    but since you say, 'We see,' YOUR SIN REMAINS."

Key Words and Phrases

9:24 _____ "give glory to God" _____

25 _____

27 _____

29 _____

31 _____

34 _____

35 _____

39 _____

others: _____

OBSERVATIONS

Segment Survey

1. The segment contains three paragraphs, each different from the other two. Read them, and record the main speakers in the conversations:

    9:24-34 _____

    9:35-38 _____

    9:39-41 _____

2. Compare the endings of the paragraphs:

    9:34 _____

    9:38 _____

    9:41 _____

3. Compare the opening and closing verses of the segment, as to sinners:

    9:24 _____

    9:41 _____

Paragraph Analysis

9:24-34

1. Compare the two opening statements of the Pharisees (verse 24):

    "give _____ "

    "we know _____ "

2. As of verse 25, what did the man *not* know?

_____

Where in the segment does a change take place?

_____

3. Compare what the Pharisees knew and what they did not know (verse 29).

_____

_____

4. Who did most of the speaking at this time (verses 24-34)? What impact did this make?

_____

What was the outcome?

_____

9:35-38

1. What was Jesus' main concern for the man?

_____

2. How did Jesus identify Himself? Compare this with the Pharisees' "this man."

_____

_____

3. What was the man's deep desire?

_____

What kept him from believing?

_____

4. What experience brought about worship?

_____

9:39-41

Compare this paragraph with the preceding one.

_____

_____

_____

Related Verses

Joshua 7:19_____

_____

Matthew 9:12,13_____

_____

John 3:13-15_____

_____

John 3:17_____

_____

John 5:14_____

_____

John 5:45-47_____

_____

INTERPRETATIONS

1. "Give glory to God" (9:24). What do you think the Pharisees meant by this? (Cf. Joshua 7:19.)

_____

_____

2. "We do not know where He is from" (9:29). The Pharisees said they did not know who Jesus was because they did not know where He was from. How did the man show them that they had enough light to know Jesus' origin?

_____

_____

_____

3. "They put him out" (9:34). Compare this with what the man's parents had feared (9:22).

_____

_____

4. "That I may believe in Him?" (9:36). What kind of belief is this? (Cf. 9:38.)

_____

_____

5. "Judgment" (9:39). How does this word relate to what is before and to what follows?

_____

_____

What was sinful about the Pharisees' boast, "We see"?_____

_____

APPLICATIONS

1. What do you learn about personal evangelism from Jesus, as recorded in 9:35-38? Discuss this with your group. (TBS#7)

_____

_____

_____

_____

_____

2. When you are speaking to an unsaved person about becoming a Christian, how do you show that *saving faith* is needed?

_____

_____

_____

Summary of Passage

For a second time the Pharisees question the man about how he was healed and who did it. The man says his healer is not a sinner, as they contend, but a man from God. Enraged, they throw him out of the meeting-place.

Jesus hears about his expulsion, finds him and talks to him about believing in the Son of Man. Jesus identifies Himself as *that One*, and the man believes in Him. Jesus later turns to the Pharisees and rebukes their self-righteousness.

Memory Verse   9:35

Looking Ahead

Jesus teaches the allegory of the Good Shepherd and His flock.

SETTING The setting is Jerusalem. Probably Jesus is still talking to the people of the preceding chapter, which includes the Pharisees, the healed blind man and his parents.

Book of John: LIFE IN JESUS, THE SON OF GOD

P R O L O G U E	SIGNS WROUGHT			SELF REVEALED		E P I L 21: O 25 G U E
	PUBLIC MINISTRY -3 YEARS-		(GREAT) (PAUSE) ▶	PRIVATE MINISTRY -FEW DAYS-		
	ERA OF INCARNATION BEGINS	YEARS OF CONFLICT	DAY OF PREPARATION	HOUR OF SACRIFICE	DAWN OF VICTORY	
1:1	1:19	5:1	12:36b	18:1	20:1	21:1

THE GOOD SHEPHERD

1 "TRULY, TRULY, I say to you,
   He who does not enter BY THE DOOR
      into the fold of THE SHEEP,
   but climbs up SOME OTHER WAY,
      he is a **thief** and a **robber.**
2 "But he who enters BY THE DOOR
      is a SHEPHERD OF THE SHEEP.
3 "To him the doorkeeper opens;
   and THE SHEEP **hear** HIS VOICE;
   and
      (1) he **calls** his sheep **by name**, and
      (2) **leads** them out.
4 "When he puts forth all his own,
   he **goes before them,**
   and THE SHEEP **follow** him,
   because ⟶ they **know** HIS VOICE.
5 "And a stranger they simply **will not follow,**
               but will **flee** from him,
   because ⟶ they do **not know**
               the VOICE of strangers."
6 This figure of speech
               JESUS spoke to them,
   but they did **not understand**
      what those things were
      which HE had been saying to them.

ALLEGORY

7 JESUS therefore said to them again,
   "TRULY, TRULY, I say to you,
   I AM THE DOOR of the SHEEP.
8 "ALL who came before ME
   are thieves and robbers,
   but THE SHEEP did not **hear** them.
9 "I AM THE DOOR;
   if ANYONE **enters through ME,**
   he
      (1) shall be SAVED, and
      (2) shall go in and out, and
      (3) find pasture.

DOOR

10 "The thief comes
      only to
         (1) steal, and
         (2) kill, and
         (3) destroy;
   I CAME
   that they
         (1) might have LIFE, and
         (2) might have it ABUNDANTLY.

11 "I AM THE GOOD SHEPHERD;
   the **good shepherd lays down HIS LIFE**
               for THE SHEEP.

GOOD SHEPHERD

12 "He who is
         (1) a hireling, and
         (2) not a shepherd,
         (3) who is not the owner
               of THE SHEEP,
      beholds THE WOLF coming,
   and leaves THE SHEEP, and flees,
   and THE WOLF
         (1) snatches them, and
         (2) scatters them.
13 He flees because he is a hireling,
            and is **not concerned about the sheep.**"

HIRELING

Key Words and Phrases

10:1 ___ "sheep"

   1 _____

   2 _____

   3 _____

   4 _____

   7 _____

   10 _____

   11 _____

others: _____

OBSERVATIONS
Segment Survey

1. This segment has five paragraphs. Using the outline shown, read the paragraphs, observing general content.
2. Note how verse 11 is a transition verse, linking what goes before and after.
3. What are the two key "I am's" of the segment?
_____
_____

Paragraph Analysis
10:1-6
1. What verses are about the shepherd?
_____

List the main descriptions.
_____
_____
_____

2. Compare what Jesus said about the thief (verse 1) and the stranger (verse 5).
_____
_____

3. What impression did the allegory make on the people? _____
_____

10:7-9
1. Why does the paragraph open with, "Jesus therefore"? _____
_____

2. Record the progression of Jesus' interpretation of the allegory:
   verse 7b—door _____
   verse 8—thieves _____
   verse 9—door _____

3. What are the three outcomes of entering through Christ? Compare this with 10:10b.

_____

_____

Compare 14:6. _____

_____

10:10
Compare the objectives of the two comings.

_____

_____

10:11
What words relate this key verse to the lines before (verse 10b) and after (verse 12a)?

_____

10:12,13
Compare the destructive works of the hireling and the wolf. _____

_____

Related Verses

Psalm 23:1 _____

_____

Isaiah 40:11 _____

_____

Ezekiel 34:23_____

_____

John 12:47 _____

_____

John 14:6_____

_____

Hebrews 13:20,21_____

_____

1 Peter 5:4 _____

_____

INTERPRETATIONS

The allegory of 10:1-6 is a figure of speech. Jesus uses an extended picture to teach some main truths about His ministry for sinners; every object of that picture, however, is not intended to be interpreted. As you study the passage, look for the main symbols and metaphors. The best clue for this is to look for the symbols Jesus interprets.

Jesus' ministry could be described in various ways. That accounts for mixed metaphors in the allegory: e.g. Jesus is "the door" and He is also "the good Shepherd."

1. Whom does Jesus identify as thieves and robbers (10:8)? Whom do you think He had in mind?_____

Did Pharisees and other hostile religious leaders match the descriptions of the hireling (10:12)?

_____

If so, how?_____

_____

2. Mark on the textual re-creation chart the various ministries of Christ for His sheep.

3. What is abundant living, according to verses 9 and 10?_____

_____

APPLICATIONS

The two ministries of Christ which are prominent in this passage are salvation for the sinner and abundant life for the Christian (10:9,10). Read the following verses for what they teach about abundant living—e.g., descriptions, requirements, power and blessings. Apply these to your own life, and record the applications:

Colossians 2:6_____

_____

Romans 6:1-16_____

_____

Psalm 37:1-7,34 _____

_____

John 15:7-11_____

_____

1 John 1:9_____

_____

Ephesians 6:10-17 _____

_____

Summary of Passage

Jesus teaches His hearers the allegory of the Good Shepherd and His flock. The people do not understand the figure of speech, and so He interprets it for them. He is the door into the fold for the sheep, and all who enter through Him are saved and have abundant life. He is the Good Shepherd who gives His life for the sheep. The thieves, robbers, hirelings and wolves are out to scatter and kill the sheep; but Jesus came to give life.

Memory Verse   10:11

Looking Ahead

Jesus concludes His teaching about the Good Shepherd, with mixed reactions from the people.

SETTING The place is still Jerusalem, possibly in the Temple. Jesus concludes His talk to the Jews about the Good Shepherd.

ONE FLOCK

14 "I AM THE GOOD SHEPHERD;
   and
       (1) I **know** MY OWN, and
       (2) MY OWN **know** ME,
15 even as
       (1) THE FATHER **knows** ME and
       (2) I **know** THE FATHER;
   and I **lay down** MY LIFE for THE SHEEP.
16 "And I have OTHER SHEEP,
     which are not of this fold;
   I **must** bring them also,
   and
       (1) they shall **hear MY VOICE**; and
       (2) they shall **become**
          ONE FLOCK with ONE SHEPHERD.
17 "For this reason
      THE FATHER **loves Me**,
   because I **lay down** MY LIFE
      that I may take it again.
18 "No one has taken it away from Me,
   but I **lay it down**
      on MY OWN INITIATIVE.
   I have AUTHORITY
      to **take it up again**.
   This commandment
      I received from MY FATHER."

19 There arose a division again
        among the JEWS
        because of THESE WORDS.
20 And **many** of them were saying,
   "He has a **demon**,
   and is **insane**;
   WHY do you **listen** to Him?"
21 Others were saying,
   "These are not the sayings
      of one **demon-possessed**.
   A **demon** cannot open the eyes
      of the BLIND,
      can he?"

(margin: ONE FLOCK / DIVIDED JEWS)

Key Words and Phrases

10:14 _"I know My own"_____
  15 _____
  16 _____
  17 _____
  18 _____
  18 _____
  19 _____
  20 _____
others: _____

OBSERVATIONS

Segment Survey

1. The segment contains two very different paragraphs. What is the tone of each?
_____
_____

P R O L O G U E	SIGNS WROUGHT		SELF REVEALED		E P I L O G U E
	PUBLIC MINISTRY -3 YEARS-	(GREAT) (PAUSE) ▶	PRIVATE MINISTRY -FEW DAYS-		
	ERA OF INCARNATION BEGINS	YEARS OF CONFLICT	DAY OF PREPARATION	HOUR OF SACRIFICE	DAWN OF VICTORY
1:1	1:19	5:1	12:36b	18:1	20:1	21:1

2. Compare the spoken words in each paragraph.
_____
_____

3. Compare "Father" (10:18) and "demon" (10:21).
_____
_____

Paragraph Analysis

10:14-18

1. Compare the words that follow "I am the Good Shepherd" with the words that follow the same statement in 14:11.
_____
_____

2. What did Jesus intend to teach by using "even as" (verses 14b-15a)?
_____
_____

3. Compare "other sheep," "this fold," and "one flock" (verse 16).
_____
_____
_____
_____

4. Why does the Father love the Son?
_____
_____

5. Observe the words Jesus used when telling about laying down His life. What did each reveal about His action?

   "my own initiative"_____
   "authority"_____
   "commandment" _____

10:19-21

1. What were the two reactions of the Jews?
_____
_____
_____

What kind of answer is given to the question "Why?"_____
_____
_____

2. Relate verse 21b to 9:3.
_____
_____
_____

Related Verses

Matthew 11:27-29 _____

_____

John 2:19 _____

_____

John 3:14 _____

_____

John 17:24 _____

_____

John 19:11 _____

_____

Ephesians 2:11-16 _____

_____

Ephesians 3:1-6 _____

_____

INTERPRETATIONS

1. "I know...even as" (10:14,15a). The measuring stick, "even as," does not intend to teach that the fellowship of verse 14 is as close (or perfect) as the Father-Son relationship, but that the former *reflects* the divine fellowship.

2. "I have other sheep, which are not of this fold" (10:16). From this statement we may interpret "fold" to be Israel. (Cf. 10:1.) So the "other sheep" are believing non-Jews. The gospel was first preached to Israel, then to the Gentiles (Romans 1:16). So when the Gentiles hear Jesus' voice and believe, a union takes place: fold + other sheep = one flock. How is this taught by 10:16?

_____

_____

_____

_____

_____

3. "I have authority to take it up again" (10:18). What does the phrase "take it up again" mean, in the context of the phrase "lay it down"?

_____

_____

_____

_____

See 2:19. The Father gave His Son unto death, and the Son gave Himself. Likewise, the Father raised the Son, and the Son took back His own life.

APPLICATIONS

Read the first paragraph again and observe what it teaches about fellowship with Jesus. Examine your own life, and arrive at ratings for these:

(1) How well do you *know* Jesus? How can you improve this?

_____

_____

_____

_____

_____

_____

_____

(2) How alert are you in hearing His voice each day? What can help you to be more alert?

_____

_____

_____

_____

_____

_____

(3) How faithfully do you follow Jesus as your Shepherd? What helps you to walk close to Him?

_____

_____

_____

_____

_____

_____

_____

Summary of Passage

Jesus teaches more about Himself as the Good Shepherd. He says He has other sheep (non-Jews) who are not of the fold of Israel, who will hear His voice and become His own, in one flock. His Father loves Him and has given Him the right to give His life and to take it back again. And He has offered Himself to do this.

The Jewish listeners react in two different ways: Some say Jesus has a demon, others acknowledge that a healer of blindness can't have a demon.

Memory Verse   10:16

Looking Ahead

Jesus talks more to the Jews in the Temple, and they try to stone Him.

SETTING It is winter time (December), during the eight-day Feast of the Dedication. Jesus is in the Temple, in Solomon's porch. The Jews challenge Jesus again to claim that He is the Messiah.

Book of John: LIFE IN JESUS, THE SON OF GOD

P R O L O G U E	SIGNS WROUGHT		SELF REVEALED		E P I L O G U E 21: 25
	PUBLIC MINISTRY -3 YEARS-	(GREAT) (PAUSE) ▶	PRIVATE MINISTRY -FEW DAYS-		
	ERA OF INCARNATION BEGINS	YEARS OF CONFLICT	DAY OF PREPARATION	HOUR OF SACRIFICE	DAWN OF VICTORY
1:1	1:19	5:1	12:36b	18:1	20:1	21:1

"ARE YOU THE CHRIST?"

22 At that time the **Feast of the Dedication**
          took place at JERUSALEM;
23 it was **winter**,
          and Jesus was walking in the TEMPLE
                in the portico of SOLOMON.
24 The JEWS therefore gathered around HIM,
          and were saying to HIM,
              "**How long** will you keep us **in suspense**?
          If you are THE CHRIST,
                    tell us plainly."
25 JESUS answered them,
              "I told you, and
              you **DO NOT BELIEVE**;
              the works that I do in my Father's name,
                    these **bear witness** of ME.
26 "But you **DO NOT BELIEVE**,
          because   you are not of MY SHEEP.
27 (1) MY SHEEP **hear** My voice and
      (2) I **know** them, and
      (3) they **follow** ME; and
28 (4) I **give** ETERNAL LIFE to them; and
      (5) they shall **never perish**, and
      (6) no one shall **snatch** them out of My hand.
29 "MY FATHER,
              who has **given them to ME**,
                    is greater than all;
          and no one is able to **snatch** them
                          out of the Father's hand.
30 "I and THE FATHER are ONE."

[right margin:] MY SHEEP

---

31 The JEWS took up stones again **to stone HIM**.
32 JESUS answered them,
          "I showed you many good works
                from the FATHER;
          for which of them are you stoning ME?"
33 The JEWS answered HIM,
              "For a good work we do not **stone You**,
          but for BLASPHEMY;
          and because YOU,   being A MAN,
                    make Yourself out to be GOD."
34 JESUS answered them,
          "Has it not been written in YOUR LAW,
              'I said, YOU ARE GODS'?   [Psalm 82:6]
35 "If he called them gods,
                to whom the WORD of GOD came
                (and THE SCRIPTURE cannot be broken),
36 do you say of HIM, whom THE FATHER sanctified
                          and sent into the world,
              'You are BLASPHEMING,'
          because I said, 'I AM THE SON OF GOD'?
37 "If I do not **the works** of MY FATHER,
                    do not BELIEVE ME;
38 but if I **do** them,
          though you **do not** BELIEVE ME,
          BELIEVE THE WORKS,
                that you may **know** and **understand**
                that THE FATHER is IN ME,
                    and I in THE FATHER."
39 Therefore they were seeking **AGAIN** to SEIZE HIM;
                and He **eluded their grasp**.

[right margin:] MY FATHER'S WORKS

Key Words and Phrases

10:24 "If you are the Christ" _____
    25 _____
    28 _____
    29 _____
    31 _____
    33 _____
    38 _____
    39 _____
others: _____

OBSERVATIONS

Segment Survey

1. What prominent names in 10:22 and 23 frame the setting of the segment?

_____

_____

2. Who asks the question in the first paragraph?

_____

Who asks the question in the second paragraph?

_____

3. How much does Jesus talk about His sheep in the first paragraph?

_____

_____

How much does He talk about His Father's works in the second paragraph?

_____

_____

4. How does the confrontation conclude (10:39)?

_____

Paragraph Analysis

10:22-30

1. What was the tone of the Jews' question and demand (verse 24)? _____

2. Jesus had answered their question earlier. (Cf. 8:56-58.) What was the Jews' deep problem?

_____

_____

3. What did Jesus teach them about His sheep? Note the alternating occurrence of "they" and "I" in the six statements of verses 27 and 28.

_____

_____

4. Why do you think He spoke to them so much about His sheep?

_____

_____

10:31-39

1. Compare the opening and closing verses of the paragraph. _____

How do you explain Jesus' ability to elude their grasp?_____

_____

2. How did the Jews justify their attempts to stone Jesus? _____

_____

3. What comparison did Jesus make to expose their error (verses 34-36)?

_____

_____

4. What two kinds of belief did Jesus cite (verse 38)?_____

_____

Why did He do this?_____

_____

Related Verses

Leviticus 24:14-16_____

_____

Mark 14:61-64_____

_____

John 5:18_____

_____

John 14:11 _____

_____

Romans 8:38,39 _____

_____

Romans 11:29_____

_____

1 Peter 1:4,5_____

INTERPRETATIONS

1. "Feast of the Dedication" (10:22). This was not one of the three annual pilgrim feasts. It was the Jews' patriotic celebration, which commemorated the Temple's cleansing after deliverance from the pagan Syrians in 165 B.C.

2. What did Jesus say about His sheep (10:26-29) that told His listeners they were not in that fold?

_____

_____

3. What does 10:28 and 29 teach about eternal life?

_____

4. "You, being a man, make Yourself out to be God" (10:33). What recent statement had Jesus made that caused the Jews to make this charge?

_____

Compare this with 10:36.

_____

5. "'I said, YOU ARE GODS'" (10:34). Human judges were called "gods" in Psalm 82:6. How did Jesus press an *a fortiori* ("all-the-stronger") argument from this?

_____

APPLICATIONS

1. If you are a believer, what is the *foundation* of your Christian faith? Is it the person of Jesus, or His works, or both? How is Christian *living* affected by what the foundation is?

_____

_____

_____

2. Jesus gives assurance of eternal life to His sheep. List some ways this assurance affects your daily walk.

_____

_____

_____

_____

_____

_____

Summary of Passage

At the Feast of the Dedication the Jews again challenge Jesus' claim to being the Christ. He charges that they don't believe His claim because they are not of His sheep. His Father has given Him these sheep, and He and the Father are One. "That's blasphemy," they say, and so they try to stone Him. He further rebukes their unbelief, and they try to seize Him; but He eludes their grasp.

Memory Verses
10:27,28

Looking Ahead

Jesus crosses the Jordan to Perea, and begins a short ministry there.

SETTING Jesus crosses the Jordan to Perea, and goes to the area of John the Baptist's earlier baptizing ministry. Word reaches Him from Bethany of Judea that Lazarus, the brother of Mary and Martha, is sick.

Book of John: LIFE IN JESUS, THE SON OF GOD

P R O L O G U E	SIGNS WROUGHT			SELF REVEALED			E P I L O G U E
	PUBLIC MINISTRY -3 YEARS-		(GREAT) (PAUSE) ▶	PRIVATE MINISTRY -FEW DAYS-			21: 25
	ERA OF INCARNATION BEGINS	YEARS OF CONFLICT	DAY OF PREPARATION	HOUR OF SACRIFICE	DAWN OF VICTORY		
1:1	1:19	5:1	12:36b	18:1	20:1		21:1

FOR GOD'S GLORY

10:40 And HE went away **again** BEYOND THE JORDAN
       to the place where JOHN was **first baptizing**;
       and HE WAS STAYING THERE.
41 And MANY CAME TO HIM
             and were saying,
       "While JOHN performed NO SIGN,
       yet EVERYTHING JOHN said
          about THIS MAN WAS TRUE."
42 And MANY BELIEVED IN HIM there.

—beyond the Jordan—

11:1 Now a certain man was **sick**,
                LAZARUS of BETHANY,
       of the village of MARY and her sister MARTHA.
2 And it was the MARY who
       (1) **anointed** the LORD with ointment, and
       (2) **wiped** His feet with her hair,
       whose brother LAZARUS was **sick**.   [Mark 14:3-9]
3 The SISTERS therefore sent to HIM, saying,
       "LORD, BEHOLD,
       he whom **YOU LOVE** is sick."
4 But when JESUS heard it, HE said,
       "**This sickness** is **not** unto DEATH,
             but for the GLORY OF GOD,
       that the SON OF GOD may be GLORIFIED by it."

GLORY

5 Now JESUS LOVED MARTHA, and
             her sister, and
             LAZARUS.
6 When therefore HE heard that he was **sick**,
       HE stayed then two days longer
             in the place where HE was.
7 Then after this HE said to the DISCIPLES,
       "Let us **go to JUDEA** again."
8 The DISCIPLES said to HIM,
       "RABBI, the JEWS were just now
             seeking to stone You;
       and are You GOING THERE AGAIN?"
9 JESUS answered,
       "Are there not twelve hours in the DAY?
       If anyone WALKS in the DAY,
             he does **not stumble,**
       because he sees THE LIGHT OF THIS WORLD.
10 "But if anyone WALKS in the NIGHT,
             he **stumbles,**
       because THE LIGHT is **not in him**."

LIGHT

11 This HE said,
       and after that HE said to them,
       "OUR FRIEND LAZARUS has **fallen asleep**;
12 The DISCIPLES therefore said to HIM,
       "LORD, if he has **fallen asleep,**
             he will RECOVER."
13 Now JESUS had spoken of His DEATH;
       but they thought
             that HE was speaking of **literal sleep**.
14 Then JESUS therefore said to them **PLAINLY**,
       "**LAZARUS IS DEAD,**
15 and I am **glad** for your sakes
       that **I was not there,**
       so that ➡ YOU MAY BELIEVE;
       but **let us go to him**."
16 THOMAS therefore, who is called DIDYMUS,
       said to his fellow DISCIPLES,
       "**Let us also go,**
       that we may die with Him."

SLEEP

Key Words and Phrases

10:41 "many came to Him"

11:2 _____

3 _____

4 _____

8 _____

9 _____

10 _____

11 _____

others: _____

OBSERVATIONS

Segment Survey

1. The first of the four paragraphs provides the setting—a place on the east side of the Jordan. Read the paragraph. Then read the opening verse in the second paragraph, which gives background information for the miracle Jesus will perform at Bethany.

2. The second, third and fourth paragraphs form one continuous narrative. Read them, and try to determine why new paragraphs start at verses 5 and 11. Identify these three prominent subjects:

GLORY (second paragraph) _____

LIGHT (third paragraph) _____

SLEEP (fourth paragraph) _____

Paragraph Analysis

10:40-42

1. Compare the two references to *many* people.

_____

What brought on the change?

_____

2. Compare 10:41 and 42 with 10:37-39.

_____

11:1-4

1. Did the sisters ask Jesus to come and heal Lazarus?

2. What do you learn here about

   (a) JESUS' LOVE? _____

_____

_____

    (b) GOD'S GLORY?_____

_____

_____

3. Relate 11:4 to 11:15; 9:3; and 7:18.

_____

_____

11:5-10

1. Why do you think John reported the fact of Jesus' love for the sisters and brother (verse 5)?

2. Does John indicate why Jesus stayed in Perea for two days after he heard the news about

Lazarus?_____ Does 11:17 provide a

clue?_____ If so, what is it?_____

_____

_____

3. In your own words, how did Jesus answer the disciples' question in verse 8?

_____

_____

11:11-16

1. What was Lazarus' state?

_____

Did Jesus say He would bring Lazarus back to

life?_____ If He did not, what clue did He give to indicate that He would do this?

_____

2. Account for Thomas' words (verse 16).

_____

_____

Related Verses

Mark 14:3-9 _____

_____

Luke 10:38-42_____

_____

John 2:11_____

_____

John 9:3-5_____

_____

John 12:1-9_____

_____

Acts 7:60_____

_____

1 Thessalonians 4:13 _____

_____

INTERPRETATIONS

1. "This sickness is not unto death" (11:4). In view of 11:14, what did Jesus *not* mean by this

statement?_____

Then what did He mean by the remainder of the

statement (11:4b)?_____

_____

2. "He stayed then two days longer" (11:6). The messenger's journey from Bethany to Perea (twenty miles) took about one day; then Jesus delayed two days; then Jesus' journey to Bethany was one day. By the time Jesus arrived at Lazarus' tomb, Lazarus had been entombed four days. So he was already dead when Jesus first heard the news of his sickness. Why, then, do you think Jesus tarried in Perea for those two

days?_____

3. What kind of belief did Jesus have in mind when He spoke to the disciples (11:15)?

4. "That we may die with Him" (11:16). Thomas was referring to Jesus, not Lazarus. What was he thinking of? (Cf. 11:8.)

APPLICATIONS

1. How strong is your faith that Jesus loves you? How deep and intimate do you think Jesus' love

is?_____

How can this support you in your sorrows and trying circumstances?

_____

2. If Jesus is your Lord, you must submit to His rule in your daily walk. Among other things, you must not walk "in the night" (11:10). Cite some examples of this kind of walking that you need to avoid, to keep you from stumbling.

_____

_____

_____

Summary of Passage

While Jesus is ministering in Perea, He learns that Lazarus, brother of Mary and Martha, is sick. He responds that this sickness is for the glory of God. He stays in Perea two more days, and then tells His disciples that He must return to Bethany, to awaken Lazarus out of sleep—that is, out of death. He is glad that the disciples will witness this awakening, for they will believe. The disciples fear for Jesus' life in going back to the enemies in Judea. Thomas urges them, "Let's go and die with Him."

Memory Verses   11:9,10

Looking Ahead

Jesus arrives at Bethany, four days after Lazarus has died. He ministers primarily to Martha and Mary.

SETTING Jesus arrives at the outskirts of Bethany, when He meets Martha, who has come out to see Him. After a short visit she returns home to get Mary, who comes to where Jesus is.

Book of John: LIFE IN JESUS, THE SON OF GOD

P R O L O G U E	SIGNS WROUGHT			SELF REVEALED		E P I L O G U E
	PUBLIC MINISTRY -3 YEARS-		(GREAT) (PAUSE) ▶	PRIVATE MINISTRY -FEW DAYS-		
	ERA OF INCARNATION BEGINS	YEARS OF CONFLICT	DAY OF PREPARATION	HOUR OF SACRIFICE	DAWN OF VICTORY	
1:1	1:19	5:1	12:36b	18:1	20:1	21:1

THE RESURRECTION AND THE LIFE

17 So when JESUS CAME,
    He found
      that he had already been **in the tomb** four days.
18   Now BETHANY was near JERUSALEM,
        about two miles off;
19 and MANY of the JEWS
      had **come** to MARTHA and MARY,
      to **CONSOLE THEM** concerning their brother.
20 MARTHA therefore,
      when she heard that JESUS WAS COMING,
  WENT TO MEET HIM;
      but MARY still **sat in the house.**
21 MARTHA therefore said to JESUS,
    "LORD, IF YOU HAD BEEN HERE,
    MY BROTHER **would not have died.**
22 "Even now I know that
    WHATEVER **You ask** of GOD,
      GOD will give You."
23 JESUS said to her,
    "Your BROTHER SHALL RISE AGAIN."
24 MARTHA said to HIM,
    "I know that he will RISE AGAIN
    in the **resurrection** on the **last day.**"
25 JESUS said to her,
    "I AM THE RESURRECTION, AND THE LIFE;
    he who BELIEVES IN ME shall LIVE
           even if he dies,
26 and everyone who lives and BELIEVES IN ME
    shall NEVER DIE.
    Do you BELIEVE THIS?"
27 She said to HIM,
    "Yes LORD; I HAVE BELIEVED that
    YOU are THE CHRIST, the SON OF GOD,
      even HE who comes into the **world.**"

MARTHA & JESUS

28 And when she had said this, she
    (1) went away, and
    (2) called MARY her sister, saying **secretly,**
    "THE TEACHER is here, and is **calling for you.**"
29 And when she heard it,
    she **arose quickly,** and was COMING TO HIM.
30 Now Jesus had not yet COME into the village,
    but was still in the place where MARTHA met Him.
31 The JEWS then who were with her in the house,
        and CONSOLING HER,
    when they saw that MARY rose up quickly
      and went out,
      followed her,
      supposing that she was going to the TOMB
      to **weep** there.

MARTHA & MARY

32 Therefore, when MARY CAME **where JESUS was,**
    she saw Him, and FELL AT HIS FEET,
    saying to Him, "LORD, IF YOU HAD BEEN HERE,
    MY BROTHER **would not have died.**"
33 When JESUS therefore saw her **weeping,**
    and the JEWS who came with her, **also weeping,**
    He was
      (1) **deeply moved in spirit,** and
      (2) was **troubled,**
34 and said, "Where have you laid him?"
    They said to Him, "LORD, COME and see."
35   JESUS WEPT.
36 And so the JEWS were saying,
    "BEHOLD **how He loved him!**"

MARY & JESUS

37 But **some** of them said,
    "Could not THIS MAN,
    who opened the eyes of him who was **blind,**
      have kept this man also from **dying?**"

Key Words and Phrases

11:17 "in the tomb four days" _____

  19 _____

  21 _____

  22 _____

  23 _____

  25 _____

  28 _____

  35 _____

others: _____

OBSERVATIONS

Segment Survey

1. The segment contains three paragraphs of different lengths and content. How does the first line introduce the passage?

_____

_____

2. Who is conversing in the first paragraph?

_____

How much did Martha talk?

_____

3. Is there much conversation in the second and third paragraphs? Whom does John quote in the

second paragraph?_____

Who are the speakers of the third paragraph?

_____

4. Compare the conclusion of the first paragraph (11:27) with the conclusion of the third paragraph (11:37).

_____

_____

Paragraph Analysis

11:17-27

1. What faith did Martha express in each of these verses?

    verse 21_____

    verse 22_____

    verse 24_____

    verse 27_____

2. Did Jesus tell Martha that He would raise Lazarus from the tomb at this time? What *did* He say (verse 23)?

What was Martha's response (verse 24)?
_____
_____

11:28-31
What do you learn about Mary from this paragraph?_____

11:32-37
1. Compare Mary's only quoted words to Jesus (verse 32) with Martha's first words to Jesus (verse 21). _____

Compare Jesus' response in each case.
_____
_____

2. What do you learn about Jesus from this paragraph?_____

3. What kind of faith is expressed in verse 37?
_____

Related Verses
Psalm 17:15 _____

Luke 19:41_____

John 20:31 _____
_____

Romans 6:8,9_____

1 Corinthians 15:20,57_____
_____

Colossians 1:18_____
_____

1 Thessalonians 4:16 _____
_____

Hebrews 5:7 _____
_____

INTERPRETATIONS
1. "In the tomb four days" (11:17). Do you think the two-day delay (11:6) was intentional to bring about Jesus' arrival after decomposition had set in?
2. "Whatever You ask of God, God will give You" (11:22). The messenger(s) may have carried Jesus' words in 11:4 back to Mary and Martha. If so, do you think Mary was referring to this when she spoke in 11:22? Explain.

3. "I am the resurrection and the life" (11:25). What does this testimony add to the other six "I am's" in John? (The seven "I am's": 6:35; 8:12; 10:9; 10:11; 11:25; 14:6; 15:5.)
_____

4. "Shall never die" (11:26). To what kind of death does this refer? _____
To what kind of death does the word "dies" in 11:25 refer?_____
5. What does 11:27 reveal about Mary's heart? Relate this to 20:31. _____

APPLICATIONS
1. The critical dilemma of sinful humankind is this: "I want to live, but I must die." How is Jesus the answer to the dilemma?
_____

What must the sinner do to be liberated?
_____

2. How should Jesus' dwelling in your heart make a difference in your daily walk?
_____

What are the implications of Jesus' testimony, "I am...THE LIFE," and how does this truth affect you?_____
_____

In what ways can your life be a better witness that Jesus indwells you?
_____

Summary of Passage
Jesus arrives at the outskirts of Bethany, and Mary comes to meet Him there. Lazarus has been dead four days. Mary tells Jesus that if He had been here, Lazarus would not have died. Jesus assures her that Lazarus shall rise again because He, the resurrection and the life, gives eternal life to all who believe.

Mary brings Martha to Jesus, and both Mary and Jesus weep. The Jews say, "See how He loved him!"

Memory Verses 11:25,26

Looking Ahead
Jesus raises Lazarus from the dead.

SETTING Jesus comes to the tomb where Lazarus is buried. Mary, Martha and many Jewish mourners witness the miracle which Jesus performs.

Book of John: LIFE IN JESUS, THE SON OF GOD

P R O L O G U E	SIGNS WROUGHT			SELF REVEALED		E P I L O G U E 21: 25
	PUBLIC MINISTRY -3 YEARS-	(GREAT) (PAUSE) ▶		PRIVATE MINISTRY -FEW DAYS-		
	ERA OF INCARNATION BEGINS	YEARS OF CONFLICT	DAY OF PREPARATION	HOUR OF SACRIFICE	DAWN OF VICTORY	
1:1	1:19	5:1	12:36b	18:1	20:1	21:1

"COME FORTH"

38 JESUS therefore **again** being **deeply** moved **within,**
     CAME TO THE TOMB.
   Now it was a cave,
        and a stone was lying against it.
39 JESUS said,
   "**Remove the stone.**"
   MARTHA, the sister of the deceased, said to Him,
   "LORD, by this time there will be a **stench;**
        for he has been dead four days."
40 JESUS said to her,
   "Did not **I say to you,**
    if you **BELIEVE,**
        you will SEE the GLORY OF GOD?"
41 And so they removed the stone.
   And JESUS raised His eyes, and said,
   "FATHER, **I thank Thee**
        that **Thou heardest Me.**
42 "And I knew that **Thou hearest Me** always;
   but because of the people standing around
                              I said it,
   that they may BELIEVE
        that Thou didst send Me."

PREPARATION

43 And when He had said these things,
      He **cried out** with a **loud voice,**
   "LAZARUS, **come forth.**"
44 HE who had died
      CAME FORTH,
      bound hand and foot with wrappings;
   and his face was wrapped around with a cloth.
   JESUS said to them,
        "UNBIND HIM, and
        LET HIM GO."

EVENT

45 MANY therefore of the JEWS,
      who had come to MARY
      and BEHELD **what HE had done,**
           BELIEVED IN HIM.
46 But SOME of them
           went away to the PHARISEES,
      and told them the **things which JESUS had done.**

EFFECTS

Key Words and Phrases

11:38 "deeply moved within" _____

   39 _____

   40 _____

   41 _____

   42 _____

   43 _____

   44 _____

   45 _____

others: _____

_____

OBSERVATIONS

Segment Survey

1. As you read the segment, be sensitive to what must have been the emotions of everyone as the action proceeded. What is the overall tone of the account?

Compare the three paragraphs, beginning with the outline shown:

   11:38-42—PREPARATION _____

   _____

   11:43,44—EVENT _____

   _____

   11:45,46—EFFECTS _____

   _____

2. Does John report any reaction from Mary and Martha after the miracle?_____
Can you think of any reason for this? (See 12:1-11, John's last reference to Lazarus' sisters.)

Paragraph Analysis

11:38-42
1. Whose feelings are reported in this paragraph?

_____

2. John's reporting of this miracle is pressed into just nine verses (11:38-46). The action is brief, as are the spoken words. To whom does Jesus speak in this paragraph? Then to whom does He speak in the second paragraph?

   verse 39_____

   verse 40_____

   verses 41 and 42_____

   verse 43_____

3. Why do you think Jesus spoke the words of verse 40 to Martha? Were His words a rebuke, a reminder, or what?

_____

4. The statement, "I said it" (verse 42) may read "I said this" (NIV). What was Jesus referring to by the word "it" ("this")?

_____

_____

11:43,44
What are your impressions of this miracle? Imagine you are an onlooker when it happened.

_____

_____

_____

_____

11:45,46

1. What were the two effects of the miracle? Compare the first one with 11:42.

_____

_____

2. In view of the first word "But" of verse 46, what do you think was in the hearts of these reporters?

_____

_____

Related Verses

John 5:25,28,29 _____

_____

John 5:36,37; 7:16,17; 8:18,27-29; 10:37,38

_____

_____

John 11:4,23 _____

_____

John 11:25,26 _____

_____

John 12:1-11 _____

_____

John 20:7 _____

_____

1 Thessalonians 4:16 _____

_____

INTERPRETATIONS

1. "Did not I say to you" (11:40). The next words of Jesus are a summary of what He had said earlier to the sisters directly or through the messenger. See 11:4,23,25 and 26.

2. "If you believe, you will see" (11:40). Was the performance of the miracle dependent on Martha's faith? If not, what did Jesus mean?

_____

_____

3. "Because of the people standing around I said it" (11:42). A possible interpretation is that "it" refers to Jesus' words in verse 40, assuming that the Jews overheard those words. If "it" refers to the words, "Father, I thank Thee that Thou heardest Me," how would such words point to the truth "that Thou didst send Me"?

_____

_____

4. "Come forth" (11:43). The command translates two adverbs: "hither, out!"

5. "Beheld what He had done" (11:45). What does the word "beheld" suggest?

_____

_____

6. Compare 11:46 with 11:47-48.

_____

_____

APPLICATIONS

Three prominent truths stand out in this passage. What does each of these have to do with your own personal life? If you are studying with a group, you may want to share testimonies about these.

1. The humanity of Jesus: _____

_____

_____

_____

_____

2. The glory of God: _____

_____

_____

_____

_____

3. Faith in Jesus' power: _____

_____

_____

_____

Summary of Passage

Jesus comes to Lazarus' tomb, deeply moved. He asks that the stone be removed, but Martha is concerned about the bad odor. Jesus reminds her that if she believed, she would see the glory of God. He prays to His Father, and calls out with a loud voice into the open tomb, "Lazarus, come out!" He comes forth, bound with wrappings and a cloth. Attendants remove these.

Many Jews behold the miracle in amazement, and believe in Him. Others go away and report it to the Pharisees.

A Memory Verse   11:44

Looking Ahead

The Jewish leaders plan together to kill Jesus.

SETTING The setting changes with each paragraph:

11:47-53—a meeting of the Sanhedrin ("council") in Jerusalem;

11:54—a village called Ephraim, possibly north of Bethany;

11:55-57—Jerusalem, just before the Passover.

ONE MAN SHOULD DIE

47 Therefore
    (1) the CHIEF PRIESTS and
    (2) the PHARISEES
convened a **council**, and were saying,
"What are **we doing**?
For THIS MAN is **performing many SIGNS.**
48 "If we let Him go on like this,
    ALL MEN will **BELIEVE IN HIM,**
    and the ROMANS will come
    and take away both
    (1) our place and
    (2) our nation."
49 But a certain one of them,
    CAIAPHAS, who was **high priest** that year,
    said to them,
    (1) "You know nothing at all, nor
50 (2) do you take into account that
    it is expedient for you
    that ONE MAN should **die for the people,**
    and that the WHOLE NATION should **not perish."**
51 Now this he did not say
          on his own initiative;
    but being **high priest** that year,
    he PROPHESIED that
JESUS WAS GOING TO DIE FOR THE NATION,
52 and **not** for the nation only,
    but that He might **also**
    GATHER TOGETHER into ONE
    the CHILDREN OF GOD who are scattered abroad.
53 So **from that day on**
    THEY PLANNED TOGETHER to KILL HIM.

(margin: PLANNING)

54 JESUS therefore
    no longer continued to walk publicly
          among the JEWS,
    but **went away** from there
    to the country near the wilderness,
    into a city called EPHRAIM;
    and there He stayed with THE DISCIPLES.

(margin: HIDING)

55 Now the PASSOVER of the JEWS was at hand,
    and MANY went up to JERUSALEM
          out of the country
    before the PASSOVER,
    to **purify** themselves.
56 Therefore they were **seeking** for JESUS,
    and were saying to one another,
    as they stood in the TEMPLE,
    "What do you think;
    that He will **not** come to the FEAST at all?"
57 Now the CHIEF PRIESTS and PHARISEES
    had given **ORDERS** that
    if anyone knew **where HE WAS,**
    he should report it,
    that they might SEIZE HIM.

(margin: SEEKING)

Book of John: LIFE IN JESUS, THE SON OF GOD

P R O L O G U E	SIGNS WROUGHT			SELF REVEALED		E P I L O G U E
	PUBLIC MINISTRY -3 YEARS-		(GREAT) (PAUSE) ▶	PRIVATE MINISTRY -FEW DAYS-		
	ERA OF INCARNATION BEGINS	YEARS OF CONFLICT	DAY OF PREPARATION	HOUR OF SACRIFICE	DAWN OF VICTORY	
1:1	1:19	5:1	12:36b	18:1	20:1	21:1

Key Words and Phrases

11:47 ___"What are we doing?"___

48 _____

49 _____

50 _____

51 _____

52 _____

53 _____

57 _____

others: _____

OBSERVATIONS

Segment Survey

1. The three paragraphs are very different as to setting and action, but all point to the one theme: getting Jesus killed.
2. Read each paragraph, and record the setting, characters, and action.

	SETTING	CHARACTERS	ACTION
11:47-53			
11:54			
11:55-57			

3. Compare the opening verse and the concluding verse. _____
_____

Paragraph Analysis

11:47-53

1. What were the three parts of the council's dilemma?

    (a) 11:47b_____

    (b) 11:48a_____

    (c) 11:48b_____

2. Read verses 49-53 in the Living Bible or a similar paraphrase.

3. In Caiaphas' view, what needed to happen to save the Jewish nation ("our nation") from destruction by the Roman powers?

_____
_____

4. What is John's commentary on Caiaphas' advice? _____
_____

How does John apply the prophecy universally?

_____

_____

_____

5. How successful was Caiaphas' strong advice, according to verse 53?

_____

_____

_____

11:54
1. Why do you think Jesus avoided public exposure in the Jerusalem area at this time?

_____

2. How does the last phrase of verse 54 suggest a ministry that Jesus wanted to perform at this time?

_____

11:55-57
1. Read verse 57 first. What is the strength of the "orders" the Jewish rulers had given?

_____

_____

2. What was prophetic about this combination: PASSOVER; PURIFY; JESUS; TEMPLE (verses 55 and 56)? _____

_____

_____

_____

3. Do you think the people expected Jesus to make *some* appearance in Jerusalem at the feast? Explain._____

_____

_____

Related Verses
Luke 17:11—19:28 (events between John 11:54 and 11:55)_____

_____

John 10:16 _____

_____

John 18:14 _____

_____

Romans 5:6-8_____

_____

Romans 11:25,26_____

_____

1 Peter 1:10-12 _____

INTERPRETATIONS
1. "The Romans will come" (11:48). The Jews knew the mind and power of Rome. In just a few decades the Roman army would destroy Jerusalem (A.D. 70). What did the council suppose would bring on such judgment (11:48a)?

_____

_____

If they recognized this, why do you think Caiaphas reprimanded them so harshly

(11:49,50)?_____
2. Unknown to Caiaphas, his prophecy had a deeper meaning (11:51,52). What was that?

_____

3. "They planned together" (11:53). Who are

"they"? _____
Since most of the high priests were Sadducees, what is significant about their planning together

with the Pharisees?_____

_____

4. "Before the Passover, to purify themselves" (11:55). Many Jewish people traveled to Jerusalem early to observe the purification rites of Passover before the larger crowds arrived.

APPLICATIONS
1. Jesus died for the nation of Israel (11:51). He also died for non-Jews (11:52). Jesus died for *you*. Reflect more on this. How should knowing this deepen your gratitude and desire to serve Him?

_____

2. Jesus was always teaching His disciples, preparing them especially to be His witnesses after His death (11:54). In what ways can you learn at the feet of Jesus to make you a better disciple? (TBS#7)

_____

_____

_____

_____

Summary of Passage
The Sanhedrin council is intensely disturbed that Jesus continues to perform miracles. Their leader, Caiaphas, warns that the only way to save their Jewish nation from the threat of Rome is to kill Jesus. So they begin to plan to do this. Jesus and His disciples retreat to a desert.

Some time later, just before the Passover week, the crowds begin arriving in Jerusalem. They wonder if Jesus will appear, because the Sanhedrin has given orders to report His presence.

Memory Verse   11:48

Looking Ahead
Jesus spends time with Mary and Martha and their brother Lazarus whom He had raised from the dead.

SETTING Six days before the Passover, Jesus and His disciples return to Bethany, where He spends time with Mary and Martha and their brother Lazarus. The gathering is in the home of "Simon the leper" (Matthew 26:6). Many Jews come to the house when they hear that Jesus and Lazarus are there.

ANOINTED FOR BURIAL

1 JESUS, therefore, six days before the PASSOVER,
    came to BETHANY,
      where LAZARUS was,
        whom JESUS had **RAISED from the DEAD.**
2 So they made Him a **supper** there,
    and MARTHA was **serving;**
    but LAZARUS was one of those
      reclining at the table **with Him.**
3 MARY therefore
    took a pound
      of very costly perfume of pure nard, and
      (1) **anointed the feet of JESUS**, and
      (2) **wiped His feet** with her hair;
        and the house was **filled**
          with the FRAGRANCE OF THE PERFUME.

FRIENDS

---

4 But JUDAS ISCARIOT,
    one of HIS DISCIPLES,
      who was **intending** to BETRAY HIM,
5 said, "Why was this perfume **not sold**
    for three hundred denarii,
    and given to poor people?"
6 Now he said this,
    not because he was **concerned about** the poor,
    but because he was a thief,
    and as he had the money box,
    he used to **pilfer** what was put into it.
7 JESUS therefore said,
    "**Let her alone,**
      in order that she may keep it
        for the DAY OF MY BURIAL.
8 "For the **poor you always have** with you,
    but **you do not always HAVE ME.**"

THIEF

---

9 The GREAT MULTITUDE therefore
      OF THE JEWS
    learned that **He was there;**
    and THEY CAME,
      not for JESUS' sake only,
      but that they might **also see LAZARUS,**
        whom He RAISED FROM THE DEAD.
10 BUT the CHIEF PRIESTS
    took COUNSEL
    that they might **put LAZARUS to death also;**
11   ▶ BECAUSE on account of him
    MANY of the JEWS
      were **going away,**
        and were BELIEVING IN JESUS.

MURDERERS

Key Words and Phrases

12:2 _"serving"_ _____
  2 _____
  3 _____
  3 _____
  4 _____
  5 _____
  7 _____

Book of John: LIFE IN JESUS, THE SON OF GOD

P R O L O G U E	SIGNS WROUGHT			SELF REVEALED			E P I L O G U E 21: 25
	PUBLIC MINISTRY -3 YEARS-		(GREAT) (PAUSE) ▶	PRIVATE MINISTRY -FEW DAYS-			
	ERA OF INCARNATION BEGINS	YEARS OF CONFLICT	DAY OF PREPARATION	HOUR OF SACRIFICE	DAWN OF VICTORY		
1:1	1:19	5:1	12:36b	18:1	20:1		21:1

    8 _____
others: _____

OBSERVATIONS

Segment Survey

1. Relate each paragraph of the segment to its preceding paragraph, in view of each connecting word:
    "therefore" (12:1) _____
    "but" (12:4) _____
    "therefore" (12:9) _____
2. Compare the tone and atmosphere of the three paragraphs. _____
_____
_____

3. What three phrases of this segment especially stand out to you?
_____
_____
_____

Paragraph Analysis

12:1-3
1. Compare what the two sisters and brother were doing individually while Jesus visited with them. _____
_____
_____

2. Which activity does John describe with more words?
_____
Why? _____
_____

12:4-8
1. What three descriptions does John give of Judas Iscariot?
_____
_____

2. What was dishonest about Judas' question (12:5)? _____
3. Compare Judas' welfare plan with Mary's act.
_____
_____

4. With whom did Jesus compare Himself, as reported in this paragraph?

What does the comparison teach?

_____

_____

12:9-11

1. Who is the central person of this paragraph?

_____

2. How did Lazarus' living presence aggravate the problem in 11:47 and 48?

_____

_____

3. Compare 12:10 with 11:53.

_____

_____

Related Verses

Matthew 26:7 _____

_____

Matthew 26:8 _____

_____

Matthew 26:13 _____

_____

Mark 8:31 _____

_____

Mark 14:1,2 _____

_____

Luke 10:39 _____

_____

John 12:17-19 _____

_____

INTERPRETATIONS

1. "Very costly perfume of pure nard" (12:3). Judas said that this pound of ointment could be sold for three hundred denarii, which was a laborer's *annual wage* (cf. Mark 14:5). "Pure nard" (genuine spikenard) was an aromatic herb grown in the highlands of the Himalayas. The ointment was extracted from this.

2. "Anointed the feet of Jesus" (12:3). This was Mary's act of devotion. Compare this with what Martha was doing (12:2). Do you think one activity was more important than the other in Jesus' eyes? Explain.

_____

_____

3. "In order that she may keep it for the day of My burial" (12:7). Matthew's account interprets the meaning: "She did it to prepare Me for burial" (Matthew 26:12). Among other things it was a symbolic anticipation of what Jesus knew was near: His day of burial.

4. "Believing in Jesus" (12:11). What brought on this belief? Compare 20:30 and 31.

_____

APPLICATIONS

1. What ministries for Jesus do you read about in this passage? Are you doing some or all of these now for Him? If so, what fruits are you enjoying from them?

_____

_____

_____

_____

_____

_____

2. What do you learn about devotion and worship here? How can you improve this important part of your Christian life?

_____

_____

_____

_____

_____

_____

_____

_____

_____

_____

_____

_____

Summary of Passage

Six days before the Passover Jesus is visiting at supper with Mary, Martha and Lazarus in a home in Bethany. Martha is serving, Lazarus is reclining with Jesus, and Mary is anointing Jesus' feet with expensive perfume. Judas Iscariot objects, saying that Mary's act is a waste of much money which could be given to poor people. Jesus defends her devotion as preparation for burial.

Multitudes come to the house to see Jesus and Lazarus, and many believe in Jesus because of Lazarus. From then on, Jesus' opponents want to kill Lazarus also.

Memory Verses   12:7,8

Looking Ahead

Jesus makes His final entry into Jerusalem.

SETTING Jesus spent Saturday in Bethany (12:1-11). Now, on Sunday (12:12), He makes His final entry into Jerusalem, from the east, with His disciples. Multitudes are crowded around Him.

Book of John: LIFE IN JESUS, THE SON OF GOD

P R O L O G U E	SIGNS WROUGHT			SELF REVEALED		E P I L O G U E
	PUBLIC MINISTRY -3 YEARS-	(GREAT) (PAUSE) ▶		PRIVATE MINISTRY -FEW DAYS-		21: 25
	ERA OF INCARNATION BEGINS	YEARS OF CONFLICT	DAY OF PREPARATION	HOUR OF SACRIFICE	DAWN OF VICTORY	
1:1	1:19	5:1	12:36b	18:1	20:1	21:1

"YOUR KING COMES"

12 On the next day
    the GREAT MULTITUDE
        who had come to the FEAST,
           when they heard
               that JESUS WAS COMING
                       TO JERUSALEM,
13 (1) **took** the branches of the palm trees, and
   (2) **went out** to MEET HIM, and
   (3) **began to cry out**,
      "HOSANNA:
      Blessed is He
    who COMES IN THE NAME OF THE LORD,
        even THE KING OF ISRAEL."
14 And JESUS,
    finding a young donkey, **sat on it;**
  as it is written,
15 "Fear not, daughter of ZION;
    BEHOLD,
  YOUR KING COMES sitting on a donkey's colt."
                        [Zechariah 9:9]

ARRIVAL

16 These things
    HIS DISCIPLES **did not understand** at the first;
  but when JESUS WAS GLORIFIED,
    then they remembered
  that these things were **written of Him,**
  and that they had done these things to Him.

REFLECTIONS

17 And so
    the MULTITUDE who were **with Him**
  when He called LAZARUS out of the **tomb,**
    and RAISED HIM FROM THE DEAD,
  were **bearing Him witness.**
18 For this cause also
    the MULTITUDE went and **MET HIM,**
  because   ▸ they heard
       that He had PERFORMED THIS SIGN.
19 The PHARISEES therefore said **to one another,**
  "You see that **you are not doing any good;**
  LOOK ▸ THE WORLD HAS GONE AFTER HIM."

REACTIONS

Key Words and Phrases

12:12 "coming to Jerusalem" _____

   13 _____

   13 _____

   13 _____

   14 _____

   15 _____

   16 _____

   19 _____

others: _____

_____

OBSERVATIONS

Segment Survey

1. The segment is only eight verses long, but the pictures of the narrative are numerous and multicolored.

2. Read each paragraph, referring to the outline as you read. In your own words, what is the contribution of each paragraph?

     12:12-15_____

     12:16 _____

     12:17-19_____

3. Compare the opening verse with the concluding verse._____

_____

_____

Paragraph Analysis

12:12-15

1. What is the prominent title given to Jesus in this paragraph? _____

By what names are His subjects identified?

_____

_____

2. How did the people identify Jesus' deity?

_____

3. How did the prophet Zechariah identify Jesus' humanity?_____

_____

12:16

1. What does John's commentary reveal about the disciples' grasp of Messianic Scripture at this time in Jesus' ministry?

_____

_____

2. When did they see the light?

_____

3. How do you explain this?

_____

_____

12:17-19

1. Read the first two words "And so" as "Now" (NIV). Who had been spreading the word about Jesus' raising Lazarus from the dead?

_____

_____

Who were now going out to meet Him?

_____

How does this explain the Pharisees' reference to "the world" (verse 19)?

_____

2. How do you think John learned about the Pharisees' reaction (verse 19)?

_____

3. Compare the exclamations in verses 13 and 19b.

_____

Related Verses

Leviticus 23:40 _____

Psalm 118:25,26 _____

Isaiah 62:10,11 _____

Matthew 21:4,5 _____

Matthew 21:10-17 _____

Mark 11:1-11 _____

Luke 19:37-44 _____

INTERPRETATIONS

1. "Jesus was coming to Jerusalem" (12:12). How does this fact teach that Jesus *voluntarily* gave Himself unto death?

_____

2. Waving palm branches symbolized joy. What was joyful about the crowd's chant (12:13b)?

_____

3. "Hosanna" (12:13). Literally, this Hebrew term means "save, I pray," or "save now." When the crowds shouted "Hosanna" to Jesus, it was both a prayer and a note of praise for the King's coming.

4. "King of Israel" (12:13). If Jesus should be crowned King of Israel, how would this affect the Jews' subjection to Rome's rule?

_____

5. "Your King comes sitting on a donkey's colt" (12:15). What did this manner of arrival teach about Jesus' objective? Compare the word "gentle" in Matthew 21:5.

6. How did this entry into Jerusalem show Jesus as the promised Messiah?

_____

APPLICATIONS

1. A line of one of our Christian songs reads, "King of my life, I crown Thee now." What does it mean to you that Jesus is your King? How does this affect your daily walk?

_____

What do you learn from this passage about Jesus as King?

_____

2. The gospel is good news for the whole world. Why is that?

_____

What makes your witness of the gospel attractive to unsaved souls?

_____

Summary of Passage

On His way from Bethany to Jerusalem, Jesus mounts a donkey's colt, as Zechariah had prophesied centuries earlier (Zechariah 9:9). A great multitude presses around Jesus on the journey, spreading palm branches on the road, and hailing Him as King of Israel. Many of them were eye-witnesses when He raised Lazarus. The enthusiasm and excitement keep growing, but the Pharisees are troubled that "the world has gone after Him."

Memory Verse   12:13b
Looking Ahead

Jesus ministers to some Greeks in Jerusalem.

SETTING This is the concluding passage of the section of John's Gospel called YEARS OF CONFLICT. (See survey chart.) Jesus is in Jerusalem, talking with some Greeks and some of His disciples. In just a few days He will be in the hands of His captors and facing crucifixion.

Book of John: LIFE IN JESUS, THE SON OF GOD

PROLOGUE	SIGNS WROUGHT		SELF REVEALED			EPILOGUE 21:25
	PUBLIC MINISTRY -3 YEARS-	(GREAT) (PAUSE) ▶	PRIVATE MINISTRY -FEW DAYS-			
	ERA OF INCARNATION BEGINS	YEARS OF CONFLICT	DAY OF PREPARATION	HOUR OF SACRIFICE	DAWN OF VICTORY	
1:1	1:19	5:1	12:36b	18:1	20:1	21:1

THE HOUR HAS COME

20 Now there were CERTAIN GREEKS among those
who were going up to **WORSHIP** at the FEAST;
21 these therefore **came to PHILIP,**
who was from BETHSAIDA of GALILEE,
and began to ask him, saying,
"Sir, WE WISH TO SEE JESUS."
22 PHILIP came and told ANDREW;
ANDREW came, and PHILIP,
and **THEY TOLD JESUS.**
23 And JESUS answered them, saying,
"THE HOUR HAS COME
for the SON OF MAN to be **GLORIFIED**.
24 "Truly, truly, I say to you,
unless a grain of wheat **falls** into the earth and **dies,**
it **remains** by itself **alone;**
but if IT DIES,
IT BEARS MUCH FRUIT.
25 "He who **loves** HIS LIFE **loses it;**
and he who **hates** HIS LIFE in this world
shall keep it to LIFE ETERNAL.
26 "If any one **serves** Me,
let him **follow** Me;
and where I am, there shall **my servant** also be;
if anyone **serves** Me,
the FATHER will **honor him.**

DEATH FOR LIFE

27 "Now My soul has become **troubled;**
and what shall I say?
'FATHER, save Me from THIS HOUR'?
But for this purpose I came to THIS HOUR.
28 "FATHER, **glorify Thy name.**"
There came therefore a **voice out of heaven:**
"I (1) **have** both glorified it, and
(2) **will** glorify it again."
29 The MULTITUDE therefore,
who stood by and heard it,
were saying that **it had thundered**;
others were saying,
"An ANGEL has spoken to Him."
30 JESUS answered and said,
"THIS VOICE has not come **for My sake,**
but **for your sakes.**
31 "NOW judgment is upon this world;
NOW the ruler of this world shall be cast out.
32 "And I, if I be lifted up from the earth,
WILL DRAW ALL MEN TO MYSELF."
33 But He was saying this
to indicate the **kind** of DEATH
by which He was to DIE.
34 The MULTITUDE therefore answered Him,
"We have heard out of THE LAW
that THE CHRIST is to **remain forever;**
and how can You say,
'The SON OF MAN must be lifted up'?
WHO IS THIS SON OF MAN?"

CROSS FOR FOLLOWERS

35 JESUS therefore said to them,
"For a **little while** longer, THE LIGHT is among you.
WALK while you have THE LIGHT,
that DARKNESS may not overtake you;
he who walks in the DARKNESS
does not know where he goes.
36a "While you have THE LIGHT,
BELIEVE **IN THE LIGHT,**
in order that you may become **SONS OF LIGHT.**"

LIGHT FOR WALKING

Key Words and Phrases

12:20 "Greeks" ______

21 ______

23 ______

24 ______

25 ______

26 ______

28 ______

29 ______

others: ______

OBSERVATIONS

Segment Survey

1. First read the passage to observe the different ones with whom Jesus is talking.
2. Then read each paragraph, and try to identify a main theme of each. Compare your conclusions with the outline shown.
3. Compare "we wish to see Jesus" (12:21) with "while you have the light" (12:36a).

______

______

4. By what names and titles is Jesus referred to in the passage? ______

______

______

Paragraph Analysis

12:20-26

1. What do you learn about the Greek (Gentile) inquirers from verses 20 and 21?

______

______

2. The text does not state that Jesus spoke the words in verses 12ff. directly to the Greeks, but they must have gotten the reply at least indirectly, otherwise verses 20-22 would seem unrelated. What do you think they wanted to learn from Jesus? ______

______

3. Assuming salvation was on their minds, study Jesus' response in verses 23-26. Observe: glory for Jesus (verse 23) and honor for followers of

Jesus (verse 26). What did Jesus teach between those statements, as to

(a) the Savior (verse 24)? _____

_____

(b) the saved ones (verses 25 and 26)?_____

_____

12:27-34

1. What did Jesus desire and pray for (verses 27 and 28)?_____

2. How did God demonstrate to the multitudes the importance of what Jesus prayed for?

_____

3. What kind of death did Jesus prophesy in verse 32?_____
How was His death related to the truths in verse 31?_____

_____

12:35,36a

How was Jesus' appeal related to what He had just said? _____

_____

Related Verses

Matthew 26:39_____

_____

Luke 9:23-26 _____

_____

Luke 24:26_____

_____

John 1:29_____

_____

John 7:30; 8:20 _____

_____

Ephesians 2:2_____

_____

Ephesians 6:12 _____

INTERPRETATIONS

1. "Greeks...going up to worship at the feast" (12:20). These Gentiles had given up idolatry for the worship of the one true God, the God of Israel. What do verses 21, 26 and 32 teach about the gospel for Gentiles in Jesus' day?

_____

_____

_____

2. "The hour has come" (12:23). Do you recall earlier times when Jesus had said that His hour had *not* come yet? Compare 12:23 with 13:1-3.

_____

_____

3. "He who hates his life in this world" (12:25). All are sinners—no one is righteous. So the way to life eternal begins not at love for the sinful life but at the heart's confession, "God be merciful to me a sinner." It is surrender to Jesus, who said that He is the resurrection and the life (11:25).

4. "We have heard out of the Law..." (12:34). These people interpreted some Old Testament Scriptures as teaching that the Messiah was to remain forever, once He arrived on the scene. See Psalm 110:4; Isaiah 9:7; Ezekiel 37:25; Daniel 7:14. They overlooked the prophecies of Jesus' suffering and death (e.g., Isaiah 53).

5. "Son of Man" (12:34). This was Jesus' favorite title for Himself. It appears thirteen times in John's account: 1:51; 3:13,14; 5:27; 6:27; 6:53; 6:62; 8:28; 9:35; 12:23; 12:34a,b; and 13:31.

APPLICATIONS

1. How would you witness to an unsaved person who says he *wishes to see Jesus*? How could you use the response of Jesus, as recorded in 12:23-26?

_____

2. Christians are to *follow* Jesus and *serve* Him. How do these activities differ? Cite some examples in everyday living.

_____

How faithful are you in these? (TBS#6)

_____

Summary of Passage

Some Greeks who have come to worship at the feast tell Philip they want to see Jesus. Jesus gives them a long message about Himself, the coming hour and manner of His death, and about who can be His followers. Many who overhear Him do not understand what He is talking about. "Who is this Son of Man?" is their big question.

A Memory Verse   12:26

Looking Ahead

Jesus withdraws from the unbelieving multitudes in preparation for the last week ahead.

DAY of PREPARATION
12:36b–17:26

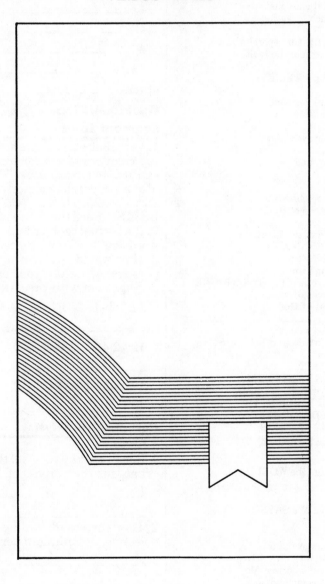

SETTING This point in John's gospel marks the "great pause" of Jesus' ministry (12:36b; see survey chart). It is Tuesday of Passion Week. Ahead of Jesus are a few days of private ministry in Jerusalem with His disciples, then His death and resurrection.

"WHO HAS BELIEVED?"

36b   These things JESUS spoke,
     and HE DEPARTED
        and HID HIMSELF FROM THEM.
37 But though He had **performed so many SIGNS**
            BEFORE THEM,
  yet they were **NOT BELIEVING IN HIM**;
38 that the word of ISAIAH the prophet
     might be **fulfilled,** which he spoke,
     "LORD,
         (1) who has BELIEVED our report? and
         (2) to whom has the arm of the LORD
     been REVEALED?"   [Isaiah 6:10]
39 For this cause they could not BELIEVE,
     for ISAIAH said again,
40 "(1) He has **blinded** their eyes, and
     (2) He **hardened** their heart;
     lest they
        (a) **see** with their eyes, and
        (b) **perceive** with their heart, and
        (c) be **converted,** and
        (d) I **heal** them."   [Isaiah 6:10]
41 These things ISAIAH said,
     because ⟶ He SAW HIS GLORY,
        and he spoke of Him.

NON-BELIEVERS

42 Nevertheless MANY even of the RULERS
            BELIEVED IN HIM,
  but because of the PHARISEES
     they were **not confessing Him,**
        lest they should be **put out** of the SYNAGOGUE;
43 for they loved the **approval of men**
     rather than the **approval of God.**

QUALIFIED BELIEVERS

44 And JESUS **cried out** and said,
     "He who **BELIEVES IN ME** does not believe in Me,
  but IN HIM who sent Me.
45 "And he who **BEHOLDS ME**
        beholds the ONE who sent Me.
46 "**I have come** as LIGHT into the WORLD,
     that everyone who **BELIEVES IN ME**
        may not remain in DARKNESS.
47 "And if anyone **hears** MY SAYINGS,
        and does not keep them,
     I do not judge him;
     for I did **not** come **to judge** the WORLD,
            but to save the WORLD.
48 "He who **rejects ME,**
     and **does not receive** MY SAYINGS,
     has one who judges him;
     THE WORD I spoke
        is what will judge him at the last day.
49 "For I did not speak on My own initiative,
  but THE FATHER Himself who sent Me
        has given Me commandment,
        what to say, and what to speak.
50 "And I know that
        HIS COMMANDMENT IS ETERNAL LIFE;
     therefore the things I speak,
        I speak just as THE FATHER has told Me."

OBJECT OF BELIEF

Book of John: LIFE IN JESUS, THE SON OF GOD

P R O L O G U E	SIGNS WROUGHT		SELF REVEALED		E P I L O G U E
	PUBLIC MINISTRY -3 YEARS-	(GREAT) (PAUSE) ▶	PRIVATE MINISTRY -FEW DAYS-		21: 25
	ERA OF INCARNATION BEGINS	YEARS OF CONFLICT	DAY OF PREPARATION	HOUR OF SACRIFICE	DAWN OF VICTORY
1:1	1:19	5:1	12:36b	18:1	20:1	21:1

Key Words and Phrases

12:36b "hid Himself" _____

37 _____

38 _____

40 _____

41 _____

42 _____

46 _____

48 _____

others: _____

OBSERVATIONS

Segment Survey

1. Verse 36b acts as a transition from the preceding chapters to the remainder of the book. We call it *The Great Pause.* The entire segment is also a transition, connecting 1:1—12:36a with 13:1—21:25. The subject of this segment is BELIEF. Read the entire segment, and underline in the textual re-creation each appearance of the word "believe" (and its cognates).
2. How would you identify the theme of each paragraph? Record your own conclusions, comparing them with the outline shown:

     12:36b-41 NON-BELIEVERS_____

     _____

     12:42,43 QUALIFIED BELIEVERS_____

     _____

     12:44-50 OBJECT OF BELIEF _____

Paragraph Analysis

12:36b-41

1. Recall the key verses of this gospel: 20:30,31. What was the purpose of Jesus' signs?

_____

_____

2. How successful was Jesus in fulfilling that objective, according to verse 37?

_____

_____

3. What does verse 37 reveal about the hearts of these people?_____

_____

4. What was John's purpose in the remaining verses of the paragraph?

_____

_____

5. In their hearts, did these people *want* to believe in Jesus? Had the "report" of God's grace reached them (verse 38b)?_____

When they refused God's message, what did God do (verse 40a)?_____

What did they fail to receive, because of their hardening (verse 40b)?

_____

12:42-43
What kind of faith do you think the rulers had, in view of verses 42 and 43?

_____

12:44-50
Record everything (directly or indirectly related) that Jesus teaches here about *believing in Him*.

_____

Related Verses

Exodus 8:32; 9:12_____

Matthew 7:21-23_____

Matthew 13:14,15 _____

John 1:7-9_____

John 12:11 _____

Acts 28:26,27_____

1 John 2:25 _____

INTERPRETATIONS
1. "He hardened their heart" (12:40). Just as the Lord hardened the heart of Pharaoh who had already hardened his own heart (Exodus 8:32; 9:12), so the Lord hardened the hearts of the people who chose to reject Jesus' message and signs which He gave as His invitation to them.
2. What comparison does John make in verse 43? How does this help to identify whether a person is a true believer in Christ?

_____

3. "Believes...in Him who sent Me" (12:44). Why do you think Jesus put His Father before Him in every aspect of His ministry (12:44-50)?

_____

4. "The word...is what will judge him" (12:48). Why is judgment by this word so incontestable?

_____

APPLICATIONS
1. Why is it easy to love the approval of men?

_____

How does this conflict with loving the approval of God? _____

_____

2. What kinds of sacrifices must be made to live pleasing to God? (TBS#6)

_____

Why is this the *real, happy* life?

_____

Summary of Passage
Jesus has reached the end of His public ministry of teaching the multitudes. He has performed many miracles, but most people have not believed in Him because of their hardened hearts. Some rulers have believed, but not genuinely, because they love the approval of men and not the approval of God.

Over and over again Jesus has taught that to believe in Him is to believe in God who sent Him. His Father's commandment is eternal life.

Memory Verse   12:48

Looking Ahead
Jesus washes the feet of His disciples.

SETTING It is Thursday evening of Passion Week. Jesus and His disciples are gathered in an upper room of a house in Jerusalem to eat the Passover meal. This event is known now as the Last Supper (Luke 22:7-16).

All the events described in chapters 13–19 take place within only twenty-four hours.

WASHED BY JESUS

1 Now before the FEAST of the PASSOVER,
    JESUS knowing that HIS HOUR HAD COME
    that He should depart **out of** this WORLD
                to the FATHER,
    having **LOVED** HIS OWN who were in the WORLD,
    He **LOVED** them to the end.
2 And during supper,
    the DEVIL having already put into the heart
    of JUDAS ISCARIOT, the son of SIMON,
    to **betray Him,**
3 JESUS, knowing
    (1) that the FATHER had given all things
                into HIS HANDS, and
    (2) that HE had come forth from GOD, and
    (3) was going back to GOD,
4 ROSE from supper, and
    LAID ASIDE His garments; and
      taking a towel,
      girded Himself about.
5 Then He poured water into the basin,
    and began to **WASH the DISCIPLES' FEET,**
        and to **WIPE THEM**
    with the towel with which he was girded.

(margin: JESUS' LOVE)

6 And so He **came to Simon Peter.**
    He said to Him,
      "LORD, do You wash my feet?"
7 JESUS answered and said to him,
    "What I do you do not **realize now;**
    but you shall **understand hereafter."**
8   PETER said to Him,
      "NEVER shall You wash my feet!"
    JESUS answered him,
    "If I do **not** wash you,
      you have **no part** with Me."
9 SIMON PETER said to Him,
    "LORD, not my **feet** only,
      but also my **hands** and my **head."**
10 JESUS said to him,
    "He who has bathed needs only to wash his **feet,**
      but is COMPLETELY CLEAN;
    and you are CLEAN, but **not all of you."**
11 For He knew the one who was BETRAYING HIM;
    for this reason He said,
      "Not all of you are CLEAN."

(margin: PETER'S CONFUSION)

Key Words and Phrases

13:1   "loved them to the end"

2 _____

2 _____

3 _____

4 _____

5 _____

8 _____

10 _____

Book of John: LIFE IN JESUS, THE SON OF GOD

P R O L O G U E	SIGNS WROUGHT		SELF REVEALED		E P I L 21: O 25 G U E
	PUBLIC MINISTRY -3 YEARS-	(GREAT) (PAUSE) ▶	PRIVATE MINISTRY -FEW DAYS-		
	ERA OF INCARNATION BEGINS	YEARS OF CONFLICT	DAY OF PREPARATION	HOUR OF SACRIFICE	DAWN OF VICTORY
1:1	1:19	5:1	12:36b	18:1	20:1	21:1

others: _____

OBSERVATIONS

Segment Survey

1. Who are the characters in the first verse?

_____

Compare this with the last verse.

_____

_____

2. Who is the main person of the first paragraph?

_____

With whom does Jesus converse in the second

paragraph?_____

3. What is the main theme of each paragraph?

  13:1-5 _____

  13:6-11 _____

Paragraph Analysis

13:1-5

1. There are two parallel statements in this paragraph, beginning with the name JESUS. Record the gist of each:

verse 1   JESUS, KNOWING _____

_____

LOVED _____

verses 3,4   JESUS, KNOWING_____

_____

ROSE _____

In each statement, how does what Jesus *knew* lead into what He *did* (loved, rose)?

_____

_____

_____

2. What does this paragraph teach about Jesus?

_____

_____

13:6-11

1. Account for the change from Peter's question (verse 6) to his objection (verse 8).

_____

_____

2. What brought Peter to a point of acceptance?

_____

_____

3. How is verse 10a a description of an oriental traveler visiting in a house?

_____

_____

What kind of cleanliness did Jesus mean by "you are clean, but not all of you" (verse 10)?

_____

_____

4. Compare verse 11 with verse 2.

_____

_____

_____

Related Verses

Luke 22:7-16 _____

_____

John 6:70,71 _____

_____

John 12:23 _____

_____

John 15:3 _____

_____

John 19:30 _____

_____

Philippians 2:7 _____

_____

1 John 1:9 _____

_____

INTERPRETATIONS

1. "He loved them to the end" (13:1). NIV translates, "He now showed them the full extent of His love." How was this about to be demonstrated?

_____

_____

2. Compare the devil's relation to Judas (13:2) with the Father's relation to Jesus (13:3).

_____

_____

3. How was humility exemplified in Jesus' actions with His disciples (13:4,5)?

_____

_____

Compare this with the disciples' vain discussions of greatness (Matthew 20:20-28; Luke 22:24-27).

_____

_____

4. "Completely clean" (13:10). The spiritual meaning of the parable is that the believer's

eternal *standing* is righteous ("completely clean") because he has been regenerated and sanctified, but his daily *state* is one of need of daily cleansing by Christ ("only to wash his feet"). See 1 John 1:9.

APPLICATIONS

What does this passage teach you about

HUMBLE CHRISTIAN SERVICE? (TBS#1)

_____

_____

_____

_____

_____

_____

_____

THE CLEANSED LIFE? (TBS#2)

_____

_____

_____

_____

_____

_____

_____

Think of ways to be a better follower of Jesus in these areas.

Summary of Passage

Jesus is eating the Passover meal with His disciples. The devil has already put into Judas' heart to betray Him. Jesus is aware that soon He will be in glory with His Father. So now He demonstrates His love for His disciples by washing their feet. Peter objects to Jesus' performing this lowly service, but Jesus assures Peter that he needs all the ministries that Jesus can give him, including daily spiritual cleansing.

Memory Verse 13:1

Looking Ahead

Jesus exhorts His disciples to serve each other.

SETTING The setting is the same as that of the preceding passage. This segment continues the Upper Room discourse of Jesus.

Book of John: LIFE IN JESUS, THE SON OF GOD

P R O L O G U E	SIGNS WROUGHT			SELF REVEALED		E P I L O G U E 21: 25
	PUBLIC MINISTRY -3 YEARS-		(GREAT) (PAUSE) ▶	PRIVATE MINISTRY -FEW DAYS-		
	ERA OF INCARNATION BEGINS	YEARS OF CONFLICT	DAY OF PREPARATION	HOUR OF SACRIFICE	DAWN OF VICTORY	
1:1	1:19	5:1	12:36b	18:1	20:1	21:1

"DO AS I DID"

12 And so when He had
     (1) **washed their feet**, and
     (2) taken His garments, and
     (3) reclined at the table again,
  He said to them,
  "Do you know what **I have done to you?**
13 "You call Me TEACHER,
    and LORD;
  and you are right; for SO I AM.
14 "If I then, the LORD and the TEACHER,
  washed your feet,
  you also ought to **wash one another's feet.**
15 "For I gave you **an example**
  that you also should DO AS I DID TO YOU.
16 "Truly, truly, I say to you,
  a SLAVE is not greater than his MASTER;
  neither is one who is SENT
    greater than the one who sent him.
17 "If you know these things,
  you are BLESSED IF YOU DO THEM.

EXAMPLE OF CHRIST

18 "I do not speak of all of you.
  I know the ONES I HAVE CHOSEN;
  but it is that the Scripture may be fulfilled,
    'He who eats My bread
    has lifted up his heel against Me.'   [Psalm 41:9]
19 "From now on
  I am telling you **before it comes to pass,**
  so that **when it does occur,**
  YOU MAY BELIEVE that I AM HE.
20 "Truly, truly, I say to you,
  he who **receives** WHOMEVER I SEND
          receives ME;
  and he who **receives** ME
        receives HIM WHO SENT ME."

CHOSEN ONES OF CHRIST

Key Words and Phrases

13:13 ____ "Teacher and Lord" ____

  14 _____

  15 _____

  16 _____

  17 _____

  18 _____

  19 _____

  20 _____

others: _____

OBSERVATIONS

Segment Survey

1. The segment is a short but powerful passage on believers' relationships to each other and to Christ. According to the first paragraph, what should be the relationship of Christian to Christian? _____
_____
_____

2. According to the second paragraph, what is the believer's relationship to Christ?
_____

3. Does God the Father appear in this segment?
_____ If so, where? _____
_____

Paragraph Analysis

13:12-17

1. Compare "Do you know" (verse 12) with "If you know" (verse 17).
_____
_____

2. What is the strength of the small word "do" in verses 15 and 17?
_____
_____

3. What titles in this paragraph refer to Christ?
_____
_____

Which titles refer to the disciples?
_____
_____

4. What was Jesus' basis for using the word "ought" in His appeal of verse 14?
_____
_____

5. How did Jesus' words in verse 16 strengthen the appeal in verses 14 and 15?
_____
_____

6. Compare the disciples' *word* (verse 13) and *deed* (verse 15).
_____
_____
_____
_____

13:18-20

1. The first line of verse 18 brings another person into Jesus' discourse. Who is that (cf. verse 18b)?
_____

2. In three ways Jesus tried to reassure His disciples about their relationship to Him in the face of the coming betrayal. Record how He did this:

    verse 18 _____
_____

verse 19_____

_____

verse 20_____

_____

Related Verses

Matthew 10:24_____

_____

Matthew 10:40_____

_____

Luke 6:13_____

_____

Luke 22:24,27_____

_____

Ephesians 4:32 _____

_____

1 Timothy 5:10 _____

_____

James 2:14-26_____

INTERPRETATIONS

1. "I gave you an example" (13:15). Jesus *did* something, and that was the example. What did this act exemplify?

_____

_____

_____

_____

2. "One who is sent" (13:16). The word "apostle" means *one who is sent*. The disciples knew that Jesus was thinking of them as apostles when He said that one who is sent is not greater than the one who sent him.

3. "Scripture may be fulfilled" (13:18). How would it help the disciples to know that the betrayal by Judas had been prophesied in the Old Testament (Psalm 41:9)?

_____

_____

_____

_____

4. In this part of His discourse Jesus talks more about Himself and His disciples than about Judas. How would that help the disciples?

_____

_____

_____

_____

APPLICATIONS

1. If you are a Christian, Jesus is your Lord, Teacher and Master. He has given you examples for living. Record some of the prominent ones you have already learned from the Gospel of John. _____

_____

_____

_____

_____

_____

_____

_____

_____

_____

_____

_____

2. Why does happiness come from doing the Lord's commandments (13:17)?

_____

_____

_____

_____

_____

3. Jesus knows the ones He has chosen (13:18). How does such a truth motivate you in your service for Him?

_____

_____

_____

_____

Summary of Passage

After Jesus finishes washing His disciples' feet, He appeals to them to follow His example, as their Teacher, Lord and Master. He promises happiness in doing for each other what He does for them.

He forewarns that one of them will betray Him, as prophesied by Scripture. He wants His disciples not to be disturbed over this, but to be assured that He is always in control, and that their ministry will always have its roots in God.

Memory Verse   13:14

Looking Ahead

Jesus identifies His betrayer, and He predicts Peter's triple denial of Him.

SETTING Jesus is still with His disciples in the Upper Room, teaching and answering questions.

"WHERE ARE YOU GOING?"

21 When JESUS had said this,
    He became **troubled in spirit,**
      and testified, and said,
    "Truly, truly, I say to you,
      that one of you will BETRAY ME."
22 The DISCIPLES began looking at one another,
    at a loss to know **of which one** he was speaking.
23 There was reclining on JESUS' breast
    one of His DISCIPLES, whom JESUS LOVED.
24 SIMON PETER therefore gestured to him,
    and said to him,
    "Tell us **who it is** of whom He is speaking."
25 He, leaning back thus on JESUS' breast,
    said to Him, **"LORD, WHO IS IT?"**
26 JESUS therefore answered,
    "That is **the one for whom I shall dip the morsel,**
    and **give it to him."**
    So **when** He had dipped the morsel,
      He took and gave it to JUDAS,
        the son of Simon Iscariot.

27 And after the morsel,
      SATAN then entered into him.
    JESUS therefore said to him,
      "WHAT YOU DO, DO QUICKLY."
28 Now **no one** of those reclining at table
    knew for what purpose He had said this to him.
29 For some were supposing,
      because JUDAS had the money box,
    that JESUS was saying to him,
    "Buy the things we have need of for the FEAST";
    or else, that he should give something to the poor.
30   And so after receiving the morsel
    he went out immediately;
    AND IT WAS NIGHT.

31 When therefore **he had gone out,**
    JESUS SAID, "NOW is the SON OF MAN **glorified,**
      and GOD is **glorified** in HIM;
32 if GOD is glorified in HIM,
    GOD
      (1) will also **glorify HIM** in HIMSELF, and
      (2) will **glorify** HIM immediately.
33 "Little children,
    I am with you a little while longer.
    You shall seek ME;
    and as I said to the JEWS,
      'Where I am going, you cannot come.'
34 "A NEW COMMANDMENT I give to you,
    that you LOVE ONE ANOTHER,
    even as I have LOVED YOU,
    that you also LOVE ONE ANOTHER.
35 "By this ALL MEN will **know**
    that you are MY DISCIPLES,
    if you have LOVE FOR ONE ANOTHER."

36 SIMON PETER said to Him,
    "LORD, **where** are You going?"
    JESUS answered, "**Where** I go,
    you **cannot follow** ME now;
    but you shall follow later."
37 PETER said to Him,
    "LORD, why can I **not follow** You right now?
      I will lay down my life for You."
38 JESUS answered,
    "Will you **lay down your life for Me?**
    TRULY, TRULY, I say to you,
      a cock shall not crow,
      until you DENY ME three times."

(side labels, top to bottom: JUDAS, SATAN, SON OF MAN, PETER)

Book of John: LIFE IN JESUS, THE SON OF GOD

P R O L O G U E	SIGNS WROUGHT			SELF REVEALED		E P I L O G U E
	PUBLIC MINISTRY -3 YEARS-		(GREAT) (PAUSE) ▶	PRIVATE MINISTRY -FEW DAYS-		21: 25
	ERA OF INCARNATION BEGINS	YEARS OF CONFLICT	DAY OF PREPARATION	HOUR OF SACRIFICE	DAWN OF VICTORY	
1:1	1:19	5:1	12:36b	18:1	20:1	21:1

Key Words and Phrases

13:21   "troubled in spirit" _____

   25 _____

   27 _____

   30 _____

   31 _____

   34 _____

   36 _____

   38 _____

others: _____

OBSERVATIONS

Segment Survey

1. As you read this long segment of four paragraphs, what tone or atmosphere do you sense? _____

2. Observe on the chart that the segment is divided into two main sections. What is different about the two? _____

3. Record the main theme of each paragraph:

   13:21-26 JUDAS _____

   13:27-30 SATAN _____

   13:31-35 SON OF MAN _____

   13:36-38 PETER _____

Paragraph Analysis

13:21-26

1. Did Jesus speak the name "Judas" at this time? Why do you think He chose to reveal the betrayer as He did: first, in a general way (verse 21), then by a sign (verse 26)? (Cf. Matthew 26:25.) _____

2. What was the disciples' logical question (verses 22-25)? _____

Why do you think they did not suspect Judas?

_____

_____

13:27-30
1. What two domains of power appear in verse 27?

_____

_____

What is significant about Jesus' command?

_____

2. Compare verse 30 with those two domains of

power. _____

13:31-35
What are the two main subjects of this paragraph (verses 31,32,34,35)?

_____

_____

13:36-38
1. Measure Peter's loyalty to Christ on the basis of his vow (verse 37b) and his experience (verse 38).

_____

_____

2. What was Peter's basic sin, as revealed in this

paragraph? _____

Related Verses

Matthew 26:22,24,25,33,34 _____

_____

Mark 13:35 _____

Mark 14:20,30 _____

_____

Luke 22:22,31-34 _____

_____

John 7:33 _____

_____

John 12:27 _____

_____

John 21:16-23 _____

_____

INTERPRETATIONS
1. "One of His disciples, whom Jesus loved" (13:23). Most Bible students identify this man as the author, John.
2. "Dipped the morsel" (13:26). At a feast, a morsel of bread was dipped in sauce and extended to a person as a token of friendship. Since Jesus gave this to Judas, what does it reveal

about Him? _____

_____

3. "Satan then entered into him" (13:27). How do you think John learned this?

_____

4. "Glorified" (13;31). Father and Son glorify each other in every aspect of Christ's ministry: passion, resurrection, ascension, and coronation. Compare John 12:23,24,31-33.
5. "A new commandment" (13:34). Why did Jesus call His words "a new commandment?"

_____

6. "A cock shall not crow, until..." (13:38). Roosters crowed during the third watch, about 12-3 A.M. So at least by 3 A.M. Peter would have denied Jesus three times. What was Jesus' implied prediction in 13:38a?

_____

APPLICATIONS
1. What do you derive from this narrative that will help you become a better servant of

Jesus Christ? _____

_____

_____

2. How should Christians regard enemies of the

gospel? _____

_____

3. According to Jesus, how important is it for believers to love one another? Do you know a Christian you do not love as you should? How does this affect your Christian witness?

_____

_____

Summary of Passage
At night, at the supper table, Jesus tells His disciples that one of them will betray Him. He indicates who it is by giving him a dipped morsel of bread. Satan enters Judas, and Judas immediately leaves the scene.

Jesus then reminds His disciples of His departure, and tells them that glory awaits Him and His Father. He gives them the new commandment to love one another as He has loved them. Jesus predicts that Peter will deny Him within a few hours, even though Peter vows he would die to protect Jesus from His enemies.

Memory Verse   13:35

Looking Ahead
Jesus begins a series of discourses in response to His disciples' questions.

SETTING The scene is still the Upper Room in Jerusalem. Jesus begins His farewell discourses, which may have been delivered as three units:

14:1-31   The Father's House

15:1–16:4a   The Vine and the Branches

16:4b-33   Promises of Jesus

"I AM THE WAY"

1 "Let not YOUR HEART be troubled;
    BELIEVE IN GOD,
    BELIEVE also IN ME.
2 In My FATHER'S house are many dwelling places;
    if it were not so, I would have told you;
    for I GO TO PREPARE A PLACE FOR YOU.
3 "And if I go and prepare a place for you,
    I will
        (1) come again and
        (2) receive you to MYSELF;
    that ⟶ where I am,
                there you may be also.
4 "And you know the WAY where I am going."

5 THOMAS said to Him,
    "LORD, we do not know WHERE You are going,
    how do we know the WAY?"
6 JESUS said to him,
    "I am
        (1) THE WAY, and
        (2) THE TRUTH, and
        (3) THE LIFE;
    no one comes to THE FATHER, but through Me.
7 "If you had known Me,
        you would have known MY FATHER also;
    from now on you
        (1) know HIM, and
        (2) have seen HIM."

8 PHILIP said to Him,
    "LORD, show us the FATHER,
        and it is enough for us."
9 JESUS said to him,
    "Have I been so long with you,
    and yet you have not come to know Me, PHILIP?
    He who has seen ME has seen the FATHER;
    how do you say,
            'Show us the FATHER'?
10 "Do you not BELIEVE
    that
        (1) I am in the FATHER, and
        (2) the FATHER is in ME?
    The words that I say to you
            I do not speak on My own initiative,
    but the FATHER abiding in ME does HIS WORKS.
11 "BELIEVE ME that
        (1) I am in the FATHER, and
        (2) the FATHER in ME;
        otherwise BELIEVE on account of the WORKS
                        themselves.

12 "TRULY, TRULY, I say to you,
    he who BELIEVES IN ME,
    the works that I do shall he do also;
    and greater works than these shall he do;
    because ⟶ I GO TO THE FATHER.
13 "And WHATEVER you ask in My Name,
            THAT will I DO,
    that ⟶ THE FATHER may be GLORIFIED
                in the SON.

(vertical labels: HEAVEN / THE WAY / THE FATHER / PETITIONS)

Book of John: LIFE IN JESUS, THE SON OF GOD

P R O L O G U E	SIGNS WROUGHT			SELF REVEALED		E P I L O G U E 21:25
	PUBLIC MINISTRY -3 YEARS-		(GREAT) (PAUSE) ▶	PRIVATE MINISTRY -FEW DAYS-		
	ERA OF INCARNATION BEGINS	YEARS OF CONFLICT	DAY OF PREPARATION	HOUR OF SACRIFICE	DAWN OF VICTORY	
1:1	1:19	5:1	12:36b	18:1	20:1	21:1

14 "If you ask Me anything in My Name,
            I will do it."

Key Words and Phrases

14:2 ____ "many dwelling places"

   3 _____

   4 _____

   6 _____

   7 _____

   9 _____

  10 _____

  12 _____

others: _____

OBSERVATIONS

Segment Survey

This segment is divided into four paragraphs. Read each paragraph, and record the main theme of each. Compare your conclusions with the outline shown.

   14:1-4 _____

   14:5-7 _____

   14:8-11 _____

   14:12-14 _____

How does each paragraph lead into the next one?

_____

_____

_____

Is Jesus talking to unbelievers or believers? What is the tone of each paragraph?

_____

Overall, what is He trying to do?

_____

_____

Paragraph Analysis

14:1-4

1. How does the first line show the disciples' feelings? _____

2. Study the paragraph carefully. Record these parts:

   a. two statements of fact _____

_____

   b. three promises _____

_____

_____

_____

c. two commands_____

d. one exhortation_____

3. How comforting should Jesus' words have been?

14:5-7

1. Thomas had two questions. What were they?

_____

_____

2. How did Jesus answer the two questions?

_____

_____

14:8-11

List the things Jesus taught about His relationship to the Father.

_____

_____

_____

14:12-14

1. Where would Jesus be when the disciples would be doing the "greater works"?

_____

2. What question did Jesus anticipate and answer (verses 13,14)?_____

_____

Related Verses

Exodus 33:17_____

_____

John 1:18_____

_____

John 14:27_____

_____

John 16:22-24_____

_____

Philippians 1:21-24_____

_____

1 Thessalonians 4:13-18_____

_____

Hebrews 10:19,20_____

_____

INTERPRETATIONS

1. "Believe" (14:1). How is trust in God and Jesus balm for troubled hearts?

_____

2. "Where I am" (14:3). What does this reveal about heaven?

_____

3. "Greater works than these shall he do" (14:12). This is not greater quality but greater (wider) outreach. How would this promise reassure the disciples after Jesus ascended into heaven?

4. "In My name" (14:13). The petitions must be those which Jesus wants to see accomplished for the glory of God. Why is this a necessary limitation on "whatever" (14:13)?

APPLICATIONS

1. What does this passage teach you about faith and prayer? How can you strengthen these two vital parts of your Christian life? (TBS#4)

_____

_____

_____

2. How can you use Jesus' words of verse 6 in your witness to an unsaved person? If you are studying with a group, discuss this among yourselves._____

_____

_____

Summary of Passage

Jesus reassures His disciples, who are troubled in heart, by promising to bring them to His Father's house, and to dwell with them. He answers Thomas' questions about where Jesus is going and how to get there. Jesus answers Philip, who wants to really know the Father. "I'm going to My Father, but while I'm gone you'll be having a wider ministry than I have had, to His glory," Jesus declares.

Memory Verse   14:13

Looking Ahead

Jesus continues His farewell discourses, instructing His disciples.

SETTING The scene is still the Upper Room in Jerusalem. Jesus is instructing His disciples through His farewell discourses.

NEVER ALONE

15 "If you LOVE ME,
　　you will keep MY COMMANDMENTS.

16 "And I will ask the FATHER,
　　and He will give you ANOTHER HELPER,
　　that He may be with you forever;

17 that is THE SPIRIT OF TRUTH,
　　　　whom the world cannot receive,
　　　　because it does not behold Him or know Him,
　　but you know Him
　　because
　　　　　(1) He abides with you, and
　　　　　(2) will be in you.

18 "I will not leave you as ORPHANS;
　　I will come to you.

19 "After a little while
　　　the world will behold Me no more;
　　　but you will behold Me;
　　because I live, YOU SHALL LIVE ALSO.

20 "In that day
　　you shall know that I am in MY FATHER,
　　　　and you in Me, and I in you.

21 "He who has MY COMMANDMENTS,
　　　and keeps them,
　　he it is who LOVES ME;
　　and he who LOVES ME
　　　shall be LOVED by MY FATHER,
　　and I will LOVE HIM,
　　and will disclose Myself to him."

22 JUDAS (not ISCARIOT) said to Him,
　　"LORD, what then has happened
　　that You are going to disclose Yourself to us,
　　　　　and not to the WORLD?"

23 JESUS answered and said to him,
　　"If anyone LOVES ME,
　　　　　he will keep MY WORD;
　　and MY FATHER will LOVE him;
　　and We will
　　　　　(1) come to him, and
　　　　　(2) make Our abode with him.

24 "He who does not LOVE ME
　　　　　does not keep MY WORDS;
　　and THE WORD which you hear is not MINE,
　　but the FATHER'S who sent Me.

25 "These things I have spoken to you,
　　　　　while ABIDING WITH YOU.

26 "But the HELPER, THE HOLY SPIRIT,
　　whom the FATHER will send in My name,
　　He will
　　　　　(1) teach you all things and
　　　　　(2) bring to your remembrance
　　　　　　　all that I said to you.

27 "Peace I leave with you;
　　　My peace I give to you;
　　not as the world gives, do I give to you.
　　Let not your heart be troubled,
　　　　　　nor let it be fearful.

28 "You heard that I said to you,
　　'I go away, and I will come to you.'
　　If you LOVED ME, you would have REJOICED,
　　　because I go to the FATHER;
　　　　for the FATHER is greater than I.

29 "And now I have told you
　　　　　　before it comes to pass,
　　that when it comes to pass, YOU MAY BELIEVE.

(margin tabs: SPIRIT-COMPANION / LIFE & LOVE / SPIRIT-TEACHER / PEACE & JOY)

Book of John: LIFE IN JESUS, THE SON OF GOD

P R O L O G U E	SIGNS WROUGHT			SELF REVEALED			E P I L O G U E
	PUBLIC MINISTRY -3 YEARS-		(GREAT) (PAUSE) ▶	PRIVATE MINISTRY -FEW DAYS-			21: 25
	ERA OF INCARNATION BEGINS	YEARS OF CONFLICT	DAY OF PREPARATION	HOUR OF SACRIFICE	DAWN OF VICTORY		
1:1	1:19	5:1	12:36b	18:1	20:1		21:1

30 "I will not speak much more with you,
　　　for the RULER OF THE WORLD is coming,
　　　　　and he has nothing in Me;

31　　　but ⟶ that THE WORLD may know
　　　　　　　　　that I LOVE THE FATHER,
　　　　　and ⟶ as the FATHER
　　　　　　　　　gave me COMMANDMENT,
　　　　　　　EVEN SO I DO.
　　　　　　　Arise, LET US GO from here."

Key Words and Phrases

14:16 "Helper" _____

　17 _____

　18 _____

　21 _____

　23 _____

　26 _____

　27 _____

　30 _____

others: _____

OBSERVATIONS

Segment Survey

1. This passage completes the first of three farewell discourses (14:1-31). How does the last line of the segment indicate a conclusion to this discourse?

_____

2. What two paragraphs are about the Holy Spirit?

_____
_____

3. What prominent subjects do you observe in the other two paragraphs? Compare those paragraphs. (Note the words shown in the outline: LOVE; PEACE.) _____

_____

4. What was Jesus' main objective in sharing these words with His disciples?

Paragraph Analysis

14:15-17

1. What did Jesus teach about the Holy Spirit (verses 16,17)? _____

_____

2. How is the Spirit's ministry related to the subject of verse 15?

_____
_____

3. Compare verses 15, 21a and 23a.

_____

_____

14:18-24

1. What did Jesus teach about the future (verses 18-20)?_____

2. What is the key repeated word in verses 21-24?

_____

3. What are the three combinations of love in verses 21-24?_____

_____

How is this related to verses 18-20?

_____

14:25-26

What need is implied in verse 26, and how does the Holy Spirit meet that need?

_____

_____

14:27-31

1. Compare "I go away" (verse 28) and "the ruler of the world is coming" (verse 30).

_____

_____

2. What need does this suggest, and how had Jesus offered solutions?_____

_____

Related Verses

John 2:22 _____

_____

John 12:31_____

_____

John 15:26_____

_____

John 16:7,13 _____

_____

1 Corinthians 2:9-14_____

_____

Ephesians 6:23_____

_____

INTERPRETATIONS

1. According to 14:15, what is the key to obeying the Lord's commandments?

_____

2. "Helper" (14:16). The Greek word is *paraclete* ("called to the side"). It is rendered in various ways by translators (e.g., "Comforter," KJ; "Counselor," NIV). The Holy Spirit gives the believer whatever help is needed. Read these verses where the same root appears: Matthew 2:18; 5:4; Luke 16:25; Acts 16:40; 1 Corinthians 14:31; 2 Corinthians 1:4; 7:6. Relate all of this to "with you" (John 14:16) and "in you" (14:17)._____

_____

3. According to 14:21, what determines that a saved person receives love from the Father and from Jesus? Is this different from God's love in John 3:16?_____ If so, how? (Cf. 14:23; Romans 8:28.)_____

_____

4. "He will teach you all things" (14:26). Why would this be an important ministry of the Spirit?

_____

5. "Ruler of the world" (14:30). This is Satan. Judas and the captors, agents of Satan, were on their way to take Jesus. But Jesus looked upon ultimate victory, and so said, "He has no effect on me" (14:30b, NIV).

6. "Arise, let us go from here" (14:31b). This marked the end of the first discourse. The second discourse (15:1–16:4a) begins without any reference to movement or travel. There may have been delay in actually leaving the house; then came the departure in 18:1.

APPLICATIONS

1. Jesus gave prominence here to the vital ministry of the Holy Spirit in the life of the believer. How can you apply these truths to your life and ministry now? (TBS#3)_____

_____

2. Your love for Jesus determines your obedience to His Word. What is your testimony on this?

_____

_____

Summary of Passage

Jesus gives further assurance and comfort to His disciples, saying that after He has left them and gone to His Father, the Spirit will be their Helper and teacher, abiding *with* them and *in* them. If they love Christ and His Father, they will keep His Word; and for that, He and His Father will love them with special love.

After Jesus has gone to His Father, then Satan, the ruler of the world, will come. But Jesus' children need not fear, for He will come back again.

Memory Verse   14:27

Looking Ahead

Jesus begins His second farewell discourse to His disciples.

117

SETTING Jesus is probably still in the Upper Room in Jerusalem, exhorting His disciples, and teaching them more things that are on His heart. Note on the survey chart that it is still the "day of preparation" for Jesus, as He reveals Himself in a private ministry to the disciples.

Book of John: LIFE IN JESUS, THE SON OF GOD

P R O L O G U E	SIGNS WROUGHT			SELF REVEALED		E P I 21: L 25 O G U E
	PUBLIC MINISTRY -3 YEARS-		(GREAT) (PAUSE) ▶	PRIVATE MINISTRY -FEW DAYS-		
	ERA OF INCARNATION BEGINS	YEARS OF CONFLICT	DAY OF PREPARATION	HOUR OF SACRIFICE	DAWN OF VICTORY	
1:1	1:19	5:1	12:36b	18:1	20:1	21:1

ABIDING IN THE VINE

TRUE VINE

1 "I AM THE TRUE VINE,
    and **My FATHER** is the **vinedresser**.
2 "Every branch in Me that does not bear fruit,
        He takes away;
    and every branch that bears fruit,
        He prunes it,
        that it may bear more fruit.
3 "You are already **clean**
    because of the WORD which I have spoken to you.

ABIDING IN THE VINE

4 "ABIDE IN ME, and **I in you.**
    As the branch **cannot bear fruit** of itself,
        unless it **abides in the vine**,
    so neither can you, unless YOU **ABIDE IN ME.**
5 "I AM THE VINE, you are the **branches**;
        he who ABIDES IN ME, and **I in him,**
        he bears much fruit;
    for apart from Me YOU CAN DO NOTHING.
6 "If anyone does **NOT ABIDE IN ME**,
    (1) he is thrown away as a branch, and dries up; and
    (2) they gather them, and
    (3) cast them into **THE FIRE**, and they are BURNED.
7 "If
    (1) you ABIDE IN ME, and
    (2) **MY WORDS ABIDE IN YOU,**
    ask **whatever you wish,**
        and it shall be done for you.
8 "By this is MY FATHER GLORIFIED,
            that you bear much fruit,
        and so prove to be MY DISCIPLES.

BELOVED FRIENDS

9 "Just as the FATHER has **loved Me,**
        I have also **loved you;**
    ABIDE IN MY LOVE.
10 "If you **keep MY COMMANDMENTS,**
    you will **ABIDE IN MY LOVE.**
        just as **I** have kept
        MY FATHER'S COMMANDMENTS,
    and **ABIDE IN HIS** LOVE.
11 "These things I have spoken to you,
    that MY JOY may be in you,
    and that YOUR JOY may be made **full.**
12 "This is MY COMMANDMENT,
    that you **LOVE ONE ANOTHER,**
    just as **I have loved you.**
13 "Greater love has no one than this, that one lay down
                his life for his friends.
14 "You are MY FRIENDS,
    if you **do** what I **command** you.
15 "No longer do I call you **slaves,**
    for the slave does not know what his master is doing;
        but I have called you FRIENDS,
    for all things that I have heard from MY FATHER
            I have **made known to you.**
16 "You did not choose Me,
    but I
    (1) CHOSE YOU, and
    (2) APPOINTED YOU,
        that you should go and **bear fruit,**
    and that **your fruit should remain;**
    that   whatever you ask of THE FATHER
                in MY Name,
        He may give to you.

17 "This I COMMAND YOU,
        that you **LOVE ONE ANOTHER.**"

Key Words and Phrases

15:1 _____ "vine" _____
2 _____
3 _____
4 _____
6 _____
9 _____
14 _____
16 _____
others: _____

OBSERVATIONS

Segment Survey

1. The segment is divided into three paragraphs of unequal lengths.
2. First, read the passage as a whole, observing the repeated words "vine," "abide," "branch," and "fruit." How would you state the main theme of the segment? _____

3. Note the outline: TRUE VINE, ABIDING IN THE VINE; BELOVED FRIENDS. How does this outline represent a natural progression of thought in the segment? _____

Paragraph Analysis

15:1-3
1. Who are the persons represented in Jesus' illustration by
    the vine? _____
    the vinedresser? _____
    a fruit-bearing branch? _____
    an unfruitful branch? _____
2. What does the word "true" suggest in the title, "True Vine"? _____
_____

3. How are the disciples identified in verse 3?
_____
_____

15:4-8
1. Read the first line as "Abide in Me, and I will abide in you."

118

2. Record the truths Jesus taught about abiding in the vine:

_____

_____

_____

3. Whom does "much fruit" magnify: the branch, the vine, or the vinedresser?

_____

15:9-17
1. Compare verses 9 and 17 regarding the activity of love._____

_____

2. How does Jesus relate *joy* and *friendship* to the abiding life (verses 11-15)?

_____

_____

3. Compare verses 16 and 17.

_____

_____

Related Verses

Isaiah 5:1-7_____

_____

Ezekiel 15:6_____

_____

Matthew 7:7ff._____

_____

1 Corinthians 3:11-15 _____

_____

Galatians 5:22 _____

_____

Colossians 3:16_____

_____

1 John 3:16,24 _____

_____

INTERPRETATIONS
1. "Vinedresser" (15:1). The vinedresser was both owner and caretaker of the vineyard.
2. "He takes away" (15:2). The unproductive believer who does not bring forth fruits of the Spirit (Galatians 5:22) may be set aside temporarily, or even removed through death (1 Corinthians 11:30).
3. "He prunes it" (15:2). The Greek verb translated "prunes" means *cleanses*. (Cf. Hebrews 10:2.) This explains the word "clean" in verse 3. How does that spiritual cleansing come about (15:3b)?

_____

4. The NIV reading of 15:6 is preferred: "...he is like a branch that is thrown away and withers; such branches are picked up, thrown into the fire

and burned." Relate this to verse 2.

_____

_____

_____

5. "I chose you" (15:16). Relate this truth to the other parts of the verse:

   bearing fruit_____

_____

   asking petitions _____

APPLICATIONS
1. In everyday Christian living, what is the difference between "fruit," "more fruit," and "much fruit"?

_____

_____

Do you see growth in your own personal life? For example, what about your goals and motivations?

_____

_____

_____

_____

2. A key to abiding in Christ is having His Word abide in the heart. What can you do to keep this Word ministry alive and healthy?

_____

_____

_____

_____

_____

_____

_____

Summary of Passage

Jesus identifies Himself as the true vine and His disciples as branches. They are to abide in Him and let His Word abide in them, so that they will bring forth much fruit to the glory of His Father.

Jesus tells His disciples that they are His beloved friends, and that He wants them to have full joy. He chose them to bear fruit with the Father's help.

Memory Verse   15:5

Looking Ahead

Jesus talks to His disciples about their enemies.

SETTING Jesus continues talking with His disciples in the house.

THE WORLD'S HATRED

18 "If the **world hates you**,
     you know that **it has hated Me** before it hated you.
19 "If you were **of the world**,
         the world would **love its own**;
   but because you are not of the world,
         but **I chose you out** of the world,
       THEREFORE THE WORLD HATES YOU.
20 "Remember the word that I said to you,
     'A SLAVE is not greater than **his MASTER.**'
                     [John 13:16]
   If they **persecuted Me**,
     they will also **persecute you**;
   if they **kept MY WORD**,
     they will keep yours also.
21 "But **all these things** they will **do to you**
         for MY NAME'S SAKE,
   because   they **do not know**
     the ONE WHO SENT ME.

(margin: WORLD HATES BELIEVERS)

22 "If I had not **come** and **spoken** to them,
         they would not have sin,
   but now they have **no excuse** for their **sin.**
23 "He who **hates ME**
   hates MY FATHER also.
24 "If I had not done among them the **works**
       which no one else did,
     they would not have sin;
   but now they have both
   (1) **seen** and
   (2) **hated ME.**
25 "**But they have done this**
   in order that the word may be fulfilled
       that is written in their Law,
       '**they HATED ME without a cause.**'
         [Psalm 35:19; Psalm 69:4]

(margin: WORLD HATES GOD)

26 "When THE HELPER comes,
   whom I will **send to you** from THE FATHER,
   that is THE SPIRIT OF TRUTH,
     who proceeds from THE FATHER,
   He will **bear witness of Me**,
27 and you will **bear witness** also,
     because you have been **with Me**
     from the beginning.

(margin: SPIRIT'S HELP)

16:1 "These things I have spoken to you,
     that you may be kept from stumbling.
2 "They will make you **OUTCASTS**
         FROM THE SYNAGOGUE,
   but an hour is COMING for **everyone**
     who **kills you** to think that he is offering
                 service to GOD.
3 "And these things they will do,
   because   they have **NOT KNOWN** THE FATHER,
                 OR ME.
4a "But these things I have spoken to you,
     that when THEIR HOUR comes,
   you may REMEMBER that **I told you** of them."

(margin: JESUS' FOREWARNING)

Key Words and Phrases

15:18 ___"world hates you"___

   20 _____

   22 _____

   24 _____

   26 _____

Book of John: LIFE IN JESUS, THE SON OF GOD

P R O L O G U E	SIGNS WROUGHT			SELF REVEALED			E P I L O G U E
	PUBLIC MINISTRY -3 YEARS-		(GREAT) (PAUSE) ▶	PRIVATE MINISTRY -FEW DAYS-			21: 25
	ERA OF INCARNATION BEGINS	YEARS OF CONFLICT	DAY OF PREPARATION	HOUR OF SACRIFICE		DAWN OF VICTORY	
1:1	1:19	5:1	12:36b	18:1		20:1	21:1

   25 _____

16:1 _____

   4 _____

others: _____

OBSERVATIONS

Segment Survey

1. What is the common subject of the first two paragraphs? _____

Compare 15:18 with the last line of 15:25.
_____
_____
_____

2. What common objective of Jesus shows in the last two paragraphs? _____
_____
_____

Whose help is available in each paragraph?
_____
_____

Paragraph Analysis

15:18-21

1. What is the key repeated statement of Jesus (four words) in this paragraph?
_____

2. List the reasons Jesus gave as to why the world hated the disciples:

     verse 19 _____
     verse 20 _____
     verse 21a _____
     verse 21b _____

3. Jesus had a reason for saying that "a slave is not greater than his master" (verse 20). How did that truth relate to the two "if" situations in the remainder of verse 20?

     (1) _____
     (2) _____

15:22-25

1. Who are the two objects of the world's hatred in this paragraph? _____
_____
_____

Are these hatreds the cause of hating the disciples? (Answer this in the light of 15:21.)

2. Read "they would not have sin" (verses 22,24) as "they would not be guilty of sin" (NIV).

3. Compare Jesus' references to His words (verse 22) and works (verse 24). How does each statement lead into a reference about the world's hatred of Him and His Father?

WORDS (verse 22) _____

WORKS (verse 24) _____

4. How does the last line of verse 25 conclude the paragraph? _____

15:26,27
Why do you think Jesus spoke these words in this context? _____

16:1-4
1. Why did Jesus speak these words (verse 1)?

2. How did He expand on the hate campaign?

Related Verses

Matthew 10:22 _____

Matthew 11:6 _____

Matthew 24:9 _____

John 9:22 _____

Acts 7:57-60 _____

Acts 26:9-11 _____

INTERPRETATIONS
1. To whom was Jesus referring when He used the term, "the world" (e.g. 15:18)? Compare 1 John 2:15; 5:4. (If you have access to an exhaustive concordance, locate other New Testament verses which refer to this world.) _____

2. What do verses 22-25 teach about accountability

for spiritual enlightenment given by God? How is this accentuated by the quotation, "They hated Me without a cause" (15:25)?

_____

3. In your own words, what kind of help would the Spirit give to the disciples after Jesus had returned to His Father (15:26,27)?

_____

4. Compare 16:2b with Paul's testimony in Acts 26:9-18. _____

APPLICATIONS
1. Have you experienced persecution from the world for being a Christian? If so, what have your reactions been? Have you identified that persecution with Jesus and His Father? Why is such an identification a help and bulwark for such trying times? _____

2. One of the Spirit's ministries is to give believers words to speak on special occasions of need. (Cf. John 15:26,27 and Mark 13:11.) Who should be magnified when such words are spoken? See 15:26,27.

_____

Summary of Passage

The world hates the Lord's disciples because Jesus has chosen them out of this world. Jesus ministers to the world by word and deed, but they still hate Him and His Father without a cause.

In times of persecution, even unto death, the believer can claim the help of the Holy Spirit to testify about Jesus his Savior. This will keep the believer from going astray in such severe testing.

Memory Verse   15:19

Looking Ahead

Jesus talks more about His going away and about the Spirit's coming.

SETTING This passage begins Jesus' third farewell discourse. He and His disciples are still in the house in Jerusalem, possibly still in the Upper Room.

Book of John: LIFE IN JESUS, THE SON OF GOD

P R O L O G U E	SIGNS WROUGHT			SELF REVEALED		E P I L O G U E
	PUBLIC MINISTRY -3 YEARS-		(GREAT) (PAUSE) ▶	PRIVATE MINISTRY -FEW DAYS-		
	ERA OF INCARNATION BEGINS	YEARS OF CONFLICT	DAY OF PREPARATION	HOUR OF SACRIFICE	DAWN OF VICTORY	
1:1	1:19	5:1	12:36b	18:1	20:1	21:1

THE SPIRIT WILL COME

4b "And these things I did not say to you
                              at the beginning,
              because I WAS WITH YOU.
5 "But now I AM GOING
                    to HIM WHO SENT ME;
       and none of you asks Me,
                        'Where are You going?'
6 "But because I have said these things to you,
              SORROW HAS FILLED YOUR HEART.
7 "But I tell you the truth,
       it is to **your advantage** that I GO AWAY;
       for if I do **not** go away,
              THE HELPER shall **not come to you**;
       but if I go, I will SEND HIM TO YOU.
8 "And He, when He comes,
       will convict the WORLD concerning
       (1) SIN, and
       (2) RIGHTEOUSNESS, and
       (3) JUDGMENT;
9 (1) concerning SIN,
              because they do not BELIEVE IN ME; and
10 (2) concerning RIGHTEOUSNESS,
              because I go to THE FATHER,
              and you no longer **behold Me**; and
11 (3) concerning JUDGMENT,
              because the RULER OF THIS WORLD
              has been **judged**.

CONVICTER OF UNBELIEVERS

12 "I have many more things to say to you,
       but you cannot bear them **now**.
13 "But when He, THE SPIRIT OF TRUTH, comes,
       HE will **guide you** into **all the truth**;
       for He will not speak on His own initiative;
       but whatever He **hears**,
       He **will speak**;
       and He will **disclose to you** WHAT IS TO COME.
14 "He shall GLORIFY ME;
       for He
       (1) shall take of Mine, and
       (2) shall **disclose** it to you.
15 "All things that THE FATHER has are MINE;
       therefore I said,
       that He
       (1) takes of Mine, and
       (2) will disclose it to you."

GUIDE OF BELIEVERS

Key Words and Phrases

16:5 _"I am going"_____
    6_____
    7_____
    8_____
    9_____
    10_____
    11_____
    14_____
others:_____
_____

OBSERVATIONS

Segment Survey

1. The segment has two paragraphs. Who is the main person in the segment?
_____

2. Which of His ministries are prominent in each paragraph?
    16:4b-11 _____
    _____
    16:12-15 _____
    _____

3. Compare the opening verse of each paragraph.
_____
_____

Paragraph Analysis

16:4b-11
1. Whose departure did Jesus talk about (verses 4b-7a)? _____
2. Why was Jesus' departure necessary?
_____
_____

What benefit would come because of it? Relate this to verse 6._____

3. What ministry would the Spirit have after He came?_____
_____

4. How would unbelievers be convicted with respect to sin, righteousness and judgment (verse 8)? Compare Acts 2:36,37 (sin); Acts 3:14,15 (righteousness); John 12:31,32 (judgment).
_____
_____
_____

16:12-15
1. Record the ministries of the Spirit that Jesus promised here. _____
_____
_____
_____

What is significant about the first ministry mentioned in verse 14? _____
_____

2. What title did Jesus give the Spirit?

_____

Compare this with the title in 16:7.

_____

_____

3. How does the Trinity appear in verse 15?

_____

_____

_____

Related Verses

John 7:37-39 _____

_____

Acts 2:22-24 _____

_____

Acts 7:51-57 _____

_____

Romans 1:3,4 _____

_____

Colossians 2:15 _____

_____

1 Timothy 3:16 _____

_____

Revelation 20:10 _____

_____

INTERPRETATIONS

1. "None of you asks Me, 'Where are You going?'" (16:5). Jesus did not forget Peter's and Thomas' earlier questions (13:36; 14:5). Those questions arose out of their concern over being separated from Him, rather than because they were genuinely interested in His destination. Now Jesus wants to direct their attention primarily to His returning to His *Father*.

2. "I will send Him to you" (16:7). This prophecy was fulfilled on the day of Pentecost. Read Acts 2:1ff.

3. Read verses 8-11 again. Paraphrase what you think is the intended meaning of each statement after the word "because" (verses 9,10,11):

   (1) concerning SIN,

because _____

_____

   (2) concerning RIGHTEOUSNESS,

because _____

_____

   (3) concerning JUDGMENT,

because _____

4. "The ruler of this world [now stands] condemned" (16:11 NIV). At the cross, Satan's power over sin

was judged; at the resurrection, his power over death was broken.

APPLICATIONS

1. As you witness to unbelievers about Christ and His invitation to them to be saved, how important do you think it is for them to recognize that they are sinners in need of salvation?

_____

_____

_____

_____

_____

_____

What convicting work does the Holy Spirit perform when a sinner considers his spiritual state?

_____

_____

_____

Why must you depend on that when you witness to such a person? (TBS#7)

_____

_____

_____

_____

_____

2. One of the ministries of the Holy Spirit today is to glorify Jesus. How can you use this as a test of the authenticity of any alleged work for God? (TBS#3) _____

_____

_____

_____

_____

_____

Summary of Passage

Jesus tells His disciples that He is going away, but that He will send them the Helper, the Holy Spirit. The Spirit will have a ministry to the unbelieving world—convicting unbelievers of sin, righteousness, and judgment. His ministry to believers will be to guide them, teach them, and glorify Jesus.

So Jesus' disciples need not sorrow over His leaving them.

Memory Verse   16:13

Looking Ahead

Jesus tells His disciples why their sorrow will turn to joy.

SETTING The setting is the same as that of the preceding segment. This is a continuation of Jesus' discourse.

IN A LITTLE WHILE

PROPHECY: EVENTS

16 "A little while,
and you will **no longer** BEHOLD ME;
and **again** a little while, and you will SEE ME."
17 Some of HIS DISCIPLES
therefore said to one another,
"What is this thing He is telling us,
A little while, and you will **not** BEHOLD ME;
and **again** a little while, and you will SEE ME';
and 'Because **I go to THE FATHER'?"**
[John 16:5]
18 And so they were saying,
"What is this that He says,
'A little while'?
We do not know what He is talking about."

PROPHECY: EMOTIONS

19 JESUS knew that they wished to **question Him,**
and He said to them,
"Are you deliberating together about this,
that I said, 'A little while,
and you will **not** BEHOLD ME,
and **again** a little while,
and you will SEE ME'?
20 "TRULY, TRULY, I say to you,
that you will WEEP and LAMENT,
but THE WORLD will REJOICE;
you will be SORROWFUL,
but your SORROW will be turned to JOY.
21 "Whenever a woman is in **travail** she has SORROW,
because **her hour has come;**
but when she gives birth to the child,
she **remembers** the ANGUISH **no more,**
for JOY that a child has been born into the world.
22 "Therefore you too **now** have SORROW;
but I will **see you again,**
and your heart will REJOICE,
and no one takes your JOY away from you.

EXHORTATION

23 "And **in that day**
you will ask Me no question.
TRULY, TRULY, I say to you,
if you shall ask THE FATHER **for anything,**
HE will **give it to you** IN MY NAME.
24 "Until now
you have **asked for nothing** IN MY NAME;
ASK, and
YOU WILL RECEIVE, that
YOUR JOY MAY BE MADE FULL."

Key Words and Phrases

16:16 "a little while" ____________________

17 ____________________

18 ____________________

20 ____________________

20 ____________________

21 ____________________

23 ____________________

24 ____________________

others: ____________________

____

Book of John: LIFE IN JESUS, THE SON OF GOD

PROLOGUE	SIGNS WROUGHT		SELF REVEALED			EPILOGUE 21:25
	PUBLIC MINISTRY -3 YEARS- (GREAT) (PAUSE) ▶		PRIVATE MINISTRY -FEW DAYS-			
	ERA OF INCARNATION BEGINS	YEARS OF CONFLICT	DAY OF PREPARATION	HOUR OF SACRIFICE	DAWN OF VICTORY	
1:1	1:19	5:1	12:36b	18:1	20:1	21:1

OBSERVATIONS

Segment Survey

1. What key phrase is repeated in the first paragraph? ____________________

____

Observe on the outline that this first paragraph is identified as PROPHECY: EVENTS. What are the events? ____________________

____

What is the prophecy about in the second paragraph?

____

____

2. How is the third paragraph different from the first two? ____________________

____

Do you see a command here? ____________________
Is there a command in any other part of the segment? ____________________
3. How bright and promising is verse 24?

____

____

Paragraph Analysis

16:16-18

1. Read the text of verse 16 as: "In a little while...and then in a little while...." In light of things Jesus had earlier taught His disciples, what would happen at the end of each "little while"? See 3:14; 11:25; 12:32-35. ____________________

____

____

In this connection, note that Jesus used two different words: "behold" and "see" (verses 16,17, and 19).

2. When had Jesus told His disciples that He was to "go to the Father" (verse 17)?

____

3. Where does each part of verses 16 and 17 fit into this chronological sequence (16a; 16b; 17c):

____ † cross ____ ○ resurrection ____ ▲ ascension

16:19-22

1. Why would the disciples "weep and lament" (verse 20)? ____________________
Why did they have sorrow "now" (verse 22)?

____

____

Why would the world rejoice (verse 20)?

_____

_____

2. What event would turn the disciples' sorrow

to joy?_____

16:23,24
1. According to 16:23a and 16:24a, had the disciples asked for anything from Jesus while in

His presence?_____ Would they do so later?

_____

2. Does the phrase "in that day" (verse 23) appear

anywhere else in the segment?_____
Could it refer to post-resurrection *and* post-

ascension time?_____
3. In what time period do you think Jesus was appealing to the disciples to pray in verses 23b and

24b)?_____

_____

Related Verses

Matthew 7:7,8_____

_____

Mark 16:9,10 _____

_____

Luke 24:38,51-53_____

_____

John 14:1,27 _____

_____

John 14:18-24 _____

_____

John 15:16_____

_____

Acts 2:46 _____

_____

INTERPRETATIONS

1. "A little while" (16:16). It would be a *very* little while before Jesus would be crucified—just a matter of hours, since this was already Thursday of Passion Week. Then in a little while—on the third day—Jesus would be resurrected, and the disciples would see Him again.
2. "Behold Me...see Me" (16:16). The sight verbs translate two different Greek words. In this context, the former means *to look upon as a spectator* (cf. Matthew 28:1). The latter is stronger, involving discernment (e.g. "they shall see God," Matthew 5:8). Why would post-resurrection days be a time of

discernment?_____

_____

_____

_____

APPLICATIONS

1. The difference between joy and sorrow in the disciples' life was the difference between a crucified Jesus and a risen Savior (16:20). How does the resurrected Christ make a difference in your daily walk as a Christian? Cite specific examples.

_____

_____

_____

_____

_____

_____

_____

_____

_____

_____

There is always some justifiable sorrow in the believer's experience. When this is your experience, where do you find solace and strength?

_____

_____

_____

_____

2. Have you experienced the full joy of 16:24?

_____

_____

_____

How can you appropriate this?

_____

_____

_____

Summary of Passage

Jesus tells His disciples that in a little while they will not see Him (He will be in the tomb). Then in a little while they will see Him again (in His resurrection body). Their sorrow at not seeing Him will be turned to joy when they see Him again.

When Jesus has gone to the Father, His disciples will always have the joy of prayer access to the Father through Jesus' name, asking for the supply of needs.

Memory Verse 16:24

Looking Ahead

Jesus promises His disciples blessings through prayer.

SETTING These are Jesus' last words to His disciples before He prays to His Father (chapter 17). He is still in the house in Jerusalem. He will not leave the city until He has prayed (18:1).

Book of John: LIFE IN JESUS, THE SON OF GOD

P R O L O G U E	SIGNS WROUGHT			SELF REVEALED		E P I L O G U E 21 :25
	PUBLIC MINISTRY -3 YEARS-		(GREAT) (PAUSE) ▶	PRIVATE MINISTRY -FEW DAYS-		
	ERA OF INCARNATION BEGINS	YEARS OF CONFLICT	DAY OF PREPARATION	HOUR OF SACRIFICE	DAWN OF VICTORY	
1:1	1:19	5:1	12:36b	18:1	20:1	21:1

PEACE IN JESUS

25 "These things I have spoken to you
      in figurative language;
   an hour is coming,
  when I will speak
   no more to you in figurative language,
  but will tell you plainly of THE FATHER.
26 "In that day you will ASK IN MY NAME;
   and I do not say to you
   that I will request THE FATHER on your behalf;
27 for THE FATHER HIMSELF loves you,
  because you
   (1) have loved Me, and
   (2) have BELIEVED
  that I came forth from THE FATHER.
28 "(1) I came forth from THE FATHER, and
  (2) have come into the WORLD;
  (3) I am leaving the WORLD again, and
  (4) going to THE FATHER."

29 HIS DISCIPLES said,
  "Lo, now You are speaking plainly,
  and are not using a figure of speech.
30 "Now we know that You know all things,
  and have no need for anyone to question You;
   by this WE BELIEVE
    that YOU CAME FROM GOD."
31 JESUS answered them,
  "DO YOU NOW BELIEVE?
32 "Behold,
  an hour is coming, and has already come,
  for you to be scattered, each to his own home,
   and to leave Me ALONE;
  and yet I am NOT ALONE,
    because THE FATHER is with Me.

33   "These things I have spoken to you,
    that in Me YOU MAY HAVE PEACE.
  In the world you have tribulation,
   but take courage;
     I have overcome the world."

(side labels: FATHER / JESUS / PEACE & COURAGE)

Key Words and Phrases

16:25 ___"an hour is coming"___

25 _____

26 _____

27 _____

28 _____

30 _____

33 _____

others: _____

OBSERVATIONS

Segment Survey

1. In what paragraphs is Jesus talking?

_____

_____

_____

How much talking by the disciples does John report?

_____

_____

2. Read the first two paragraphs again and arrive at a theme for each. In some ways the paragraphs are very similar, so it is difficult to distinguish them. (Note the outline: FATHER; JESUS.)

   theme of 16:25-28 _____

_____

   theme of 16:29-32 _____

_____

3. How is the last paragraph a conclusion to the segment? _____

Paragraph Analysis

16:25-28

1. What are the two time references in this paragraph? _____

_____

Did Jesus identify the event or period? _____
What would He be doing then?

_____

What would the disciples be doing?

_____

2. What time do you think Jesus was referring to when He spoke those words?

_____

3. What activity of the disciples do verses 26-28 describe? _____

_____

4. How did Jesus assure the disciples of their success in praying to the Father?

_____

What part would Jesus play in this?

_____

What would Jesus not have to do (verse 26b)?

_____

16:29-32

1. Begin your study of the paragraph with the central affirmation, "We believe that You came from God" (verse 30). Relate this to what Jesus had just said in verse 28. _____

_____

2. What illustration did Jesus use to show that genuine belief is the answer to problems and trials (verse 32a)?

_____

_____

16:33
1. Relate the last statement in verse 33 to the last statement in verse 32.

_____

_____

2. What are the encouraging words of the paragraph?

_____

_____

Related Verses
Matthew 26:31_____

_____

John 14:27-31 _____

_____

Acts 1:8,9; 2:1ff. _____

_____

Acts 3:6_____

_____

Romans 8:35-39_____

_____

1 John 5:4,5_____

_____

INTERPRETATIONS
1. "An hour is coming" (16:25); "in that day" (16:26). Since Jesus prophesied His "leaving the world again, and going to the Father" (16:28), here He must have been looking toward His ascension (Acts 1:9-11) and the subsequent coming of the Holy Spirit to this world. He would teach His children through the Holy Spirit.
2. Here is the Living Bible's paraphrase of 16:26b,27: "And I won't need to ask the Father to grant you these requests, for the Father himself loves you dearly because you love me and believe that I came from the Father." Why do you think Jesus said this?

_____

_____

3. "Leave Me alone" (16:32). When was Jesus left alone? _____
4. "I have overcome the world" (16:33). Why could Jesus make this claim?

_____

_____

_____

APPLICATIONS
Why is effectual prayer so vital in your Christian life? (Cf. James 5:16.) (TBS#4)

_____

_____

Jesus said that we should make petitions **in His name**. What did He mean by this?

_____

_____

_____

_____

How does this affect your prayer life, as to

motives?_____

_____

_____

methods?_____

_____

_____

fruits? _____

_____

_____

Why does your love to Jesus and the Father determine to a large extent the effectiveness of your prayer life?_____

_____

_____

_____

_____

Summary of Passage
Jesus prophesies that the time is coming when He will tell His disciples plainly about the Father. And in those days they will make their supplications directly to the Father in Jesus' name. The Father will hear and answer them, because they truly believe in Him and His Son.

Jesus says the hour is coming when He will have only the Father with Him. He encourages the disciples to be prepared for future tribulation. He has overcome the world, and they may have His peace in those experiences.

Memory Verse   16:33

Looking Ahead
Jesus prays to His Father in the presence of His disciples.

SETTING Jesus is still with His disciples, probably in the Upper Room in Jerusalem. From 18:1 we may conclude that He prayed audibly. So the disciples must have heard their Master's intercessions.

Book of John: LIFE IN JESUS, THE SON OF GOD

P R O L O G U E	SIGNS WROUGHT		SELF REVEALED			E P I L O G U E
	PUBLIC MINISTRY -3 YEARS-	(GREAT) (PAUSE) ▶	PRIVATE MINISTRY -FEW DAYS-			21: 25
	ERA OF INCARNATION BEGINS	YEARS OF CONFLICT	DAY OF PREPARATION	HOUR OF SACRIFICE	DAWN OF VICTORY	
1:1	1:19	5:1	12:36b	18:1	20:1	21:1

"GLORIFY ME WITH YOU"

(margin: DELEGATED AUTHORITY)

1 These things JESUS spoke;
     and **lifting up His eyes** to HEAVEN,
  He said, "FATHER, the hour has come;
     GLORIFY THY SON,
     that THE SON may GLORIFY THEE,
2 **even as** Thou gavest Him **authority**
         over all mankind,
that to all whom Thou hast given Him,
    ➤ He may GIVE ETERNAL LIFE.
3 "And **this** is ETERNAL LIFE
     that they may KNOW
  (1) Thee, the only TRUE GOD, and
  (2) JESUS CHRIST whom Thou hast sent.

(margin: RESTORED GLORY)

4 "I **glorified Thee** on the earth,
    having accomplished the work
     which Thou hast given Me to do.
5 "And now, GLORIFY Thou ME
    together with THYSELF, FATHER,
  with the GLORY which I had
     WITH THEE before the world was."

Key Words and Phrases

17:1   "eyes to heaven" _____

1 _____

2 _____

2 _____

3 _____

4 _____

4 _____

5 _____

others: _____

OBSERVATIONS

Segment Survey

1. Chapter 17 is known as Jesus' high-priestly prayer. In most of the prayer He intercedes for His disciples and all future believers—hence the name high-priestly prayer. The prayer has three parts:

  17:1-5   Jesus prays for Himself

  17:6-19   Jesus prays for His disciples

  17:20-26   Jesus prays for future believers

2. This first part of Jesus' prayer is very brief. It is His prayer for Himself. Observe that a new paragraph begins at verse 4. Read the segment, noting the reason for the division at verse 4.
3. What is the main repeated word of the segment?

_____

_____

Paragraph Analysis

17:1-3

1. Compare "heaven" (verse 1) and "world" (verse 5).

_____

_____

_____

What two other words appear in the segment which have reference to the domain of Jesus' ministry? _____

2. By what names did Jesus identify His Father and Himself? _____

_____

_____

3. What event was Jesus referring to in the words, "the hour has come" (verse 1)? (Cf. 2:4; 7:30; 8:20; 12:23,27; 13:1.) _____

What then is significant about the very next word in His prayer? _____

_____

_____

Why did Jesus want to be glorified (verse 1b)?

_____

4. Into what subject did this prayer for glory lead (verses 2,3)? _____

_____

_____

5. What is the way to eternal life (verse 3)?

_____

_____

_____

17:4,5

1. Compare the past tense, "I glorified Thee" (verse 4) with the earlier statement, "that the Son may glorify Thee" (verse 1). _____

_____

_____

_____

2. How had Jesus glorified His Father?

_____

_____

3. What does the phrase, "together with Thyself," tell you?_____

_____

4. What does verse 5b reveal about Jesus' public ministry on earth? _____

_____

_____

Related Verses

Matthew 28:18_____

_____

John 3:14,15; 5:39,40; 6:54,68; 10:27,28; 12:25 (eternal life)_____

_____

John 12:23_____

_____

Romans 8:34_____

_____

Philippians 2:5-11 _____

_____

1 John 5:20_____

INTERPRETATIONS

1. What does the word "glory" mean?

_____

_____

What does the phrase "glorify thy Son" (17:1) mean?

_____

_____

To measure that glory, relate it to what Jesus said about eternal life (17:2).

_____

_____

2. Compare the three references to giving in verse 2: "gavest," "given," and "give."

_____

_____

_____

_____

_____

_____

3. What did Jesus mean by the word "know" in 17:3?

_____

_____

_____

How can a sinner come to *know* the Father and Son? How can he be assured that he knows God? (Cf. 1 John 2:3-6.)_____

_____

_____

_____

_____

_____

APPLICATIONS

Using the thought starters below, tell what you learn from Jesus in this part of His prayer.

1. The few words Jesus spoke about Himself (17:1-5) compared with the many spoken about others (17:6-26) (TBS#4):

_____

_____

_____

_____

2. The humility of Jesus—surrendering glory for the earth ministry:

_____

_____

_____

_____

3. Obedience to do the Father's will (TBS#6):

_____

_____

_____

_____

_____

Summary of Passage

Jesus looks toward heaven, and prays to His Father. He says that the time of sacrifice has come, and asks the Father to restore the glory He had before the world began. He testifies that He has accomplished His earth ministry, giving eternal life to all whom the Father has given Him and who have come to know Him and the Father.

Memory Verse   17:3

Looking Ahead

Jesus prays for His disciples.

SETTING Jesus is continuing in prayer, so the setting is that of the preceding passage. The whole prayer session marks the last time the disciples are alone with Jesus before His death.

Book of John: LIFE IN JESUS, THE SON OF GOD

P R O L O G U E	SIGNS WROUGHT			SELF REVEALED		E P I L 21: O 25 G U E
	PUBLIC MINISTRY -3 YEARS-		(GREAT) (PAUSE) ▶	PRIVATE MINISTRY -FEW DAYS-		
	ERA OF INCARNATION BEGINS	YEARS OF CONFLICT	DAY OF PREPARATION	HOUR OF SACRIFICE	DAWN OF VICTORY	
1:1	1:19	5:1	12:36b	18:1	20:1	21:1

THE MEN YOU GAVE ME

6 "I **manifested** THY NAME
to the men whom Thou **gavest** Me out of the world;
THINE they were,
and Thou gavest them to Me,
and they have KEPT THY WORD.
7 "Now they have come to know
that EVERYTHING Thou hast **given** Me
IS FROM THEE;
8 for the words which Thou **gavest** Me
I have **given to them**; and they
(1) **received** them, and
(2) truly understood that
I came forth from Thee, and they
(3) **BELIEVED** that Thou didst send Me.
9 "I ASK on **their** behalf;
I DO NOT ASK on behalf of the world,
but of those whom Thou hast given Me; for
(1) they are THINE; and
10 (2) all things that are MINE are THINE, and
(3) THINE are MINE; and
(4) I have been GLORIFIED in them.
11a "And I am **no more** in the **world**;
and yet they themselves are in the **world**,
and I COME TO THEE.

I ASK ON THEIR BEHALF

11b "HOLY FATHER, keep them IN THY Name,
the NAME which Thou hast **given** Me,
that they may be one, even as We are.
12 "While I was **with them**,
I was keeping them IN THY NAME
which thou hast given Me;
and I guarded them,
and not one of them perished,
but the **son of perdition**,
that the SCRIPTURE might be FULFILLED.
[Psalm 41:9]

PROTECT THEM

13 "But now I COME TO THEE;
and these things I speak **in the world**,
that   they may have
MY JOY made FULL in themselves.
14 "I have given them THY WORD;
and the WORLD has **hated** them,
because   they are **not of the world**,
even as I am **not of the world**.
15 "I do not ask Thee
to take them **out of the world**,
but to KEEP THEM from THE EVIL ONE.
16 "They are **not of the world**,
even as I am **not of the world**.
17 "Sanctify them in THE TRUTH;
THY WORD IS TRUTH.
18 "As Thou didst send Me **into the world**,
I also have sent them **into the world**.
19 "And for their sakes I **sanctify** Myself,
that they themselves also
may be SANCTIFIED IN TRUTH."

SANCTIFY THEM

Key Words and Phrases

17:6 ___ "manifested Thy name" ___
8 _____
9 _____
11a _____
11b _____
13 _____
15 _____
19 _____
others: _____

OBSERVATIONS

Segment Survey

1. Read the entire segment. For whom was Jesus praying? _____

2. Where in the segment is the first specific prayer request? _____

What other specific requests appear in the prayer?
_____
_____
_____

3. What is the last word of the segment? _____

Compare this word with a similar one in the opening verse. _____
_____

Paragraph Analysis

17:6-11a

1. What are the first words that specifically tell that Jesus was praying in behalf of others?
_____
_____

How did He describe those men (the disciples) in verses 6-8? _____
_____
_____

What words and phrases of verses 6-8 show that the disciples were genuine believers?
_____
_____
_____

2. How did Jesus relate the disciples to Himself and the Father, in verses 6,9b-10?

_____

_____

_____

17:11b-12

1. What was Jesus' first prayer request for His disciples? _____

_____

_____

2. Compare this with His ministry for them while He was with them (verse 12).

_____

_____

17:13-19

1. What were Jesus' two prayer requests in this paragraph? _____

_____

Compare the first one with that of 17:11b.

_____

_____

2. What references did Jesus make to "the world" in this paragraph? _____

_____

_____

Related Verses

Matthew 6:13 _____

_____

John 13:10,11,18 _____

_____

Acts 1:14 _____

_____

Philippians 2:9,10 _____

_____

Hebrews 7:25 _____

_____

1 Peter 5:8 _____

_____

1 John 5:18 _____

_____

INTERPRETATIONS

1. What did Jesus mean by the statement, "I am no more in the world" (17:11a)?

_____

_____

2. The statement, "keep them in Thy name" (17:11b), is translated "protect them by the power of your name" in NIV. How is this translation reinforced by the words "guarded" (17:12) and "keep them from the evil one" (17:15)?

_____

_____

3. "Not one of them perished but..." (17:12). This is a reference to Judas. (Cf. 6:71; 13:2,18,26,30; 15:2,6.) Judas' death was at hand. Read Matthew 27:3-10 and Acts 1:18.

4. Jesus and the disciples were "not of the world" (17:14), but they were sent "into the world" (17:18). What was the difference?

_____

_____

_____

5. "Sanctify them in the truth" (17:17). The Greek word translated "sanctify" means *set apart for holy use*. How would the Father accomplish this, according to verse 17?

_____

_____

APPLICATIONS

1. How much do you pray for other Christians— family, friends, or those who are not acquaintances?

_____

What does this prayer of Jesus teach you about intercession? _____

_____

How can you become a better intercessor?

_____

_____

2. Why do Christians need divine protection from the evil one, Satan? (See 1 Peter 5:8.)

_____

3. Jesus wants you set apart (sanctified) for service in His vineyard. What does this mean to you? For example, set apart from what, and unto what? Why is this a vital requirement for Christian service? Discuss this with the other members of your study group.

Summary of Passage

Jesus prays on behalf of His disciples, whom His Father gave to Him and who have truly understood that He came from His Father. He prays for their protection from the evil one, Satan, that they may be one, even as He and the Father are one. They need this protection because they are in the world, even though they are not of it. And Jesus prays that His Father will set His disciples apart, in the truth, for holy use in the days to come.

Memory Verse   17:15

Looking Ahead

Jesus prays for the church, the body of all who believe in His Name.

SETTING This passage concludes Jesus' prayer to His Father. After praying, Jesus and His disciples leave Jerusalem and walk to the Garden of Gethsemane (18:1).

Book of John: LIFE IN JESUS, THE SON OF GOD

P R O L O G U E	SIGNS WROUGHT			SELF REVEALED			E P I L O G U E 21: 25
	PUBLIC MINISTRY -3 YEARS-		(GREAT (PAUSE) ▶	PRIVATE MINISTRY -FEW DAYS-			
	ERA OF INCARNATION BEGINS	YEARS OF CONFLICT	DAY OF PREPARATION	HOUR OF SACRIFICE	DAWN OF VICTORY		
1:1	1:19	5:1	12:36b	18:1	20:1		21:1

UNITY OF BELIEVERS

20 "I do not **ask** in behalf of these **alone**,
   but for those **also**
     who BELIEVE IN ME through **their word**;
21 that ⟶ they may ALL BE ONE;
   even as Thou, FATHER, art in Me,
       and I in Thee,
   that ⟶ they also may be IN US;
     [so] that the WORLD may BELIEVE
     that **Thou didst send Me**.
22 "And THE GLORY which Thou hast **given** Me
        I have **given** to them;
   that they may BE ONE,
   just as we ARE ONE;
23 "I IN THEM, and THOU IN ME,
   that they may be **perfected in unity**,
   [so] that the WORLD may KNOW
   that Thou
     (1) **didst send Me**, and
     (2) **didst love them**,
   even as Thou didst **love Me**.

24 "FATHER, I desire
   that they also whom Thou hast **given** Me
     be WITH ME where I am,
   in order that they may BEHOLD MY GLORY,
    which Thou hast **given** Me;
    for Thou didst **love Me**
     before the foundation of the WORLD.

25 "O RIGHTEOUS FATHER,
   although the WORLD has **not known** Thee,
   yet **I have known** Thee;
  and **these** have known that **Thou didst send Me**;
26 and I **have made** THY NAME known to them,
     and **will make it known**;
    that
    (1) the **LOVE** wherewith
      THOU DIDST LOVE ME
      may be **IN THEM**, and
    (2) **I IN THEM**."

(margin labels: INTERCESSION, TESTIMONY)

Key Words and Phrases

17:21 "all be one"
   21 _____
   22 _____
   23 _____
   23 _____
   24 _____
   25 _____
   26 _____
others: _____
_____

OBSERVATIONS
Segment Survey

1. Here Jesus is praying for all who will believe in Him—the church (17:20). The segment has two main parts: INTERCESSION and TESTIMONY. What intercessions does Jesus make in the first two paragraphs?_____
_____

2. Did Jesus request anything of His Father, as recorded in the concluding paragraph?
_____

How do these verses serve as a conclusion to His prayer?_____
_____

3. Note the words, "love Me," at the end of each paragraph.

Paragraph Analysis
17:20-23

1. Who are "these alone" and "those also" (verse 20)?
_____

2. What were Jesus' two prayer requests (verse 21)?
_____

3. To what did Jesus liken the unity that He prayed for (verse 21a)?_____
_____

4. What was His purpose in the second request (verse 21b)? _____

5. Follow the progression in verses 22 and 23, beginning with God's giving glory to Jesus. Account for the advance in each instance:

   GLORY (verse 22a)_____

   UNITY (verses 22b,23a) _____

   TESTIMONY (verse 23b)_____

6. What is the last phrase of the paragraph?
_____
_____

17:24

1. What was Jesus' request?
_____
_____
_____

2. Why did He ask for this?

_____

_____

17:25,26

1. What did Jesus testify (verse 25)?

_____

_____

2. What did He promise (verse 26a)?

_____

_____

Related Verses

John 10:16 _____

_____

John 13:35 _____

_____

1 Corinthians 12:13 _____

_____

2 Corinthians 3:18 _____

_____

Ephesians 2:19 _____

_____

Colossians 1:27 _____

_____

1 Timothy 2:5,6 _____

INTERPRETATIONS

1. "That they may all be one" (17:21). What kind of unity is this? (Cf. 1 Corinthians 12:13.)

_____

_____

What tie binds believers together? (Cf. 1 Corinthians 10:16,17; 1 John 1:3,7.)

_____

_____

2. "That they also may be in Us" (17:21). What brings believers into union with God? (Cf. John 14:16-18,23; Revelation 3:20.)

_____

_____

What kind of union is this? _____

_____

What is one practical outworking of this union (17:21b,23)? _____

_____

3. "The world has not known Thee" (17:25). "Known" has the impact of acknowledgement. (Cf. 1:10.) The world did not acknowledge God to be who He was. But Jesus knew God.

4. "I...will make it known" (17:26). NIV translates, "I...will continue to make you known."

5. Compare the two statements of the last verse (17:26): "love...in them," and "I in them."

_____

_____

_____

_____

APPLICATIONS

1. A deep desire of Jesus' heart is that the world may know that His Father sent Him into this world, because He loves sinners even as He loves His Son. Jesus knows that one of the best testimonies to the world of this divine love is the unity of the believers (17:21). Why is such a testimony powerful? _____

_____

_____

_____

_____

_____

2. What can you do as a believer to help strengthen this unity among fellow Christians?

_____

_____

_____

_____

_____

_____

_____

_____

_____

Summary of Passage

Jesus prays to His Father in behalf of all believers, that they all may be one in the Father and in the Son. He prays for this so that the world, seeing the unity of the saints, may know that the Father loves the Son and has sent His Son to sinners whom He loves.

Jesus prays also that the believers may be with Him wherever He is, to behold His glory which the Father has given Him.

Memory Verse   17:24

Looking Ahead

The enemies of Jesus come upon Him in the Garden of Gethsemane to arrest Him.

HOUR of SACRIFICE
and
DAWN of VICTORY
18:1–20:31

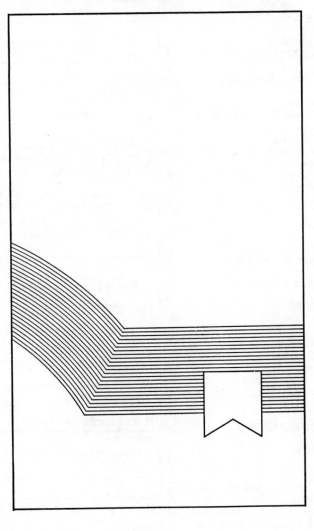

SETTING Observe on the survey chart that 18:1–19:42 of John's gospel is called HOUR OF SACRIFICE.

After singing a hymn (Mark 14:26), Jesus and His disciples leave the house, go out of the city, cross the Kidron Valley, and arrive at Gethsemane on the Mount of Olives. Jesus prays with the disciples (Mark 14:32-42). Then, Judas, a multitude of soldiers, officers, and other people come upon them.

It is early Friday morning of Passion Week.

Book of John: LIFE IN JESUS, THE SON OF GOD

P R O L O G U E	SIGNS WROUGHT			SELF REVEALED		E P I L O G U E
	PUBLIC MINISTRY -3 YEARS-		(GREAT) (PAUSE) ▶	PRIVATE MINISTRY -FEW DAYS-		21 22
	ERA OF INCARNATION BEGINS	YEARS OF CONFLICT	DAY OF PREPARATION	HOUR OF SACRIFICE	DAWN OF VICTORY	
1:1	1:19	5:1	12:36b	18:1	20:1	21:1

Key Words and Phrases

18:2 ___ "betraying Him"

3 _____

4 _____

5 _____

6 _____

9 _____

10 _____

11 _____

others: _____
_____

JUDAS CAME

1 When JESUS had spoken THESE WORDS,
　HE WENT FORTH with HIS DISCIPLES
　　over the ravine of the KIDRON,
　　　where there was a **GARDEN**,
　　into which HE HIMSELF ENTERED,
　　and HIS DISCIPLES.
2 Now JUDAS also, who was **betraying** HIM,
　knew the place;
　for JESUS had **often met there**
　　　　　　WITH HIS DISCIPLES.
3 JUDAS then, having received
　　(1) the ROMAN COHORT, and
　　(2) OFFICERS from the chief priests
　　　　　and the Pharisees,
　CAME THERE with
　　　(1) lanterns and
　　　(2) torches and
　　　(3) **weapons**.

ARRIVAL

---

4. JESUS therefore,
　　knowing all the things
　　　　　that were **coming upon Him**,
　WENT FORTH,
　　and said to them, "Whom do you seek?"
5 They answered Him,
　　"JESUS THE NAZARENE."
　He said to them,
　　"I AM HE."
　And JUDAS also who was betraying Him,
　　was standing WITH THEM.
6 When therefore He said to them, "I AM HE,"
　they **drew back**, and **fell** to the ground.
7 Again therefore He asked them,
　　"Whom do you **seek**?"
　And they said,
　　　　"JESUS THE NAZARENE."
8 JESUS answered,
　　"I told you that I AM HE;
　if therefore you **seek Me**,
　　let **these** go their way,"
9 ⟶ that the word might be fulfilled which He spoke,
　　"Of those whom THOU HAST GIVEN ME
　　　I lost not one."　　　[John 17:12]

CONFRONTATION

---

10 SIMON PETER therefore having a SWORD,
　drew it, and
　　(1) struck the high priest's slave, and
　　(2) cut off his right ear;
　　　and the slave's name was MALCHUS.
11 JESUS therefore said to PETER,
　　"Put the SWORD into the sheath;
　THE CUP which THE FATHER HAS GIVEN ME,
　　　⟶ shall I not drink it?"

VIOLENCE

OBSERVATIONS

Segment Survey

1. Note the title assigned to this segment: JUDAS CAME. What verse is this title based on?

_____

2. Observe the outline assigned to the three paragraphs. How do the paragraphs serve as the setting for Jesus' arrest? (The arrest is reported in 18:12.)

_____

_____

3. What is the extent of the action in the second paragraph? _____

_____

_____

Compare this with the action of the third paragraph.

_____

_____

Paragraph Analysis

18:1-3

1. Who are the two main persons in this paragraph?

_____

_____

2. Compare the atmosphere in the first and third verses. _____

_____

3. Compare these two statements:

"Jesus...went forth with His disciples" (verse 1).

"Judas...came...with lanterns and torches and weapons" (verse 3).

_____

_____

_____

18:4-9

1. What two parts of this paragraph reveal that what was about to happen was divinely predetermined?_____

_____

2. What is unusual about the enemies' reply to Jesus (verses 5,7)?_____

_____

3. What is significant about what verse 6 reports?

_____

4. Why do you think the confrontation was repeated (verses 7,8)?

_____

5. What does verse 8 reveal about Jesus?

_____

18:10,11

1. Compare the symbolical meaning suggested by the sword (verse 10) and the cup (verse 11) in this context. _____

2. What impact do the words, "The Father has given Me" (verse 11), have on this setting?

_____

Related Verses

Matthew 26:52-56_____

Mark 14:26-42 _____

Mark 14:44,45_____

Luke 22:35-38,51_____

John 13:1-3_____

John 13:37_____

John 17:12_____

INTERPRETATIONS

1. "Having received the Roman cohort" (18:3). NIV translates, "guiding a detachment of soldiers." A cohort was a battalion of 300-600 soldiers. We do not know precisely how many soldiers came with Judas, but Matthew reports that a "great multi-

tude" was involved (Matthew 26:47; cf. Mark 14:43; Luke 22:47).

2. "Jesus the Nazarene" (18:5). Some Bible students conclude that the enemies did not recognize Jesus because of the darkness. Otherwise they would have answered something like, "Thou art the one." What do you think?

_____

3. The title "Nazarene," when used by Jesus' enemies, was one of scorn. The prophecy of Matthew 2:23 may refer to Isaiah 11:1, where Messiah is called *netzer*—"shoot"—that is, the lowly shoot out of the roots of Jesse. The name Nazarene may be traced back to this.

4. "Fell to the ground" (18:6). What is there about John's reporting of this part of the story that points to a supernatural impact of Jesus' presence?

_____

In what way might this explain why Jesus asked His question a second time? _____

_____

APPLICATIONS

1. Jesus and His disciples had a favorite place in the garden where they often met for prayer. How can you apply this to your own personal prayer life? Why should prayer be natural, relaxing, and enjoyable? (TBS#4).

_____

2. Jesus' words, "I lost not one" (18:9) assure every believer of Jesus' power to protect and preserve all His servants. How does this truth bolster your Christian life?

_____

Summary of Passage

Jesus walks with His disciples across the Kidron Valley to a favorite spot in a garden where they have often met. Judas knows the place, and leads a multitude of soldiers and religious leaders there to confront Jesus. Jesus twice asks whom they are seeking. Each time they answer, "Jesus the Nazarene." Jesus answers, "I am He."

In the excitement of the moment, Peter cuts off the ear of the high priest's slave, and Jesus calms the scene with the words, "Shall I not drink the cup the Father has given Me?"

Memory Verse 18:11

Looking Ahead

Jesus is arrested and brought to Annas, one of the high priests, for His first trial.

SETTING It is before dawn, Friday morning. Jesus is arrested in the garden and brought to Annas for the first of His hearings. When the trials are over, He will have appeared before the Jewish religious rulers and the Roman political rulers. This is the schedule: JEWISH TRIALS—1) before Annas (John 18:12-14,19-23); 2) before Caiaphas and the Sanhedrin (John 18:24; Matthew 26:57-68); 3) before the Sanhedrin (Luke 22:66-71). ROMAN TRIALS—1) before Pilate (John 18:28-38); 2) before Herod Antipas (Luke 23:6-12); 3) before Pilate (John 18:39–19:16a).

"WHY STRIKE ME?"

12 So the ROMAN COHORT and the COMMANDER,
　　　and the OFFICERS of the JEWS,
　　(1) **arrested** JESUS and (2) **bound** Him,
13 and (3) **led** HIM to ANNAS first;
　　for he was father-in-law of CAIAPHAS,
　　　who was HIGH PRIEST that year.
14 Now CAIAPHAS was the one
　　who had advised that it was **expedient**
　　for ONE Man to DIE ON BEHALF of the PEOPLE.
　　　　　　　　　　　　　　　　[John 11:50]

15 And SIMON PETER was **following** JESUS,
　　and so was ANOTHER DISCIPLE.
　　Now that DISCIPLE was known to the HIGH PRIEST,
　　and **entered with JESUS**
　　　　into the court of the HIGH PRIEST,
16 but PETER was standing at the door outside.
　　So the other DISCIPLE, who was known
　　　　to the HIGH PRIEST,
　　went out and spoke to the DOORKEEPER,
　　　and **brought in PETER**.
17 The slave-girl therefore who kept the door
　　said to PETER, "You are not also
　　　　ONE OF THIS MAN'S DISCIPLES, ARE YOU?"
　　He said, "I am not."
18 Now the SLAVES and the OFFICERS
　　　were standing there,
　　　having made a charcoal FIRE,
　　for **it was cold** and they were **warming themselves**;
　　and PETER also was with them,
　　　standing and warming himself.

19 The HIGH PRIEST therefore **questioned JESUS**
　　about (1) HIS DISCIPLES, and
　　about (2) HIS TEACHING.
20 JESUS answered him,
　　"I have **spoken openly** to the WORLD;
　　"I always **taught** in synagogues,
　　　　　and in the TEMPLE,
　　where all the JEWS come together;
　　and I **spoke nothing in secret**.
21 "Why do you **question Me**?
　　Question those who have heard
　　　　　　　what I spoke to them;
　　BEHOLD, → these **know** what I said."
22 And when He had said this,
　　one of the OFFICERS standing by **gave JESUS a blow**,
　　saying, "Is that the way You **answer**
　　　　the HIGH PRIEST?"
23 JESUS answered him,
　　"If I have **spoken wrongly**, bear witness of the wrong;
　　but if **rightly**, WHY DO YOU STRIKE ME?"
24 ANNAS therefore sent Him bound
　　　　to CAIAPHAS the HIGH PRIEST.

(side tabs: ARREST · PETER'S FIRST DENIAL · BEFORE ANNAS)

P R O L O G U E	SIGNS WROUGHT			SELF REVEALED		E P I L O G U E
	PUBLIC MINISTRY -3 YEARS-		(GREAT) (PAUSE) ▶	PRIVATE MINISTRY -FEW DAYS-		21: 25
	ERA OF INCARNATION BEGINS	YEARS OF CONFLICT	DAY OF PREPARATION	HOUR OF SACRIFICE	DAWN OF VICTORY	
1:1	1:19	5:1	12:36b	18:1	20:1	21:1

25 Now SIMON PETER was **standing**
　　　　　　and **warming** himself.
　　They said therefore to him,
　　"You are not also ONE OF HIS DISCIPLES,
　　　ARE YOU?"
　　He **denied it**, and said, "I am not."
26 One of the slaves of the HIGH PRIEST,
　　being a relative of the one whose ear
　　　　PETER cut off,
　　said, "Did I not see you
　　　　in the GARDEN WITH HIM?"
27 PETER therefore **denied it again**;
　　and ----→ IMMEDIATELY
　　　　A COCK CROWED.

(side tab: PETER'S SECOND & THIRD DENIAL)

Key Words and Phrases

18:12 "arrested Jesus"

14 _____

15 _____

17 _____

19 _____

20 _____

23 _____

27 _____

others: _____

OBSERVATIONS

Segment Survey

1. The segment has four paragraphs, which alternate between the two main persons, Jesus and Peter. Which paragraphs are about Peter?

_____

2. What does the story of Peter contribute to the story of Jesus? _____

_____

3. How many times is Peter reported to have denied a relationship with Jesus?

_____

4. Compare the first and last verses of the segment. _____

Paragraph Analysis

18:12-14

1. After Jesus was arrested, to whom was He first brought, a Jew or a Roman?

_____

What do you think was the reason for this?

_____

2. What was John's reason for recalling what Caiaphas had advised earlier?

_____

_____

(Read 11:47-53.)

18:15-18

1. To what area did they bring Jesus?

_____

Who was with Him? _____

_____

2. What was the setting where the slaves, officers and Peter were standing?

_____

Compare this with the cold words of Peter's denial.

_____

18:19-24

1. Who was the high priest in verse 19?

_____

Compare this with verse 24. See *INTERPRETA-TIONS.* _____

_____

2. What was Jesus questioned about?

_____

3. From Jesus' reply in verses 20 and 21, of what was the high priest apparently accusing Jesus?

_____

4. How was Jesus' reply in verse 23 a rebuke to the officer (verse 22)? _____

_____

18:25-27

1. Compare these two denials with the earlier one (verse 17). _____

_____

2. What is the impact of the word "immediately" (verse 27)? _____

Related Verses

Mark 14:30 _____

_____

Mark 14:53-65 _____

_____

Mark 14:66-72 _____

_____

Luke 22:56 _____

_____

Luke 22:63-65 _____

_____

John 13:37,38 _____

_____

INTERPRETATIONS

1. "Annas" (18:13). Caiaphas (18:13) was the official high priest; Annas, his father-in-law, had been the official high priest earlier (A.D. 6-15), and was now serving with his son-in-law in an unofficial capacity. (Cf. Luke 3:2; Acts 4:5,6.)

2. Review your earlier study (*Unit 40*: 11:47-53) of Caiaphas' advice, "that it was expedient for one man to die on behalf of the people" (18:14). Was Caiaphas interested in the salvation of the world or in the preservation of Israel as a nation?

_____

3. "Court of the high priest" (18:15). This was the courtyard, outside Annas' chamber.

4. "One of this man's disciples" (18:17). What is your reaction to the slave-girl's words, "this man's"?

5. "The high priest...questioned Jesus" (18:19). This was a hearing, not a trial. The trials would take place before the Sanhedrin ("council"—NASB). (Matthew 26:57-68; Luke 22:66-71)

6. "Why do you question Me?" (18:21). Jesus challenged Annas to bring forth witnesses if he thought Jesus was guilty of anything. Why was that a fair trial procedure? _____

_____

APPLICATIONS

1. Jesus was questioned by Annas about His disciples and His teachings. Today, the unbelieving world questions Christians about their Savior, and about the doctrines they believe as truth from God. How important is it for you to have solid, clear answers to unbelievers when you witness to them about Christ? See 1 Peter 3:15-18. (TBS#7)

_____

2. Are you consistently in close fellowship with Jesus? _____ Compare John with Jesus (18:15) and Peter with the crowd (18:18). What does true loyalty measure in your spiritual life?

_____

Summary of Passage

The officers arrest Jesus and lead Him, bound, to Annas, who questions Jesus about His disciples and His teaching. Jesus challenges Annas' right to question Him, since Annas could ask first-hand witnesses about that. An officer gives Him a blow for challenging the high priest.

While this is going on, Peter is standing in the courtyard, and within a short period of time he denies three times that he is a disciple of Jesus. A cock crows immediately after the third denial.

Memory Verse   18:23

Looking Ahead

The Jews lead Jesus to Pilate for the first phase of Roman trial.

SETTING The place is the Praetorium, the headquarters of the Roman governor, Pilate. Jesus has appeared before the Jewish authorities. Now He makes His first defense before Pilate.

Book of John: LIFE IN JESUS, THE SON OF GOD

P R O L O G U E	SIGNS WROUGHT			SELF REVEALED		E P 21: L 25 O G U E
	PUBLIC MINISTRY -3 YEARS-	(GREAT) (PAUSE) ▶		PRIVATE MINISTRY -FEW DAYS-		
	ERA OF INCARNATION BEGINS	YEARS OF CONFLICT	DAY OF PREPARATION	HOUR OF SACRIFICE	DAWN OF VICTORY	
1:1	1:19	5:1	12:36b	18:1	20:1	21:1

"WHAT HAVE YOU DONE?"

28 They **led JESUS** therefore
    from CAIAPHAS into the Praetorium,   [John 18:24]
        and **it was early**;
    and they themselves did not enter
                      into the Praetorium
    in order that
    they might **not be defiled**,
    but MIGHT EAT THE PASSOVER.
29 PILATE therefore went out to them, and said,
    "What ACCUSATION do you bring
        AGAINST THIS MAN?"
30 They answered and said to him,
      "IF THIS MAN were **not an evildoer**,
    we would not have delivered Him up to you."
31 PILATE therefore said to them,
    "Take Him yourselves,
    and JUDGE HIM ➡ ACCORDING TO YOUR LAW."
        The JEWS said to him,
    "We are not permitted to **put anyone to death**;"
32 ➡ that the WORD OF JESUS
        MIGHT BE FULFILLED, which He spoke,
signifying by **what kind of death**
        He was about to die.   [John 12:32,33]

JEWS ACCUSE

33 PILATE therefore
    (1) entered again into the Praetorium, and
    (2) **summoned JESUS**, and
    (3) said to Him,
    "ARE YOU THE KING OF THE JEWS?"
34 JESUS answered,
    "Are you saying this on your own initiative,
    or did others **tell you about Me**?"
35 PILATE answered, "I am not a JEW, am I?
    Your own NATION and the CHIEF PRIESTS
        delivered You up to me;
    WHAT HAVE YOU DONE?"

PILATE QUESTIONS

36 JESUS answered,
    "MY KINGDOM IS NOT OF THIS WORLD.
    If MY KINGDOM **were of this world**,
      then My servants would be **fighting**,
      that I might not be delivered up to the JEWS;
    but as it is
  ➡ MY KINGDOM IS NOT OF THIS REALM."
37 PILATE therefore said to Him,
    "So YOU ARE A KING?"
    JESUS answered,
    "You say correctly that I AM A KING.
    For this I have been **born**, and
    for this **I have come into the world**,
        to BEAR WITNESS TO THE TRUTH.
    Everyone who is of THE TRUTH
        hears My voice."
38a PILATE said to Him,
        "What is truth?"

JESUS ANSWERS

Key Words and Phrases

18:28   "might not be defiled" _____

  28 _____

  29 _____

  30 _____

  32 _____

  33 _____

  36 _____

  37 _____

others: _____

OBSERVATIONS

Segment Survey

1. Who asks the first question of the segment?

_____

Who asks the last one? _____
How many other questions does he ask?

_____

What does this reveal about him?

_____
_____

2. Jesus is alone with Pilate in which paragraphs?

_____
_____

3. Compare the extent of Jesus' words in each paragraph.

    18:28-32: prophecy _____

_____

    18:33-35: question _____

_____

    18:36-38: answers _____

_____

Paragraph Analysis
18:28-32

1. Who are "They" (verse 28)? Where in the text of John were they last identified?

_____
_____

How is the group identified in verse 28b?

_____

2. With what words did Pilate identify Jesus (verse 29)? _____

_____
_____

3. Why did the Jews deliver Jesus to Pilate, when they should have judged Him according to their Jewish law (verses 30-32)?

_____

_____

4. Why did John add verse 32? (See *INTER-PRETATIONS*.)_____

_____

_____

18:33-35
1. Where was Pilate's meeting with Jesus?

_____

Were the accusing Jews present?

_____

_____

2. What were Pilate's three questions?

_____

_____

_____

Compare the first and the last.

_____

_____

18:36-38a
1. How did Jesus finally answer (verses 36,37a) Pilate's original question in verse 33?

_____

_____

2. How did Jesus lead into the subject of truth (verses 37b,38a)?_____

_____

Related Verses
Deuteronomy 21:22,23 _____

_____

Daniel 7:13,14,22,23,27_____

_____

Matthew 20:19_____

_____

Luke 23:2_____

_____

John 3:14 _____

_____

John 12:32,33_____

_____

John 19:12_____

_____

Galatians 3:13_____

_____

INTERPRETATIONS

1. "Praetorium" (18:28). This was the judgment-hall, the headquarters of the Roman governor, Pilate. Governors were rulers of designated territories, and were appointed by the emperor. Therefore, they were directly responsible to him. Pilate was governor of Judea, Samaria, and Old Idumea (south of Judea).

2. "That they might not be defiled" (18:28). Compare these Jews' pride of ceremonial purity with their base craving to execute Jesus.

_____

3. "We are not permitted to put anyone to death" (18:31). On occasion the Jewish authorities (Sanhedrinists) were permitted to stone a person who had violated the Temple precincts by defiling holy ground. According to Roman law, however, only the Roman authorities had the power of execution. And their method of execution was crucifixion. How does this explain the Jews' refusal of 18:31b?_____

Also, how does this explain John's commentary in 18:32, when compared with 12:32,33?

4. "My kingdom is not of this realm" (18:36). To the Roman authorities, a king of the Jews would be viewed as an insurrectionist, which Jesus was not. This is why Jesus stayed clear of the question, "Are You the King of the Jews?" (18:33).

APPLICATIONS

1. What important warning can everyone heed from the ceremonial self-righteousness of the Jews (18:28)? _____

Apply this to a situation in a Christian's life.

_____

2. Jesus' kingdom is not of this world. In what way does this affect your behavior as a believer?

_____

What things should you be surrendering to Jesus' rule? _____

Summary of Passage

The Jewish officers lead Jesus to the judgment-hall of the Roman governor, Pilate. They accuse Jesus of being a criminal, and want Rome to execute Him, since they do not have that authority. Pilate leaves them and has a private meeting with Jesus. He wants to know if Jesus is King of the Jews and if He has done any evil. Jesus affirms that He is a king, but His kingdom is not of this world. He came to this world to bear witness to the truth. Pilate asks, "What is truth?"

Memory Verse   18:37

Looking Ahead

Jesus is examined further by Pilate.

SETTING After Jesus' first hearing before Pilate (18:28-38a), Pilate sends Him to Herod Antipas for interrogation. Herod then returns Jesus to Pilate (Luke 23:6-12). The passage of this unit reports Jesus' second hearing before Pilate and the scourging and mocking He endured at the hands of the soldiers and Jewish accusers.

NO GUILT IN HIM

18:38b And when he had said this,
   he went out again to the JEWS,
   and said to them, "I FIND NO GUILT IN HIM."
39 "But you have a CUSTOM,
      that I should **release** someone for you
            at the PASSOVER;
         do you wish then that I **release for you**
            THE KING OF THE JEWS?"
40 Therefore they cried out again, saying,
      "Not this MAN,
         but BARABBAS."
      Now BARABBAS was a **robber**.

19:1 Then PILATE therefore **took JESUS**,
                  and SCOURGED HIM.
2 And the SOLDIERS
      wove a CROWN of thorns and put it on his head,
         and **arrayed** Him in a PURPLE ROBE;
3 and they began to come up to Him,
      and say, "HAIL, KING of the JEWS!"
      and to give Him **blows to the face**.
4 And PILATE came out again, and said to them,
      "BEHOLD, I am bringing Him out **to you**,
         that you may know that
            I FIND NO GUILT IN HIM."
5 JESUS therefore came out,
      wearing the CROWN OF THORNS
         and the PURPLE ROBE.
      And PILATE said to them,
         "BEHOLD, THE MAN!"

6 When therefore the CHIEF PRIESTS
            and the OFFICERS
               saw Him,
         they cried out, saying, "CRUCIFY, CRUCIFY!"
      PILATE said to them,
         "**Take Him** yourselves, and **crucify Him**,
            for I FIND NO GUILT IN HIM."
7 The JEWS answered him,
      "**We have A LAW**,
      and by that law **he ought to die**
      because He made Himself out to be
                  THE SON OF GOD."

8 When PILATE therefore heard this statement,
               he was **more afraid**;
9 and he entered into the PRAETORIUM again,
      and said to JESUS,
         "Where are You from?"
      But JESUS gave him **no answer**.
10 PILATE therefore said to Him,
      "You do not speak to me?
      Do You not know that
         (1) I have **authority** to **RELEASE** You, and
         (2) I have **authority** to **CRUCIFY** You?"
11 JESUS answered,
      "You would have **no authority** over Me,
      unless it had been given you FROM ABOVE;
      for this reason he who delivered Me up to you
                  has the GREATER SIN."

Side labels: "BARABBAS!" | SCOURGED | "CRUCIFY" | AUTHORITY

Book of John: LIFE IN JESUS, THE SON OF GOD

P R O L O G U E	SIGNS WROUGHT			SELF REVEALED		E P I L 21: O 25 G U E
	PUBLIC MINISTRY -3 YEARS-		(GREAT) (PAUSE) ▶	PRIVATE MINISTRY -FEW DAYS-		
	ERA OF INCARNATION BEGINS	YEARS OF CONFLICT	DAY OF PREPARATION	HOUR OF SACRIFICE	DAWN OF VICTORY	
1:1	1:19	5:1	12:36b	18:1	20:1	21:1

Key Words and Phrases

18:38b "no guilt in Him" _____

39 _____

40 _____

19:1 _____

2 _____

3 _____

5 _____

6 _____

others: _____

OBSERVATIONS

Segment Survey
1. Read the four paragraphs, and record the main action of each in a few words:

   18:38b-40 _____

   _____

   19:1-5 _____

   _____

   19:6,7 _____

   _____

   19:8-11 _____

2. What paragraph(s) report(s) Pilate speaking with the Jews? _____

_____

What strong statement does he repeat in each?

_____

_____

3. What paragraph(s) report(s) Jesus speaking?

_____

_____

4. What is the last reference to a person in each paragraph—who is he, and how is he identified?

_____

_____

5. Relate this segment to the key verses of John 20:30,31. _____

_____

Paragraph Analysis
18:38b-40
1. Compare Pilate with the Jews.

_____

142

2. Compare Jesus with Barabbas.

19:1-5
1. Compare what Pilate did (verse 1) with what he said (verses 4,5). _____

2. What was the tone and spirit of the soldiers' treatment of Jesus (verses 2,3)?

How did each of their acts show this?

3. What do you think Pilate intended by saying, "Behold, the man!" (verse 5)?

19:6,7
1. This paragraph is the most intense one of the segment. Identify the intense parts.

2. Compare "We have a law" (verse 7) with "you have a custom" (18:39).

3. What claim of Jesus did the Jews violently reject? (Read Matthew 26:63-65, which records Jesus' earlier claim before Caiaphas—second phase of the Jewish trial.) _____

19:8-11
1. What do you learn about Pilate from this paragraph? _____
2. Compare Jesus' "no answer" with His answer in verse 11. _____

Related Verses

Isaiah 53:5,7 _____

Matthew 20:19 _____

Mark 14:62-64 _____

Mark 15:6-8 _____

Luke 23:6-16 _____

John 5:18 _____

Acts 3:13-15 _____

INTERPRETATIONS

1. "Barabbas" (18:40). John cites one crime of which Barabbas was guilty. Read Luke 23:19, which cites two other crimes.
2. "Scourged Him" (19:1). This was cruel torture by beating, using rods or weighted whips. Most victims fainted; many died. The punishment was usually inflicted on murderers and traitors. Note how briefly John reports the scourging. What does this tell you? _____
3. "We have a law" (19:7). The law was: death for blasphemy. Read Leviticus 24:16. How did the Jews apply this to Jesus?

4. "He was the more afraid" (19:8). Why was Pilate's fear growing? _____

5. "Where are You from?" (19:9). Do you think Pilate meant geographical origin, or something else? Explain. _____

6. "He who delivered Me up to you" (19:11). This was Caiaphas, not Judas. His was the greater sin, because as ruling high priest he had delivered Jesus over to Pilate for execution.

APPLICATIONS

Jesus suffered and died for you, for your sins. Does this truth stir up any emotions in you? Think back over what Jesus suffered during the time span of this passage. Reflect on this, considering why it should have some effect on your personal life as a Christian. For example, should you be willing to experience the suffering of persecution by the world for being one of Jesus' disciples? _____
If so, what will help you persevere in the hardship? See Matthew 5:10-16. (TBS#7)

Summary of Passage

The Jews choose to release the criminal, Barabbas, rather than Jesus, in observing one of their Passover customs. So Pilate has Jesus scourged, and the soldiers in mockery put a crown of thorns on Jesus' head, and array Him in a purple robe. Pilate presents Him to the Jews, still insisting that he finds no guilt in Him. They shout, "Crucify, crucify!" and Pilate becomes more afraid. He even confronts Jesus with the claim that he has the authority to release Him or crucify Him. Jesus replies simply that all such authority originates from above.

Memory Verses 19:2,3

Looking Ahead

Jesus is crucified at Golgotha.

SETTING It is about 6 A.M., Friday. Pilate tries once more to persuade the Jews to release Jesus, but fails. The soldiers lead Jesus to Golgotha, where they crucify Him.

Book of John: LIFE IN JESUS, THE SON OF GOD

P R O L O G U E	SIGNS WROUGHT			SELF REVEALED		E P I L O G U E 21: 25
	PUBLIC MINISTRY -3 YEARS-		(GREAT) (PAUSE) ▶	PRIVATE MINISTRY -FEW DAYS-		
	ERA OF INCARNATION BEGINS	YEARS OF CONFLICT	DAY OF PREPARATION	HOUR OF SACRIFICE	DAWN OF VICTORY	
1:1	1:19	5:1	12:36b	18:1	20:1	21:1

THEY CRUCIFIED HIM

12 As a result of this
　　PILATE made efforts to **RELEASE Him,**
　　but the JEWS cried out, saying,
　　　　"If you **release** THIS MAN,
　　　　　you are **no friend of CAESAR;**
　　everyone who makes himself out to be a KING
　　　　　　opposes CAESAR."
13 When PILATE therefore heard these words,
　　　　he brought JESUS out,
　　　and sat down on the **JUDGMENT SEAT**
　　　　at a place called THE PAVEMENT,
　　　　but in Hebrew, GABBATHA.
14 Now it was the **day of preparation**
　　　　　for THE PASSOVER;
　　　it was about the sixth hour.
　　And he said to the JEWS,
　　　　"BEHOLD, YOUR KING!"
15 They therefore cried out,
　　"Away with Him, away with Him,
　　　　　　CRUCIFY HIM!"
　　PILATE said to them,
　　　　"Shall I CRUCIFY YOUR KING?"
　　　The CHIEF PRIESTS answered,
　　　"We have no king but CAESAR."
16 And so he delivered Him up to them
　　　　　to be CRUCIFIED.

17 **They took** JESUS therefore,
　　and He went out, **bearing HIS OWN CROSS,**
　　　to the place called THE PLACE OF A SKULL,
　　which is called in Hebrew GOLGOTHA;
18 There THEY CRUCIFIED HIM,
　　and with Him two other men,
　　one on either side, and JESUS in between.

19 And PILATE wrote an inscription also,
　　　　　　and put it on the **CROSS.**
　　And it was written,
　　　　"JESUS THE NAZARENE,
　　　　THE KING OF THE JEWS."
20 Therefore this inscription many of the JEWS read,
　　　for the place where JESUS was CRUCIFIED
　　　　　　was near the city;
　　and it was written in Hebrew, Latin, and in Greek.
21 And so the CHIEF PRIESTS of the JEWS
　　were saying to PILATE,
　　　"Do not write, 'THE KING OF THE JEWS';
　　　but **that He said,** 'I am THE KING OF THE JEWS.'"
22 PILATE answered,
　　"What I have written I have written."

23 THE SOLDIERS therefore,
　　　　when they had CRUCIFIED JESUS,
　　took His **outer garments** and made four parts,
　　a part to every soldier and also the **tunic;**
　　now the **tunic was seamless,** woven in **one piece.**
24 They said therefore to one another,
　　"Let us **not tear** it, but **cast lots** for it,
　　　to decide whose it shall be";
　　⟶ that the SCRIPTURE might be FULFILLED,
　　"They **divided** My **outer garments** among them,
　　and for my clothing they **cast lots.**" [Psalm 22:18]
25a Therefore THE SOLDIERS **did these things.**

(vertical side labels: GABBATHA | CRUCIFIXION | INSCRIPTION — GOLGOTHA | GARMENTS)

Key Words and Phrases

19:12 "no friend of Caesar" _____

　13 _____

　14 _____

　15 _____

　17 _____

　18 _____

　22 _____

　24 _____

others: _____

OBSERVATIONS

Segment Survey

1. Note that this segment has been divided into four paragraphs. The last three paragraphs are combined into one group, under the geographical name, GOLGOTHA. Where does the action of the first paragraph take place?

_____

2. Read each paragraph and record the main action in each:

　19:12-16 _____

　19:17,18 _____

　19:19-22 _____

　19:23-25a _____

3. What key word is repeated in this segment?

How many times does it appear?

_____

Paragraph Analysis

19:12-16

1. Compare verse 12 with verse 16.

_____

_____

_____

Then compare verse 16 with 19:11a.

_____

_____

2. Study the appearances of "king" in the paragraph. Record the connections:

　Caesar _____

　Jesus _____

　Pilate _____

　the Jews _____

19:17,18

1. What are the two strongest statements of the paragraph?_____

2. How many words does John use to report the actual crucifixion of Jesus?

What is significant about this?

19:19-22

1. Why did John include verse 20 in his account?

2. Compare the titles, NAZARENE and KING, in the inscription which Pilate put on the cross.

3. Why did the chief priests object to the inscription?_____

4. Was the inscription accurate?

19:23-25a

What is the most important part of this paragraph?

Relate this to the key verses of John.

Related Verses

Isaiah 53:12_____

Matthew 27:24,25,33,34,39,44_____

Luke 23:26-43_____

Luke 24:40 _____

John 20:25_____

Romans 11:15,25_____

Revelation 5:9,10_____

INTERPRETATIONS

1. "Caesar" (19:12). The term "Caesar" was equivalent to the title, "Emperor." The ruling Roman emperor at this time was Tiberius. What do you think was the ulterior motive of the Jews in their references to Caesar (19:12,15)?

2. "About the sixth hour" (19:14). This was about 6 A.M., Roman time. At 9 A.M., Jesus was crucified. (The "third hour" of Mark 15:25 is Jewish time.) He was on the cross for about six hours.

3. "We have no king but Caesar" (19:15). What does this reveal about the spiritual life of the chief priests?_____
What was God's relationship to true Israel?

4. "They crucified Him" (19:18). Crucifixion was slow execution. The pain and agony could last two to three days before death came. For a description of Jesus' soul agony, read Psalm 22.

5. "That the Scripture might be fulfilled" (19:24). This was just one of over 300 Old Testament prophecies fulfilled in Christ. What must an unbeliever acknowledge about this?

APPLICATIONS

1. The Jews said, "We have no king but Caesar." Change the words and apply them to yourself: "I have no king but Jesus." What should the lordship of Christ mean to you?

How can it be observed by others, in your daily walk? (Cf. 1 Corinthians 2:2; 2 Corinthians 10:3-5; Ephesians 1:20-22.)

2. Christ died to atone for your sins. He was your substitute. How often do you return thanks to Him, in word and by life? Read the following verses to help stir up gratitude in your heart: 1 Peter 1:18-20; 2:24; 3:18; Hebrews 13:12,20,21; Revelation 1:5.

Summary of Passage

Pilate tries further to release Jesus, but the Jews insist that He must be crucified because they cannot have two kings. The choice is either King Caesar or King Jesus. So Pilate delivers Jesus to the Jews to be crucified. The soldiers lead Him to Golgotha and crucify Him with two other men.

An inscription on the cross reads, "Jesus the Nazarene, the king of the Jews." The soldiers divide His garments among them and cast lots for his tunic, thereby fulfilling the prophecy of Psalm 22:18.

Memory Verses   19:17,18a

Looking Ahead

John reports the death of Jesus.

SETTING The setting for this passage is the same as the preceding one. Between the first and second paragraphs there is a three-hour period of darkness, as reported in Mark 15:33.

Book of John: LIFE IN JESUS, THE SON OF GOD

P R O L O G U E	SIGNS WROUGHT			SELF REVEALED		E P I L O G U E 21 25
	PUBLIC MINISTRY -3 YEARS-		(GREAT) (PAUSE) ▶	PRIVATE MINISTRY -FEW DAYS-		
	ERA OF INCARNATION BEGINS	YEARS OF CONFLICT	DAY OF PREPARATION	HOUR OF SACRIFICE	DAWN OF VICTORY	
1:1	1:19	5:1	12:36b	18:1	20:1	21:1

JESUS DIES

25b But there were **standing**
    by THE CROSS OF JESUS
        (1) His mother, and His mother's sister,
        (2) Mary the wife of Clopas, and
        (3) Mary Magdalene.
26 When JESUS therefore SAW His mother,
    and the **DISCIPLE whom He loved**
        standing nearby,
    He said to His mother,
        "WOMAN, BEHOLD, YOUR SON!"
27 Then He said to the DISCIPLE,
        "BEHOLD, YOUR MOTHER!"
    And from that hour
        the DISCIPLE took her into his own household.

GOODBYE

THREE HOURS OF DARKNESS (noon to 3 P.M.) (Mark 15:33)

28 After this, JESUS,
    KNOWING that **all things**
        had already been **accomplished**,
        in order that
            THE SCRIPTURE MIGHT BE FULFILLED,
    said, "I AM THIRSTY."   [Psalm 69:21]
29 A jar full of sour wine was standing there;
    so they put a sponge full of the sour wine
                upon a branch of HYSSOP,
        and brought it up to HIS MOUTH.
30 When JESUS therefore had **received** the sour wine,
    He said, "IT IS FINISHED!"
    And He **bowed His head**,
        and GAVE UP HIS SPIRIT.

DEATH

31 The JEWS therefore,
    because it was the DAY OF PREPARATION,
    so that the bodies should not remain
        on the CROSS on the SABBATH
            [Deuteronomy 21:22,23]
        (for that SABBATH was a **high day**)
            [Exodus 12:16]
    asked Pilate
        (1) that their legs might be broken, and
        (2) that they might be taken away.
32 The SOLDIERS therefore came, and broke the legs
        (1) of the first man, and
        (2) of the other man who
            was CRUCIFIED with Him;
33 but coming to JESUS,
    when they saw that HE WAS ALREADY DEAD,
        they did not break His legs;
34 but one of the SOLDIERS
        pierced His side with a spear,
    and immediately ——▶ there came out
        BLOOD AND WATER.

DEAD BODY

35 And he who has SEEN
        has BORNE WITNESS,
    and **his witness is True**;
    and he **knows** that he is telling the truth,
        so that YOU ALSO MAY BELIEVE.
36 For these things came to pass,
    that THE SCRIPTURE MIGHT BE FULFILLED,
        "Not a bone of Him shall be broken."
            [Exodus 12:46; Numbers 9:12]
37 And again another SCRIPTURE says,
        "They shall look on HIM
            whom they PIERCED."
        [Psalm 34:20; Zechariah 12:10]

TESTIMONY

Key Words and Phrases

19:26 "behold, your Son!" _____

27 _____

28 _____

30 _____

33 _____

34 _____

34 _____

35 _____

others: _____

OBSERVATIONS

Segment Survey

1. The four paragraphs of this segment continue John's reporting of Jesus' crucifixion. (Recall that John reported the *commencement* of the crucifixion with the words, "they crucified Him"—19:18.) The paragraphs differ. Read each one, and record the main theme of each.

    19:25b-27 _____

    19:28-30 _____

    19:31-34 _____

    19:35-37 _____

2. Where is the moment of Jesus' death reported?

_____

How is the last paragraph different from the other three? _____

_____

Paragraph Analysis

19:25b-27

1. What is the tone of this paragraph?

_____

Compare it with that of the previous paragraph (19:23-25a). _____

_____

2. Compare Jesus' words to His mother with those spoken to the disciple (John).

_____

_____

What do you think Jesus had in mind?

_____

_____

How is verse 27b a commentary on this?

_____

_____

19:28-30

1. First, read Psalm 69:21. What is the impact of the fulfillment of the prophecy (verses 28-30)?

2. What did Jesus' thirst reveal about the physical anguish of crucifixion?

3. Relate the words, "It is finished," to verse 28a.

Also relate them to 3:35; 13:3; and 17:4.

19:31-34

1. What was the purpose of breaking the legs of a person on the cross, according to verse 33?

2. In view of the prophecies in 19:36,37, who was in control of the soldiers' thoughts and actions?

19:35-37

1. Note how emphatic John is in reporting the fulfillment of the prophecies. How does each of the first four lines of verse 35 bring this out?

2. Relate verse 35b to the key verses of John (20:30,31).

Related Verses

Psalm 22:15

Psalm 69:20

Matthew 12:50

Mark 15:40,44,45

John 17:4

Hebrews 9:23-28

1 John 5:6-8

INTERPRETATIONS

1. "His mother's sister" (19:25b). This was probably Salome, mother of John, which explains Jesus' special relationship to John.

2. "Woman, behold your Son!" (19:26). Calling His mother, "Woman," was not cold; it was very thoughtful. Jesus wanted to spare His mother any deeper immediate sorrow in thinking about her Son's agony, so He directed her thoughts to the long-range significance of His work. From now on, she should look upon Him as her *Lord*, not her *Son*.

3. Of Jesus' seven sayings from the cross, John records three. Read all seven: 1) Luke 23:34; 2) Luke 23:43; 3) John 19:26,27; 4) Matthew 27:46; Mark 15:34; 5) John 19:28; 6) John 19:30; 7) Luke 23:46.

4. "It is finished" (19:30). The same Greek word translates "finished" and "accomplished" (19:28).

5. "That Sabbath was a high day" (19:31). The first day of the Feast of Unleavened Bread fell that year on a sabbath, so it was a "high day."

6. "Blood and water" (19:34). Jesus' body was already dead. Medical authorities say it is possible that this flow came from a ruptured heart. Read Psalm 69:20.

APPLICATIONS

1. What is significant about John's reporting of the women who stood by the cross of Jesus, especially since only one man is named?

What spiritual dimension can Christian women, especially, reinforce in the wide ministry of the church and the gospel?

2. Jesus on the cross was deeply moved by the heavy burden of sorrow which His mother was bearing. What does this reveal about Jesus as intercessor and comforter of His children?

How does it help your prayer life to know that Jesus is moved with strong compassion concerning your needs?

See Hebrews 4:14-16.

Summary of Passage

Standing by the cross of Jesus are His mother, aunt, a few other women, and John. Jesus asks His mother and John to take care of each other. When the time of His death arrives, He calls out, "I am thirsty," and they give Him some sour wine. With the words, "It is finished," He breathes His last.

The soldiers break the legs of the two criminals to speed their deaths, but because Jesus is already dead, a soldier pierces His side instead, bringing forth blood and water. All this happens in fulfillment of prophecy, that the reader may believe.

Memory Verse
19:30

Looking Ahead

Jesus is buried, and on the first day of the week His empty tomb is viewed.

SETTING Jesus' body is carried from the cross and laid in a nearby tomb. On the first day of the week (Sunday) Mary Magdalene, Peter and John find the tomb empty. On the survey chart 20:1 begins a new section (DAWN OF VICTORY). In this study unit the verse appears in the middle of the segment to contrast the death and the life.

Book of John: LIFE IN JESUS, THE SON OF GOD

P R O L O G U E	SIGNS WROUGHT			SELF REVEALED		E P I L O G U E 21: 1-25
	PUBLIC MINISTRY -3 YEARS-		(GREAT) (PAUSE) ▶	PRIVATE MINISTRY -FEW DAYS-		
	ERA OF INCARNATION BEGINS	YEARS OF CONFLICT	DAY OF PREPARATION	HOUR OF SACRIFICE	DAWN OF VICTORY	
1:1	1:19	5:1	12:36b	18:1	20:1	21:1

Key Words and Phrases

19:38 ___ "body of Jesus" _____

39 _____

41 _____

42 _____

20:2 _____

5 _____

6 _____

8 _____

others: _____

THE BODY OF JESUS

JOSEPH & NICODEMUS

38   And after these things
JOSEPH OF ARIMATHEA,
  being a DISCIPLE of JESUS,
    but a SECRET ONE, for fear of the JEWS,
  asked PILATE that he might take away
    the BODY OF JESUS;
  and PILATE granted **permission**.
He came therefore, and took away HIS BODY.
39 And NICODEMUS came also
  ↪ who had first come to Him by night;
            [John 3:1ff.]
  bringing a mixture of myrrh and aloes,
    about a hundred pounds weight.
40 And so **THEY TOOK THE BODY OF JESUS**,
  and bound it in linen wrappings with the spices,
    as is the **burial custom of the JEWS**.
41 Now in the PLACE WHERE HE WAS CRUCIFIED
    there was a GARDEN;
  and in the GARDEN A NEW TOMB,
    in which no one had yet been laid.
42 Therefore on account of the JEWISH DAY
OF PREPARATION,
  because the **tomb was nearby**,
  THEY LAID JESUS THERE.

MARY MAGDALENE

20:1   Now on the FIRST DAY OF THE WEEK
  Mary Magdalene came **early** to the tomb,
            while it was still **dark**,
  and SAW the stone already taken away from the tomb.
2 And so she ran and came
  (1) to SIMON PETER, and
  (2) to the OTHER DISCIPLE whom JESUS loved,
      and said to them,
  "They have **taken away the LORD** out of the tomb,
    and **we do not know** where they have laid HIM."

PETER & JOHN

3 PETER therefore went forth,
    and the OTHER DISCIPLE
      and they were **going to the tomb**.
4 And the two were **running together**;
    and the OTHER DISCIPLE ran ahead
      faster than PETER,
      and **came** to the tomb **first**;
5 and **stooping** and **looking** in,
    he SAW the linen wrappings lying there;
    but HE DID NOT GO IN.
6 SIMON PETER therefore also **came, following him**,
    and **entered** the tomb;
    and he BEHELD
      (1) the linen wrappings lying there, and
7 (2) the face-cloth, which had been on His head,
      not lying with the linen wrappings,
      but rolled up **in a place by itself**.
8 **Then entered in**
    therefore the OTHER DISCIPLE also,
      who had first come to the tomb, and
      (1) he SAW, and
      (2) BELIEVED.
9 For as yet they did not understand THE SCRIPTURE,
    that HE MUST RISE AGAIN FROM THE DEAD.
10 So the DISCIPLES went away again
      to their own homes.

OBSERVATIONS

Segment Survey

1. Read the segment's three paragraphs, visualizing as you read.
2. Compare the paragraphs as to

   persons: _____

   the tomb: _____

   Jesus' body: _____
3. Compare the negative references in verses 19:38 and 20:9. _____

4. Compare the prominent tone of each of the paragraphs. _____

_____

5. How does 20:10 conclude the segment?

Paragraph Analysis

19:38-42

1. Compare John's descriptions of Joseph (verse 38) and Nicodemus (verse 39).

_____

_____

2. Then observe carefully the services of Joseph and Nicodemus. What impressions do you get from reading about those services?

_____

_____

20:1,2

1. What did Mary Magdalene see?

_____

What did she tell Peter and John?

_____

2. What problem did she voice? (Note the plural "we." Compare Mark 16:1-8. Apparently while the other women entered the tomb, Mary Magdalene was running to Peter and John.)

_____

_____

_____

20:3-10

1. Who was the faster runner?

_____

Did he enter the tomb immediately? _____

If not, what did he do? _____

_____

What did he see? _____

Note: the Greek word translated "saw" means *viewed*. Would he have had a closeup look at the particulars? _____

2. Did Simon Peter enter the tomb? If so, what did he see? _____

_____

Note: the Greek word is translated "beheld." What Simon Peter saw was awesome. What was that?

_____

3. Then John entered, "and he saw, and believed." Again a different Greek word appears. Why was John so perceptive?

_____

4. Verse 9 is parenthetical. Why did John insert this here? _____

_____

Related Verses

Psalm 16:10,11 _____

_____

Matthew 16:21 _____

_____

Matthew 27:57,60-66 _____

_____

Matthew 28:1-8 _____

_____

Mark 15:43 _____

_____

Luke 23:50-52,55,56 _____

_____

Acts 20:7 _____

_____

INTERPRETATIONS

1. "Arimathea" (19:38). This town may have been located about 20 miles northwest of Jerusalem.

2. "A secret one" (19:38). Compare 7:13. Read Mark 15:43 for a description of Joseph. What had his fear been? _____

_____

Now what had that fear turned to?

_____

3. Review your earlier studies of the man Nicodemus (3:1-12; 7:50-52). What are your reflections now? Do you think Nicodemus has become a genuine believer? _____

4. "Stone already taken away" (20:1). Why had this taken place? _____

5. "The linen wrappings lying there" (20:6). Note the orderliness of the burial clothes, as described in 20:6,7. What does this tell you about the "exit" of Jesus' body from the tomb?

_____

6. "For as yet they did not understand" (20:9). NIV places verse 9 in parentheses. Some interpret John's intent as, "for they had not previously understood...." There was belief, but full understanding was slow in coming. Compare Mark 9:10; Luke 24:26; and Luke 24:45,46.

APPLICATIONS

1. The fruits of personal witness of the gospel to unsaved souls may not appear for a long time, as in the experience of Nicodemus and possibly Joseph of Arimathea. Jesus was the one who first counseled Nicodemus. What are your thoughts about the timing of the fruits of personal witnessing? (TBS#7) _____

2. God raised Jesus from the dead on the first day of the week—Sunday. Why was it natural for the early Christian church to set aside that day for worship? _____

What should be the characteristics of this day for Christians everywhere? _____

Summary of Passage

Joseph of Arimathea and Nicodemus secure the body of Jesus from Pilate and bury it in a nearby tomb.

On the first day of the week Mary Magdalene comes to the tomb and sees the stone rolled back. She runs and tells Peter and John, who run to the tomb. John views the linen wrappings from outside. Peter enters and beholds the linen wrappings and face-cloth neatly lying there—but there is no body. Then John enters, sees, and believes. (They had not fully understood from Scripture that Jesus must rise from the dead.)

Memory Verse   20:8

Looking Ahead

Jesus appears to Mary and to His disciples.

SETTING The disciples have gone to their own homes. But Mary is standing outside the tomb. Two angels, and then Jesus, appear to her. In the evening Jesus suddenly appears to the disciples gathered in one of the homes behind closed doors.

Book of John: LIFE IN JESUS, THE SON OF GOD

P R O L O G U E	SIGNS WROUGHT			SELF REVEALED		E P I L O G U E
	PUBLIC MINISTRY -3 YEARS-		(GREAT) (PAUSE) ▶	PRIVATE MINISTRY -FEW DAYS-		21: 25
	ERA OF INCARNATION BEGINS	YEARS OF CONFLICT	DAY OF PREPARATION	HOUR OF SACRIFICE	DAWN OF VICTORY	
1:1	1:19	5:1	12:36b	18:1	20:1	21:1

JESUS IN THE MIDST

11 But MARY was standing
                outside the tomb WEEPING;
    and so, as she WEPT,
    she stooped and LOOKED INTO THE TOMB;
12 and she BEHELD TWO ANGELS in white
    sitting,
        (1) one at the **head**, and
        (2) one at the **feet**,
    where the BODY of JESUS had been lying.
13 And they said to her,
    "WOMAN, why are you WEEPING?"
    She said to them,
        "Because they have **taken away** MY LORD,
        and I do **not now** where they have laid Him."
14 When she had said this, she turned around,
        and BEHELD JESUS **standing there**,
        and **did not know that** it was JESUS.
15 JESUS said to her,
    "WOMAN, why are you WEEPING?
                Whom are you SEEKING?"
    Supposing Him to be the gardener,
        she said to Him,
    "Sir, if you have carried Him away,
        tell me where you have laid Him,
            and I will take Him away."
16 JESUS said to her, "MARY!"
    She turned and said to Him in Hebrew,
        "RABBONI," (which means, TEACHER.)
17 JESUS said to her, "**Stop clinging to Me**;
    for I have **not yet ascended** to the FATHER;
    but **GO TO MY BRETHREN**, and say to them,
    'I ASCEND to MY FATHER and YOUR FATHER,
    and MY GOD and YOUR GOD.'"
18 MARY MAGDALENE came,
    announcing to the DISCIPLES,
        "I HAVE SEEN THE LORD";
            and that He had said these things to her.

(margin: MARY MAGDALENE)

19 When therefore it was **EVENING**,
    on that day, the **FIRST DAY OF THE WEEK**,
        and when the doors were shut
    where the DISCIPLES were, for **fear of the JEWS**,
    JESUS CAME
    and   STOOD IN THEIR MIDST,
    and said to them, "**Peace be with you**."
20 And when He had said this,
    He showed them both
        (1) His hands and
        (2) His side.
    THE DISCIPLES therefore REJOICED
            when they SAW THE LORD.

(margin: DISCIPLES)

21 JESUS therefore said to them again,
                "**Peace be with you**;
    as the FATHER has **sent Me**,
                I also send you."
22 And when He had said this,
                He **breathed on them**,
    and said to them, "RECEIVE THE HOLY SPIRIT.
23 "If you **forgive** the SINS of any,
        their sins **have been forgiven** them;
    if you **retain** the SINS of any,
        they have been retained."

(margin: COMMISSION)

Key Words and Phrases

20:11 ___"weeping"___

    12 _____

    13 _____

    14 _____

    16 _____

    17 _____

    19 _____

    22 _____

others: _____

OBSERVATIONS

Segment Survey
1. The segment is divided into three paragraphs. Who is the main character in the first paragraph?

_____

To whom does Jesus speak, as reported in the last two paragraphs? _____
2. How do verses 17 and 18 lead into the second paragraph? _____

3. How is the last paragraph different from the two preceding ones? _____

Paragraph Analysis
20:11-18
1. What do the two angels contribute to John's account of the empty tomb?

_____

_____

2. Compare the three appearances of "beheld" at these places:
    20:6 _____
    20:12 _____
    20:14 _____
3. What caused Mary to recognize Jesus?

_____

4. Compare the two titles Mary used in referring to Jesus (verses 16,18). _____

_____

20:19,20

Relate these parts of the story:

    (1) atmosphere _____

(2) miracle _____

(3) message _____

(4) demonstration _____

(5) effect _____

20:21-23

1. Identify the ministry of each person of the Trinity, mentioned or implied.

_____

_____

_____

2. What statement to the disciples did Jesus make immediately after saying, "Receive the Holy Spirit"?

_____

_____

What is the connection between the two statements?

_____

_____

_____

Related Verses

Psalm 122:8 _____

Matthew 16:19 _____

Matthew 28:9 _____

Mark 2:5-7 _____

Mark 16:9-14 _____

Luke 24:36-43 _____

John 14:27 _____

Hebrews 2:11,12 _____

INTERPRETATIONS

1. "Did not know that it was Jesus" (20:14). Why do you think Mary did not recognize Jesus?

_____

_____

2. "Stop clinging to Me" (20:17). Explain Jesus' reason for this restraint. Note the words "stop" and "go." _____

_____

_____

3. "Go to My brethren" (20:17). What does the relationship as "brethren" reveal about Jesus at this time? _____

_____

4. "Jesus came and stood in their midst" (20:19). How would you describe Jesus' body at this time? (Cf. 20:20.) How was it different from His pre-resurrection body? _____

_____

_____

What kind of body will a believer have in heaven? See 1 Corinthians 15:42-44; Philippians 3:21.

_____

_____

5. "If you forgive the sins of any" (20:23). Only God can forgive sins (Mark 2:7). Why?

_____

_____

_____

With the Spirit's guidance and authority ("Receive the Holy Spirit") the disciples would declare that God forgives all who repent and believe. See Luke 24:46-49.

APPLICATIONS

Jesus gave the highest authority to His servants by saying, "As the Father has sent Me, I also send you" (20:21). How do you apply this to your own life as an ambassador of Christ? (Cf. 2 Corinthians 5:20.) Think first how the Father sent His Son. (TBS#7). _____

_____

_____

Summary of Passage

Mary is standing outside the tomb and is weeping. When she looks inside, she sees two angels sitting where Jesus' body had been lying. Turning around, she beholds Jesus but doesn't recognize Him until He speaks her name. He sends her to the disciples to tell what His next major move will be.

Toward evening, Jesus suddenly appears to the disciples, who are meeting behind closed doors. He shows them His wounded hands and side, and He charges them with the proclamation of the message of forgiveness of sins.

Memory Verse 20:20

Looking Ahead

Jesus appears to Thomas, who has doubted the reports of the resurrection.

SETTING Thomas was not with the disciples when the resurrected Jesus first appeared to them. Now, eight days later, he is with them, and Jesus suddenly stands in their midst.

Book of John: LIFE IN JESUS, THE SON OF GOD

P R O L O G U E	SIGNS WROUGHT		SELF REVEALED		E P I L O G U E
	PUBLIC MINISTRY -3 YEARS-	(GREAT) (PAUSE) ▶	PRIVATE MINISTRY -FEW DAYS-		21: 25
	ERA OF INCARNATION BEGINS	YEARS OF CONFLICT	DAY OF PREPARATION	HOUR OF SACRIFICE	DAWN OF VICTORY
1:1	1:19	5:1	12:36b	18:1	20:1	21:1

"MY LORD AND MY GOD!"

24   But THOMAS, one of the TWELVE,
          called DIDYMUS,
              was not with them when **JESUS came.**
25 The other DISCIPLES therefore
          were saying to him,
          "WE HAVE SEEN THE LORD!"
          But he said to them,
          "Unless
              (1) I shall SEE in His **hands**
                      the **imprint of the nails**, and
              (2) **put my finger** into the place of the nails, and
              (3) **put my hand** into His **side**,
          I WILL NOT BELIEVE."

26 And after eight days
          again HIS DISCIPLES were inside,
          and **THOMAS with them.**
          JESUS CAME, the doors having been shut,
                  and STOOD IN THEIR MIDST,
          and said, **"Peace be with you."**
27 Then he said to THOMAS,
          "(1) Reach here your **finger**,
                  and SEE My hands; and
          (2) reach here your **hand**,
                  and put it into My **side**;
          and be not unbelieving, but BELIEVING."
28 THOMAS answered and said to Him,
                  "MY LORD AND MY GOD!"
29   JESUS said to him,
          "Because you have SEEN ME,
              have you BELIEVED?
          BLESSED are they who
                  DID NOT SEE,
                  AND YET BELIEVED."

30 **Many other signs** therefore
          JESUS ALSO PERFORMED
                  in the presence of HIS DISCIPLES,
          which are **not written in this book;**
31   but these have been written
              that YOU MAY BELIEVE
              that JESUS IS THE CHRIST,
                  THE SON OF GOD;
          and that **BELIEVING**
                  YOU MAY HAVE LIFE IN HIS NAME.

"UNLESS I SEE"

"REACH AND SEE"

BOOK'S PURPOSE

Key Words and Phrases

20:25 _"We have seen the Lord!"_____

25 _____

26 _____

27 _____

28 _____

29 _____

30 _____

31 _____

others: _____

_____

OBSERVATIONS
Segment Survey

1. The last two verses of the segment are key verses of John's gospel record. How do they serve as the conclusion to the book up to this point?

_____

_____

NOTE: In the introduction of this study guide we observed that an epilogue (chapter 21) appears after these key verses.

2. Who is the main person of the first two paragraphs? _____

3. What two exclamatory statements are in the first two paragraphs?

_____

_____

How do they set the atmosphere of CONCLUSION to the book? _____

_____

Paragraph Analysis
20:24,25

1. Compare the enthusiastic testimony of the ten disciples with the insistent unbelief of Thomas (verse 25). What made the difference?

_____

_____

2. What strikes you about Thomas' "unless" list?

_____

_____

20:26-29

1. Compare this appearance of Jesus (verse 26) with the one eight days earlier (20:19,20).

_____

_____

2. What did Jesus know about Thomas?

_____

_____

3. Compare what Jesus asked Thomas to do with Thomas' "unless" list.

_____

_____

4. Does the text report that Thomas touched Jesus?

Reflect on this.

5. What two kinds of believing do you see in verses 28 and 29? _____

_____

20:30,31
What do these key verses teach about
  the number of miracles Jesus performed:

_____

_____

  the number of Jesus' miracles that were reported:

_____

_____

  the immediate objective of the reporting:

_____

_____

  the ultimate goal desired:

_____

_____

Related Verses

Matthew 22:42-45_____

_____

Matthew 28:20_____

_____

Luke 24:39 _____

_____

John 4:48 _____

_____

John 5:28,29 _____

_____

1 Peter 1:8_____

_____

1 John 1:1 _____

_____

INTERPRETATIONS

1. "Thomas, one of the twelve" (20:24). The designation, "the twelve," was a common name for Jesus' disciples. Of course, by this time, Judas had defected.

2. Jesus gave instructions to Thomas (20:27), then devalued Thomas' kind of believing (20:29). Why do you think Jesus withheld the words of verse 29 until after Thomas' declaration of faith?

_____

_____

_____

_____

3. "My Lord and my God!" (20:28). This is a strong and explicit acknowledgment of Jesus' deity, but how can such an acknowledgment be even stronger

(20:29)? _____

_____

4. "Many other signs" (20:30). What do you consider as the climax of the miracles in John's gospel?

_____

_____

5. "That you may believe" (20:31). NIV suggests an alternate translation, "that you may continue to believe."

APPLICATIONS

This passage shows the kind of faith Jesus wants His disciples to have. In your own words, what kind of faith is it?

_____

_____

_____

_____

_____

_____

_____

How are you tempted to waver in your faith?

_____

_____

_____

_____

_____

Where do you find help for this weakness?

_____

_____

_____

_____

Read Hebrews 11 for inspiration from the lives of other believers.

Summary of Passage

Thomas is not with the disciples when Jesus appears to them behind closed doors. They excitedly tell Thomas about seeing the Lord. But Thomas insists he will not believe it is Jesus until he sees and feels His hands and side. Eight days later Jesus appears to the disciples again. This time Thomas is present. He sees Jesus and believes. "My Lord and my God!" he exclaims.

The disciples witnessed many other signs performed by Jesus, but John reports the ones he did in order to lead the reader to believe that Jesus is the Christ, the Son of God.

Memory Verses   20:30,31

Looking Ahead

Jesus appears a third time to the disciples.

EPILOGUE
21:1–25

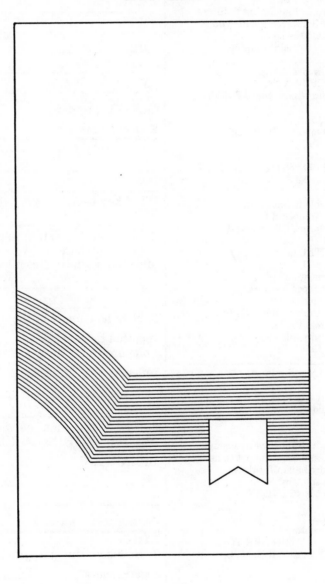

SETTING This is the third time Jesus appears to the disciples after His resurrection. The scene is the Sea of Tiberias (Galilee). Seven disciples are present.

Book of John: LIFE IN JESUS, THE SON OF GOD

P R O L O G U E	SIGNS WROUGHT		SELF REVEALED			E P I L O G U E
	PUBLIC MINISTRY -3 YEARS-	(GREAT) (PAUSE) ▶	PRIVATE MINISTRY -FEW DAYS-			2 1 2
	ERA OF INCARNATION BEGINS	YEARS OF CONFLICT	DAY OF PREPARATION	HOUR OF SACRIFICE	DAWN OF VICTORY	
1:1	1:19	5:1	12:36b	18:1	20:1	21:1

BREAKFAST WITH JESUS

1 After these things
    JESUS **manifested Himself** again to the DISCIPLES
                at the SEA of TIBERIAS;
    and **He manifested Himself in this way**.
2 There were together SIMON PETER,
    and THOMAS called DIDYMUS,
    and NATHANIEL of CANA in GALILEE,
    and the sons of ZEBEDEE, and two others
              of His DISCIPLES.
3 SIMON PETER said to them, "I am **going fishing**."
    They said to him, "We will also come **with you**."
    They went out, and got into the boat;
        and that night they caught nothing.

NOTHING

4 But when the **day** was **now breaking**,
    JESUS STOOD ON THE BEACH;
    yet the DISCIPLES did **not know** that **IT WAS JESUS**.
5   JESUS therefore said to them,
    "Children, you do not have any fish, do you?"
    They answered Him, "No."
6 And He said to them,
    "**Cast the net on the right-hand side of the boat,
        and you will find a catch**."
    They cast therefore,
    and then they were not able to haul it in
        because of the great number of fish.
7 That **disciple** therefore **whom JESUS loved**
    said to PETER, "IT IS THE LORD."
    And so when SIMON PETER heard
      that **IT WAS THE LORD**,
      he put his outer garment on
          (for he was stripped for work),
      and threw himself into the sea.
8 But the other DISCIPLES came in the little boat,
    for they were not far from the land,
      but about one hundred yards away,
    dragging the **net full of fish**.

GREAT NUMBER

9 And so when they got out upon **the land**,
    they saw
        (1) a **charcoal fire already laid**, and
        (2) **fish** placed on it, and
        (3) **bread**.
10 JESUS said to them,
    "BRING some of the fish which you have now caught."
11 SIMON PETER went up, and drew the net to land,
    full of **large fish**, a hundred and fifty-three;
    and although there were so many,
            THE NET WAS NOT TORN.
12 JESUS said to them,
    "COME and have breakfast."
    None of the DISCIPLES ventured
      to question Him,   ➞   "WHO ARE YOU?"
        knowing that IT WAS THE LORD.
13 JESUS CAME and
        (1) took the bread, and
        (2) GAVE them, and
        (3) the fish likewise.
14 This is now the third time
    that JESUS was manifested to the DISCIPLES,
        after He **was raised from the dead**.

BREAKFAST

Key Words and Phrases

21:1   "manifested Himself" _____

3 _____

3 _____

4 _____

6 _____

7 _____

12 _____

14 _____

others: _____

OBSERVATIONS

Segment Survey

1. Compare the first and last verses of the segment.
_____

_____

What key word is repeated?
_____

2. Mark on the textual re-creation where Jesus speaks. Compare the words He spoke before and after the disciples recognized who He was.
_____

_____

3. Note how many of the disciples' words are reported by John. _____
Compare this with Jesus' words. What are your reflections? _____

_____

4. How do these outline words represent this segment: NOTHING, GREAT NUMBER, BREAKFAST? _____

_____

Paragraph Analysis

21:1-3

1. How does this paragraph emphasize togetherness? _____

2. What is natural about Peter's words?
_____

3. What is the key phrase of the paragraph in light of what follows? _____

_____

21:4-8

1. What do the words "But" and "yet" contribute to the narrative?

"But":_____

_____

"yet":_____

_____

2. What miracles do you see in this paragraph?

_____

_____

3. Who was the first to recognize Jesus?

_____

How is he identified in verses 7 and 2?

_____

21:9-14

1. Go through the paragraph and mark on the textual re-creation the key verbs of Jesus' *speaking* or of His *doing* (e.g., "Bring").

_____

2. Why do you think Jesus asked the disciples to bring some fish, since He already was preparing fish and bread (21:9)?

_____

_____

3. Relate verse 12 to verse 7.

_____

_____

4. How does verse 14 conclude this segment?

_____

Related Verses

Matthew 28:7,10 _____

Mark 1:17_____

Luke 5:1-11 _____

Luke 24:16 _____

John 6_____

John 15:5 _____

John 20:19_____

John 20:26_____

INTERPRETATIONS

1. "Manifested Himself" (21:1). Read the following verses where the same Greek word appears, translated here as "manifested." This will give you an indication of the depth of the word in a context like this. John 2:11; 2 Corinthians 4:10; 2 Corinthians 5:10; Ephesians 5:13; Colossians 3:4; 1 John 4:9.

Here is a list of the passages which record the post-resurrection appearances of Jesus: 1) in Jerusalem: Mark 16:9; John 20:11-18; Matthew 28:9,10; Luke 24:13-35; Luke 24:34; 1 Corinthians 15:5; John 20:19-23; John 20:24-29; 2) in Galilee: John 21:1-14; Matthew 28:16-20; 1 Corinthians 15:6; 1 Corinthians 5:7; 3) near Jerusalem: Acts 1:4-11 (cf. Luke 24:50,51); 4) to Paul: Acts 9:3-7; Acts 22:6-10; 26:12-18; 1 Corinthians 9:1; 15:8.

2. "Sons of Zebedee" (21:2). These sons were James and the Gospel writer, John. How is John identified in 21:7? _____

3. "Fish...and bread" (21:9). The original text suggests the singular paraphrases: "the one breadcake" and "the one fish." It is singular also in verse 13. What miracle is recalled here?

_____

Why do you think Jesus made the request in 21:10?

_____

4. "The third time" (21:14). The first two appearances were reported in 20:19-23 and 20:24-29.

APPLICATIONS

Jesus is the tender, loving Savior, who knows all the needs of His followers and supplies those needs. List specific illustrations of that fact as seen in this passage. In what ways has He been your help in times of need?

_____

_____

_____

Summary of Passage

Jesus appears early one morning to seven disciples after they fail to catch any fish. Unrecognized, He instructs them as to where to cast their net, and they catch 153 fish. John exclaims, "It is the Lord."

After they bring the boat and fish to land, Jesus invites them to have breakfast with Him—fish and bread which He has been preparing on a charcoal fire. They do not ask who He is, because they know that He is the Lord.

This is Jesus' third post-resurrection appearance to His disciples.

Memory Verse   21:12

Looking Ahead

Jesus reinstates Peter to fellowship with Himself.

SETTING At the end of the breakfast (21:1-14)
Jesus talks with Peter. The apostle John is
standing nearby.

"FOLLOW ME"

15 So when they had finished breakfast,
   JESUS said to SIMON PETER,
   "SIMON, son of JOHN,
   DO YOU LOVE ME more than these?"   [agapao]
   He said to Him,
   "Yes, LORD; **You know** that **I LOVE YOU**."   [phileo]
               He said to him, "**Tend My lambs**."
16 He said to him again a second time,
   "SIMON, son of JOHN,
   DO YOU LOVE ME?"   [agapao]
   He said to him,
   "Yes, LORD; **You know** that **I LOVE YOU**."   [phileo]
           He said to him, "**Shepherd My sheep**."
17 He said to him the third time,
   "SIMON, son of JOHN,
   DO YOU LOVE ME?"   [phileo]
   PETER was grieved
   because He said to him **the third time**,
               "DO YOU LOVE ME?"
   And he said to Him,
       "LORD, **You know all things**;
           You know that **I LOVE YOU**."   [phileo]
           JESUS said to him, "**Tend My sheep**.
18 "TRULY, TRULY, I say to you,
   when you were *younger*, you used to gird yourself,
           and WALK wherever you wished;
   when you **grow old**, you will stretch out your hands,
       and someone else will GIRD YOU,
           and BRING YOU **where you do not wish to go**."
19 Now this He said,
   signifying **by what kind of death**
       HE WOULD GLORIFY GOD.
   And when He had spoken this,
   He said to him,
               "FOLLOW ME!"

20 PETER, turning around,
   saw the DISCIPLE whom JESUS LOVED
   following them; the one who also had leaned back
       on His breast at the supper,
       and said, "LORD, who is the one
           who betrays You?"
21 PETER therefore seeing him said to JESUS,
   "LORD, and WHAT ABOUT THIS MAN?"
22 JESUS said to him,
   "If **I want** him to **remain until I come**,
       WHAT IS THAT TO **YOU**?
   YOU FOLLOW ME!"
23 This saying therefore went out among the BRETHREN
   that **that DISCIPLE would not die**;
   yet JESUS did **not** say to him
               that he **would not die**;
   but only, "If **I want** him to remain until I come,
       WHAT IS THAT TO **YOU**?"

24 This is the DISCIPLE
   who **bears witness of these things**,
       and **wrote** these things;
   and **we know** that his witness is TRUE.
25 And there are **also**
   many other things which JESUS DID,
   which if they were **written in detail**,
   I suppose that **even the world itself**
   would **not contain** the books which were written.

Key Words and Phrases

21:15 _____ "love"

CHALLENGE

CORRECTION

Book of John: LIFE IN JESUS, THE SON OF GOD

P R O L O G U E	SIGNS WROUGHT		SELF REVEALED			E P I L O G U E 21: 25
	PUBLIC MINISTRY -3 YEARS-		(GREAT) (PAUSE) ▶	PRIVATE MINISTRY -FEW DAYS-		
	ERA OF INCARNATION BEGINS	YEARS OF CONFLICT	DAY OF PREPARATION	HOUR OF SACRIFICE	DAWN OF VICTORY	
1:1	1:19	5:1	12:36b	18:1	20:1	21:1

15 _____
16 _____
19 _____
19 _____
21 _____
23 _____
25 _____
others:_____

OBSERVATIONS

Segment Survey

1. How does the last paragraph serve as a conclusion to the whole book of John?

_____

2. Compare the first two paragraphs. For example, who asks the first question in each of them?

_____

3. What CHALLENGE do you see in the first

paragraph? _____
What CORRECTION do you see in the second?

_____

Paragraph Analysis

21:15-19
1. What question did Jesus ask three times?

_____

Compare Peter's three answers. Note on the chart the interchange of the two Greek words translated "love." *Agapao* means unselfish love, a love that is ready to serve. *Phileo* signifies intimate and

tender affection. _____

2. Compare Jesus' three responses with Peter's

three answers._____

_____

3. What did Jesus talk about (verses 18, 19a) after saying, "Tend My sheep"?

_____

Why do you think He introduced this subject here?

_____

Account for the timing of the next words, "Follow

Me!"_____

_____

21:20-23

1. Why do you think Peter asked the question in verse 21?_____

_____

2. What are the key phrases of Jesus' response (verse 22)?_____

_____

_____

3. What false report was circulated?

_____

_____

21:24,25

1. Identify "the disciple" and "we" (verse 24).

_____

2. Who wrote verse 25?_____
Compare verse 25 with 20:30-31.

_____

_____

Related Verses

Mark 14:27-31 _____

_____

Luke 24:34 _____

_____

John 3:35 (*agapao*) _____

_____

John 10:14,27_____

_____

John 12:23_____

_____

John 13:36-38 _____

_____

John 14:2,3_____

_____

John 18:15-18,25-27_____

_____

Hebrews 13:1 (*phileo*) _____

INTERPRETATIONS

1. "More than these" (21:15). There are two possible meanings: 1) "more than these things" (fishing); 2) "more than these disciples do."

2. "I love (*phileo*) You" (21:15). Why do you think Peter avoided the strong word *agapao*?

_____

_____

Why do you think Jesus resorted to the word *phileo* in His third question (21:17)?

3. "The third time" (21:17). Do you think Peter's three denials of Jesus accounted for Jesus' repeated questions here? _____

4. "What kind of death" (21:19). Some believe the words, "stretch out your hands," signify crucifixion. Tradition indicates Peter was crucified as a martyr. What do the words "glorify God" and "Follow Me" reveal about Jesus' deepest thoughts concerning Peter?_____

_____

5. "Until I come" (21:22). This refers to Jesus' return. What was important for Peter to do?

_____

Why was that important?

_____

_____

APPLICATIONS

1. Love for Jesus is a basic condition for fruitful Christian service. List some reasons this is so.

_____

_____

2. How can an unsaved acquaintance recognize that you love Jesus?

_____

_____

Summary of Passage

After breakfast, Jesus asks Peter three times if he truly loves Him. Peter's answers are affirmative but cautious. Jesus commissions Peter to take care of His lambs and sheep, and He calls him to follow him.

Peter asks about John, and Jesus rebukes Peter for his curiosity, reminding him of the earlier charge to follow Him.

Thus ends John's gospel record of some of the things Jesus did on earth.

Memory Verse 21:25

Some Final Questions

You have now finished your study of John. What highlights stand out in your mind?

_____

What are the two main divisions of the book?

_____

What is each one about?_____
Why did John write this book?

_____

If you were an unbeliever when you began studying this Gospel, have you come to the place of belief?

_____

If you were already a believer, have you grown and matured in your Christian faith?_____

How? _____

SELECTED SOURCES
FOR FURTHER STUDY

Bright, Bill. *Ten Basic Steps Toward Christian Maturity* (booklets). San Bernardino: Here's Life, 1965. Revised, 1983.

Griffith-Thomas, W.H. *The Apostle John: His Life and Writing.* Grand Rapids: Eerdmans, 1946.

Harrison, Everett F. *John, The Gospel of Faith.* Chicago: Moody, 1968.

Hendriksen, W. *Exposition of the Gospel According to John* in *The New Testament Commentary.* Grand Rapids: Baker, 1953.

Jensen, Irving L. *Independent Bible Study.* Chicago: Moody, 1963.

_____. *Jensen's Survey of the New Testament.* Chicago: Moody, 1981.

_____. *John.* Chicago: Moody, 1970.

_____. *Life of Christ.* Chicago: Moody, 1969.

Morgan, G. Campbell. *The Gospel According to John.* Westwood, N.J.: Revell, n.d.

Pfeiffer, Charles F., and Harrison, Everett F. (eds.) *The Wycliffe Bible Commentary.* Chicago: Moody, 1962. One-volume commentary of the whole Bible.

Tenney, Merrill C. *John: The Gospel of Belief.* Grand Rapids: Eerdmans, 1948.

Thomas, Robert L., ed. *New American Standard Exhaustive Concordance of the Bible.* Nashville: Holman, 1981.

Thomas, Robert L., and Gundry, Stanley N. *A Harmony of the Gospels.* Chicago: Moody, 1978.

Vine, W.E. *An Expository Dictionary of New Testament Words.* Westwood, N.J.: Revell, 1961.

Westcott, B.F. *The Gospel According to St. John.* Grand Rapids: Eerdmans, 1951.